Methods and Meaning
in the Novels of Stephen King

ALSO BY JAMES ARTHUR ANDERSON
AND FROM MCFARLAND

*The Linguistics of Stephen King: Layered Language
and Meaning in the Fiction* (2017)

Methods and Meaning in the Novels of Stephen King
A Constant Reader's Guide

JAMES ARTHUR ANDERSON

McFarland & Company, Inc., Publishers
Jefferson, North Carolina

LIBRARY OF CONGRESS CATALOGING-IN-PUBLICATION DATA

Names: Anderson, James Arthur, 1955– author.
Title: Methods and meaning in the novels of Stephen King :
a constant reader's guide / James Arthur Anderson.
Description: Jefferson, North Carolina : McFarland & Company, Inc.,
Publishers, 2024. | Includes bibliographical references and index.
Identifiers: LCCN 2024028548 | ISBN 9781476695051 (paperback : acid free paper) ∞
ISBN 9781476653303 (ebook)
Subjects: LCSH: King, Stephen, 1947—-Criticism and interpretation. |
LCGFT: Literary criticism.
Classification: LCC PS3561.I483 Z517 2024 | DDC 813/.54—dc23/eng/20240621
LC record available at https://lccn.loc.gov/2024028548

BRITISH LIBRARY CATALOGUING DATA ARE AVAILABLE

ISBN (print) 978-1-4766-9505-1
ISBN (ebook) 978-1-4766-5330-3

© 2024 James Arthur Anderson. All rights reserved

*No part of this book may be reproduced or transmitted in any form
or by any means, electronic or mechanical, including photocopying
or recording, or by any information storage and retrieval system,
without permission in writing from the publisher.*

Front cover images © Adobe Firefly/Shutterstock

Printed in the United States of America

*McFarland & Company, Inc., Publishers
Box 611, Jefferson, North Carolina 28640
www.mcfarlandpub.com*

To my wife Lynn Llorye
for still being there for me

Acknowledgments

I would like to gratefully acknowledge the faculty and staff of Johnson & Wales University, which generously awarded me a grant under the Faculty Research Fellowship Program to work on this project.

Table of Contents

Acknowledgments	vi
Introduction: Why Is Stephen King So Good and So Popular?	1
1. *Carrie*: Prom Night	5
2. *'Salem's Lot*: New World Vampires	11
3. *Rage*: Getting It on in the Schools	17
4. *The Shining*: Iconic Horror	21
5. *The Stand*: The Modern Plague	28
6. *The Long Walk*: Dystopian Nightmare	35
7. *The Dead Zone*: Everyman Is a Hero	39
8. *Firestarter*: Don't Play with Fire	45
9. *Roadwork*: Mental Meltdown	52
10. *Cujo*: He Tried to Be a Good Dog	57
11. *The Running Man*: Reality TV on Steroids	62
12. *Rita Hayworth and the Shawshank Redemption*: Hope Springs Eternal	68
13. *The Body*: The Birth of a Writer	72
14. *Christine*: America Loves Its Wheels	77
15. *Pet Sematary*: Sometimes Dead Is Better	83
16. *Eyes of the Dragon*: Genre-Bending Fantasy	89
17. *Thinner*: The Book That Outed Bachman	95
18. *It*: We All Float Down Here	100
19. *Misery*: The Price of Fame	106

20. *The Tommyknockers*: Mechanized Aliens	112
21. *The Dark Half*: Attack of the Pseudonym	117
22. *Needful Things*: The Downside of a Consumer Society	121
23. *Gerald's Game*: Escape Room	126
24. *Dolores Claiborne*: Justice Served	131
25. *Rose Madder*: The Fury of a Woman Scorned	136
26. *Insomnia*: Miles to Go Before I Sleep	141
27. *The Green Mile*: Rebirth of the Serial Novel	146
28. *Desperation*: Even God Has a Price	153
29. *The Regulators*: Horror in the Burbs	158
30. *Bag of Bones*: Digging Up the Past	164
31. *The Girl Who Loved Tom Gordon*: Gretel Goes It Alone	171
32. *Dreamcatcher*: A Winter's Tale	177
33. *From a Buick 8*: The One-Way Portal	183
34. *The Colorado Kid*: The Unsolved Mystery	188
35. *Cell*: The Techno-Zombie Attack	192
36. *Lisey's Story*: The Literary Best Seller	197
37. *Blaze*: Bachman Returns	203
38. *Duma Key*: Art Therapy	207
39. *Under the Dome*: Ants Under a Magnifying Glass	213
40. *11/22/63*: Changing the Past	219
41. *Joyland*: Carny from Carny	225
42. *Doctor Sleep*: Danny Torrance Grows Up	231
43. *Mr. Mercedes*: Enter, Holly Gibney	238
44. *Revival*: Reanimation and Revelation	244
45. *Finders Keepers*: The Problem with Buried Treasure	250
46. *End of Watch*: To Be or Not to Be	255
47. *The Outsider*: The Doppelgänger Effect	260
48. *Elevation*: King's Feel-Good Book	265

Table of Contents

49. *The Institute*: Suffer the Children	269
50. *Later*: I See Dead People	274
51. *Billy Summers*. The Moral Assassin	280
52. *Fairy Tale*: Once Upon a Time	286
53. *Holly*: A Journal of the Covid-19 Years	291
Conclusion: The English Professor and Constant Reader	297
Appendix 1: Theoretical Works Consulted	309
Appendix 2: Bibliography of Works about Stephen King	311
Appendix 3: A Chronology of Stephen King's Books	313
Index	315

Introduction

Why Is Stephen King So Good and So Popular?

Although I'm an English professor, that doesn't mean I don't like a good story. While I was in graduate school studying Elizabethan drama and William Faulkner so I could collect more letters to put after my name, I was also reading fantasy, science fiction, horror, and Stephen King for pleasure. After I graduated and was armed with alphabet soup and a fancy title, I began teaching writing and literature. But I still kept reading Stephen King. Never in my wildest dreams did I ever think I'd someday be *teaching* King's works—I was, after all, just a "Constant Reader." Even though most of the books I'd read for pleasure were, quite literally, disposable, King's fiction stayed with me over the years, and I found myself returning to his older works and reading them again. I couldn't get novels like *Carrie*, *The Shining*, and *Pet Sematary* out of my mind even as I read his new works as soon as they were released. So I began to wonder what was going on.

Professors are expected to do some scholarly work, even at teaching institutions such as mine, and I had published a few things on H.P. Lovecraft, the subject of my PhD dissertation. Before long, I found myself presenting papers on King at academic conferences and writing about him in journals like *Studies in Weird Fiction*. I've now published two full-length scholarly academic studies on King, taught a senior-level university seminar on his works (LIT 4800: Advanced Studies in a Major Literary Figure) which was always full, and still preorder his books. Through all of this work, I have become convinced that Stephen King is indeed worthy of the title of a "major literary figure," and my dean agreed, allowing me to teach King's work in a class usually reserved for the likes of Shakespeare, Hemingway, and Milton.

What is it about Stephen King that makes his work worthy of further study and raises his books above the level of just disposable bestsellers that one reads and then donates to the pleasure reading bin at the local library? Well, I've detailed my thoughts on this in my previous two books using the language of professors to convince critics and other professors, and you're more than welcome to purchase and read these studies if you'd like (I can certainly use the royalties). But I thought the time had come for me to share the thoughts of a professor with King's "Constant Readers" so they might be better able to respond when someone asks, usually in a condescending voice, "Why do you read that stuff?" (and the word "stuff" sounds like something that needs to be cleaned up off the bottom of your shoe after you've accidentally stepped in it on the sidewalk). In this book, I'm going to take each of King's novels in turn and explain them from the point of view of a literature professor who is also a Constant Reader. I've found some elements in King's fiction that demonstrate both his literary merit and his ability to capture and hold an audience. I will try to keep it simple and avoid unnecessary jargon, but when some literary terms are necessary, I'll explain them as simply as possible.

One of the things I'll look at in each work is the story itself. As King has said in *On Writing*, "the story is boss." According to him, people want to read a story where something actually happens, where there is a plot, conflict, and a resolution. And King is a master at producing such stories. One way he does this is by tapping into what Carl Jung called "archetypes," which could be defined as part of the human collective unconsciousness, stories that have been told and retold in new and different ways. Joseph Campbell and others have identified these types of stories in mythology and folklore from ancient times to the present. The "hero's journey" archetype, for example, can be found in *The Odyssey* and in *Star Wars*—and in some Stephen King stories, such as *The Stand*.

King also believes that a story should have a "point," a reason for being beyond mere entertainment. In other words, it should mean something and help readers to understand something about life. This, in professorial terms, involves themes and subtexts, and although this subject is the dreaded topic of so many English essay questions, every one of King's works is rich in meaning on several levels, with themes that add texture and significance to his fiction.

If, indeed, "story is boss," the story depends not just on "what happens" but also on the way it is told. This involves such things as narrative devices, foreshadowing, metaphor, style, setting, and other staples of the English professor's toolbox in teaching basic literature courses. Despite the accusation by some critics that King is "dumbing down American letters," I will show that he is, indeed, a master of his craft and asks his readers to think deeply about important subjects.

Finally, a good story must have believable, memorable characters,

Introduction 3

and, again, King has accomplished this goal in his fiction. Furthermore, once these characters have been created, King is able to tap into what evolutionary psychologists call "human universals," or, in simpler terms, basic emotions that are shared by all members of our species: fear, love, rage, and other feelings that we are all familiar with on a visceral level.

To round out the discussion, I will include a brief background of each book and what was happening in the world when it was written and a summary, just to remind readers who may have read the book in the past and may have forgotten some of the specifics. I will also include notable quotes that have become part of the popular lexicon and discuss iconic settings, characters, and ideas that have found their way into contemporary American culture.

This book is intended for those who have read King's works, so, fair warning, there will be spoilers. It is intended as a resource to be read in conjunction with King's books by students, fans, and "Constant Readers," not as a substitute for reading the books themselves. It is my hope that this study will help readers understand, appreciate, and enjoy the books on a deeper level and encourage rereading King's work more carefully and thoughtfully, especially since (in my case, anyway) the first reading is just for fun. I am convinced that each of King's books can be enjoyed and better understood by multiple readings, so I'd suggest that the Constant Reader enjoy each book as pure entertainment the first time through; indeed, the books are difficult to put down once one begins reading. That is where the book you're holding enters the picture and invites a second reading of King's work that will dig beneath the surface of just an entertaining story and reveal some of the methods and meanings beneath the madness.

I have chosen to include just King's novels and two novellas in this volume except for the Dark Tower books, which would merit a complete study of their own. I've also avoided his collaborative efforts with Peter Straub, Richard Chizmar, and his son, Owen, since having two creative talents involved does muddy the waters. Of course, some of the longer stories in his anthologies are actually the size of short novels themselves; including all of his novellas would also require another volume of its own. Perhaps if my energy holds up, I'll follow this work with a study of his remaining works, including the short story collections, at a later date.

1

Carrie

Prom Night

Background

Although *Carrie* was Stephen King's first published novel, it was the fourth book he'd written (*Rage*, *The Long Walk*, and *Blaze*, his first three, were later published under the Richard Bachman pen name). According to King, it was inspired when someone told him he couldn't write about women, and so he decided to write a scene about a high school student having her first menstrual period in the girls' shower in gym class and not knowing what it was. King claims he hated the scene and threw it in the trash. His wife Tabitha rescued the manuscript, encouraged her husband to finish it, and this launched his career. At the time of its writing, King was teaching high school English, living in a house trailer, and working with a manual typewriter. The $2,500 advance he received allowed him to buy a new car, and the first edition of 30,000 copies was released on April 5, 1974. Paperback rights sold for $400,000, and the book went on to sell over a million copies and has never gone out of print. The novel was adapted into films in 1976, 2002, and 2013 and was even adapted into a Broadway musical.

Summary and Narrative Devices

The plot of *Carrie* is well known, even by those who haven't read the book, and thus needs little repeating. It is the story of Carrie White, a high school student raised by an abusive, religious single mother and a victim of bullying and social ostracization from her peers. What makes this young woman different from other teenage victims of violence and abuse is her telekinetic abilities, which manifested themselves when she was a child and developed into a powerful force once she reached sexual maturity.

The story opens with the iconic scene of Carrie experiencing her first menstrual period in the girls' shower in gym class, with the other girls jeering at her and throwing sanitary napkins. Carrie, who has never been told about menstruation by her mother, believes she is bleeding to death in the shower and is terrified. Susan Snell, one of the girls who took part in the bullying, feels remorse afterward and convinces her boyfriend Tommy, the "all American boy," to ask Carrie to the school dance. Chris Hargensen, the "mean girl," is suspended and not allowed to attend the dance for the role she played in the incident and vows revenge on Carrie White. With the help of her boyfriend Billy and some of his friends, she arranges for Tommy and Carrie to be voted prom king and queen, and Chris and Billy drop buckets of pigs' blood on them as they accept the honor. This scene from *Carrie*, replayed in the film versions, has become an iconic symbol in American culture. After her initial shock, Carrie uses her telekinetic power to destroy the town.

The interesting part of the plot is that the reader knows what will happen. It is foreshadowed from the very beginning, as the text refers to "one of her surviving classmates" and later refers to "over two hundred deaths and the destruction of an entire town." The foreshadowing is not subtle. It is clear that something terrible is going to happen and that Carrie's powers will be the cause of it. The suspense is in the anticipation of the inevitable.

King employs an interesting style in *Carrie* that works with point of view in an unusual way. Originally, the book had been planned as a simple narrative using an omniscient (all-knowing) point of view where the reader was allowed inside the mind of all of the major characters. However, when the draft was finished, he realized the book wasn't quite long enough for a full-length novel. To solve this problem, he inserted excerpts from "reliable" sources, including the White Commission, scholarly journals, newspaper accounts, the autobiography of Susan Snell, and others to stretch the story. These additional points of view give more veracity to the story, allowing the reader to understand Carrie White on several levels and also to see how misunderstood she was. This perspective gives a 360-degree view of both Carrie and the events that led to the catastrophe and makes the supernatural seem realistic. One of King's trademarks is using the elements of fantasy and horror to bring light to real-world problems, such as bullying and the misuse of religion. For this to work, the reader has to suspend disbelief and "buy into" the supernatural element. This technique of including these made-up biographies, newspaper, journal, and magazine articles, and other similar elements into the story help the reader believe in some of the "science" behind the Carrie White case and accept the story as plausible, even if only in the fictional context of a novel.

Archetypes

Most fictional works rely on what critics refer to as narrative archetypes to appeal to readers, and Stephen King's works are no different. An archetype, in simple terms, is a storyline that has become part of what Jung calls the "collective unconscious," or, in other words, is ingrained into human understanding. *Carrie*, in fact, employs several of these archetypes that readers readily relate to, interweaving them to complete a new and different story, yet one that appeals to the reader's sense of story. The novel has elements of the "coming of age" story, the "Cinderella" story (rags to riches, only in this version, back to rags again), and the "revenge" story, which is one of the most popular genres in the modern world and a staple of Hollywood blockbusters. I will examine each of these archetypes and how they work in *Carrie*.

The coming-of-age story is a classic in literature, having been used in works ranging from the Harry Potter series to *A Portrait of the Artist as a Young Man* by James Joyce. In this archetype, a child undergoes a set of conflicts resulting in the attainment of maturity and adulthood. Carrie White begins the story as a child, and the moment of her first menstruation signals her journey into womanhood. While the blood might symbolize this womanhood, it also initiates her quest to discover and harness her supernatural powers. This begins unconsciously at first, with the lights in the girls' shower and her throwing a boy off his bike. But Carrie soon learns to strengthen and control her abilities, which allows her to force her mother's compliance and ultimately leads to the destruction of Chamberlin, Maine. Her sudden and unexpected entry into womanhood triggers the acceleration of her telekinesis to superhuman powers; unfortunately for Carrie and her fellow students, her powers grew faster than her ability to control her emotions, resulting in a catastrophic end.

Carrie is also a Cinderella story about the abused and ugly young woman who becomes a beautiful swan. Some of these "rags to riches" stories end well, as does the fairy tale, and in some the main character is returned to rags again or even worse. At the start of the novel, Carrie is under the complete control of her mother (the wicked stepmother), has no social life, is mocked by her fellow students (her stepsisters), and wears unattractive clothing and styles. Sue Snell (the fairy godmother) grants her a date with Tommy (the handsome prince) and Carrie is transformed into a princess and even crowned as a queen. Metaphorically, the coach turns into a pumpkin as the correct time is struck and the blood is dumped on her. She becomes the outcast again, losing both of her slippers in the grass outside of the high school. Unlike in the fairy tale, though, no one lives happily ever after since her prince, killed by the bucket of blood falling on his head, cannot rescue her.

Finally, and perhaps providing the most satisfaction for readers, *Carrie* is a revenge story. Revenge stories bring readers satisfaction for a number of reasons; according to evolutionary psychologists, it is part of human nature to want to see rule breakers punished. From prehistoric times, there has been a dislike of liars, cheaters, slackers, and others who fail to help the social group; such people are the first to be voted off the island, so to speak. In the narrative of popular culture, criminals and murderers are captured and punished, often killed in horrible ways as we see in countless television shows and films where the "good guy" wins. By allowing the reader inside Carrie's mind, King presents her as a sympathetic character (the "good guy") who is being tormented by a group of mean girls. Although Carrie is the social outcast, the reader takes her side, especially when she is shown to be the victim of a horrible mother—and our culture loves to embrace the underdog. When Carrie destroys the school and the town and kills her mother, then Chris and Billy, the revenge is justified, and the reader is satisfied. Sue, the fairy godmother, survives and understands Carrie's plight. Sadly, Tommy, despite his innocence, is killed not by Carrie but by her tormenters.

Themes and Subtexts

As in all of King's works, *Carrie* is rich in themes and subtexts, meanings that linger beneath the surface of the story and provide some understanding about the human condition, particularly in light of the story's time and place. The most obvious theme is bullying and abuse, both from the other students and from Margaret White. Bullying has become an unfortunate part of modern culture, particularly in America's schools (and now, on social media). King, who worked as a high school teacher while writing the novel, would be attuned to this experience and was familiar with it. In *On Writing*, he says that Carrie White is an amalgamation of two girls with whom he went to high school. The bullying of the students toward Carrie is shown realistically, and the reader is forced to endure it with her. Yet King takes this bullying to the next level, and the violence returns to raise havoc on the town and on society. When one considers that many killers, rapists, and abusers are products of abuse themselves, Carrie's metaphorical retribution is not as far-fetched as it first seems. Isolation and child abuse also form the basis of her world, personified in her mother's fanatical religious views.

Religion is a common theme in many of King's novels, ranging from the saint-like character of Mother Abigail in *The Stand* to the hypocritical preacher in *Revival*. *Carrie* specifically examines the dangers of religious extremism in the persona of Carrie's mother who is the leader of a cult of one, with her daughter as the only member of the perverse congregation. Carrie is unable to escape this cult, and once again, the reader suffers along with her. Her telekinetic powers offer a way for her to have a normal life, so she develops them to an extreme.

Although King has said that *Carrie* is a feminist book, this subtext is less obvious than bullying and religion. However, all the major players of the novel are female: Carrie, her mother, Sue, and Chris. Tommy and Billy, the "good" boy and the "bad" boy, are not so much characters as they are instruments of Sue and Chris, respectively. Carrie personifies the power of women, regardless of their beauty, and Sue represents empathy and the ability of one woman to understand another, even if she is completely different. Carrie's telekinetic abilities are the epitome of power and are best harnessed when she is bullied, abused, and held back, a metaphorical warning about underestimating women.

Blood is a major symbol of this novel, beginning with Carrie's menstrual blood, signifying womanhood, and ending with Sue's menstrual period, which, since it is two weeks late, may imply a miscarriage. Carrie cuts her finger at the prom, which foreshadows the pig's bath of blood, and Margaret White requires a blood sacrifice and cuts herself sharpening the knife with which she plans to kill her daughter. Blood, of course, is life, and in this novel it represents the loss of life. Women who bleed die. The fact that Sue's period comes late foreshadows her survival and points to a possible pregnancy, a life within her, which terminates at the end of the novel.

Human Universals

One of King's greatest talents is his ability to tap into universal emotions, identified by evolutionary psychologists as "human universals." One of these sentiments, altruism, has enabled the human species to form groups, work together, and create society. As the sociobiologist E.O. Wilson has noted, cooperative groups outperform selfish groups every time. The selfish group, Chris and her peers, is destroyed in this novel, while Sue Snell's altruism gives the reader hope, even if the ending does not turn out well. In his fiction, King repeatedly tells us that most people do want to do the right thing, and whether they succeed or fail, we admire them for it.

Rage is another human universal emotion that, although not pretty, evolved in humans to help the species survive. The noted neuroscientist

R. Douglas Fields has identified nine triggers that can make people snap. Three of them apply to Carrie White and explain destructive rage: "life or limb" (self-defense), "insult," and "stopped" (or being captured or cornered). Carrie feels attacked, insulted, and cornered—any one of which might set off a rage response. The average person can certainly appreciate how danger, insult, or being trapped could result in a violent response, one that might have saved our ancient ancestors from being injured or killed.

Evaluation

Carrie was, of course, a milestone for King in that it launched his career as a writer and steered him into the horror genre. It was also a gamechanger in breaking some taboos in horror, accurately depicting menstruation and the bullying that can occur among teenagers. Although the novel is now decades old, it still holds up today. The book uses a horror motif to examine important themes, such as feminism and religion, and bring to light cultural issues such as bullying and mental health. *Carrie* has reached the status of being a horror classic and, in my humble opinion, has made an important contribution to modern American fiction.

Interesting Fact

In the original first draft of the novel, Carrie used her powers to crash a commercial jet into the town of Chamberlain to destroy it. That scene was edited out in the final cut to make the book more realistic.

Iconic Moment

Carrie has become the prototype for the nightmare senior prom. The image of Sissy Spacek covered in pig's blood from the 1976 film version is an icon of popular culture.

Notable Quote

"Sorry is the Kool-Aid of human emotions."

2

'Salem's Lot
New World Vampires

Background

Stephen King began writing *'Salem's Lot* before *Carrie* was published. Originally titled *The Second Coming*, the novel was inspired by a dinner conversation that King had when he wondered what would happen if Dracula came to America. While it was agreed that the vampire would probably be baffled by the modern technology of a major city and probably hit by a cab, he might well prosper in a small Maine town where he could remain under the radar, so to speak. When King decided to publish *'Salem's Lot* instead of *Roadwork*, his "serious" novel, which he had also completed, he was typecast as a horror writer. "I don't care what they call me," he said in the introduction to the 2005 reprinted illustrated edition, "as long the checks don't bounce."

The novel was originally published in 1975 and was adapted into a television miniseries in 1979 and again in 2004. Although King had wanted to write a sequel to the novel, he instead incorporated that story into the Dark Tower series, where Father Callahan returns in *Wolves of Calla* and *Song of Susannah*.

Summary and Narrative Devices

'Salem's Lot is the story of what would happen if European vampires immigrated to Jerusalem's Lot, a small New England town. Ben Mears, the lead character (or protagonist in professorial terms), returns to the place of his birth to write a book about the Marsten House, an evil place with a sordid history that terrified him as a child. His real goal is to exorcise the demons of his childhood, where he either saw or imagined supernatural events. The novel develops into a love story first as Ben begins dating

Susan and thinks he is in love with her (though for all of that, he doesn't really grieve much over her death), and before long, strange things begin happening: a mutilated dog is found in the cemetery, one boy disappears and his brother develops a severe low blood count and dies, and then the town drunk also gets sick and dies. Ben and his friends Susan, Matt, Mark, and Father Callahan realize that the town has been infested with vampires who have moved into the Marsten House. Then they begin their quest to destroy the evil. It is the outline of most horror stories. Act 1: something weird is going on here. Act 2: we figure out what it is. Act 3: let's kill it.

The novel begins after the story has ended, which illustrates the differentiation between "story" and "discourse." The story, in professorial language, refers to the chronological events of the story, or what happened from the beginning to the end. Most stories aren't told in exact chronological order but move around in time, which is referred to as the "discourse," or the way the story is told. This involves the use of flashbacks, which take the reader into the past and show backstory, and foreshadowing, where we get peeks into future events that haven't happened yet. Many stories begin in medias res, a fancy Latin name for "in the middle of things," and then use flashbacks to tell the backstory of what happened before page one of the novel. When the novel opens, the vampire infestation is over and the heroes have escaped. Ben keeps an eye on the news from the area, and when he spots something unusual, he decides to return to the Lot to crush it before it gets worse. An extended flashback composes the bulk of the novel and fills in the details of the horrors that occurred.

King spends most of the first third of the book creating a town that is realistic in the most minute details. Although the Marsten House dominates the town from its position on the hill, we are shown details of the more mundane areas as well. In fact, the reader is given a virtual tour of the town, complete with street names, specific places, some, like the junkyard, that are described in panoramic detail. The town's history is also presented in detail, as if being told by an omniscient town elder who knows of every event in Jerusalem's Lot from the day of its founding in 1765 until the present narrative moment when the story is being told. It is revealed that Jointner Avenue was named for a local member of Congress who died of syphilis. The political system of the town is presented (the town has three selectmen, and the volunteer fire department was allotted $300 per year), and there was no public works department.

The townspeople as well become living entities, with even minor characters having intricate and intimate backstories. King's omniscient narrator enters the minds of Richie, the 11-year-old bully; Dud Rogers, the town dump custodian who was obsessed with rats; and the school bus driver, Charlie Rhodes, who runs his bus with an iron fist. This character-building technique creates a "real" place, a perfect canvas where the supernatural can then be painted and believed. King seduces his audience into believing that Jerusalem's Lot is a real place on a map, with real people living quite ordinary lives. Once you believe that Father Callahan is an alcoholic and that Mark Petrie builds models of Frankenstein as a hobby, then the appearance of vampires becomes real as well. In fact, the vampires do not directly appear until well into the book. Barlow's name is not mentioned until chapter 4, and the old vampire doesn't appear until chapter 10. By that time, the reader is fully invested in the belief that 'Salem's Lot exists, and so anything within it must also exist. The reader has "suspended disbelief" and is now convinced that vampires live in the Lot.

Archetypes

Shirley Jackson's *The Haunting of Hill House* is what English professors call the "objective correlative" for the novel. That's a fancy name for saying the book was inspired by and based on the concept of Jackson's novel. The idea is based on the concept of the "evil place," which serves as a breeding ground for evil entities, such as vampires in this case, which are naturally attracted to places like 'Salem's Lot.

Of course, Bram Stoker's *Dracula*, the classic vampire novel, is also an archetype for the book. *Dracula* basically set up all the rules for the vampire myth, rules that can either be followed or, as later authors did, intentionally broken according to the dictates of their particular universe. Stoker brought vampire legends into popular culture and made them familiar to just about everyone on the planet, thereby setting up the subgenre of the vampire story that has become a mainstay of horror fiction. King's contribution takes the vampire from the old world of Gothic castles into the new world of a small, American town.

Themes and Subtexts

As a Constant Reader, I see *'Salem's Lot* as an exciting vampire story with some likable (and some unlikable) characters struggling to defeat evil. The book has enough suspense to keep me turning the pages, wondering who is going to live and who will be turned into the undead. But as an English professor, I see this novel as more than just the transportation of the Gothic tradition to the New World. In addition to this being an entertaining story suitable for a fun read on a summer afternoon, I see lots of things going on just beneath the surface of the pond, so to speak.

One of the things I do as a professor is place this book in the context of the time it was written. When I originally read the novel in the late 1970s, it was contemporary fiction. Now, over 45 years later, this novel displays a slice of history, and this history influences its meaning.

'Salem's Lot was written between 1972 and 1975 during a time of corruption in American politics, including Richard Nixon and the Watergate controversy, and the book reflects this theme in the microcosm of a small Maine town. During the 1970s, it seemed like corruption and decay were everywhere, from the war in Vietnam to political scandals on the daily news. 'Salem's Lot offers a microcosm of that decay as it presents a corrupt town that is destroyed from within by an outside evil that silently enters into its body like a plague.

The creation of real characters with real sins helps to make the story believable, as I've said, but in this case, they also contribute to the meaning of the novel. The corruption that had pervaded American politics is shown to exist even in the smallest, most mundane New England town. Small-town life and corruption infects everyone, even everyday people. The priest is a drunk; Bonny Sawyer is having an illicit affair with a much younger man; and Lawrence Crockett, the town's insurance real estate agent, is a cheat and reads books with titles such as *Satan's Sex Slaves*. All these characters offer a peek into the corruption of the 1970s and the secrets that everyday people hold close. Every character in the book has demons, great or small. Ben has the guilty memories of his wife's death, George Middler has to keep his secret in a time and place where homosexuality was not accepted (even though the entire town knows), and Sandy McDougal is physically abusive of her child. Even Mark Petrie secretly builds monster models. This theme depicts a corrupt town, a corrupt state, a corrupt nation, and even a corrupt world capable of harboring vampires for centuries.

Theme is often misunderstood as "the moral of the story." Fairy tales have morals and novels have themes. A theme is much more complex and multilayered than a moral and sometimes even contradicts itself. One school of criticism, the deconstructionists, says that language always contradicts itself because of its fluid nature. For example, the word "love" describes the way I feel about my wife, my sons, my dog, my job, the work of Stephen King, and shrimp cocktail, to name just a few objects of my affection. So if I can't make my meaning clear with a simple word, how can writers expect to write a story that specifically expresses their meaning? Therefore, stories may have multiple themes, and each of these themes may be interpreted in more than one way. Such is the case with Stephen King's novels.

Religion is a fairly consistent theme in King's books. As mentioned in the previous chapter, it plays a role in *Carrie*. It appears again in *'Salem's Lot* only with a different interpretation as King looks at all of the different facets of religion in his books.

'Salem's Lot pits good against evil, with good involving the trappings of religion and evil involving undead vampires. There are no religious fanatics in this novel as in *Carrie*, but there are believers and doubters, and these two groups do not fall into the usual stereotypes. It is more a matter of faith than it is of position. The priest, for example, lacks the faith necessary to defeat Barlow. His crucifix, sanctioned by the power of the church, is easily destroyed by the vampire once he causes Father Callahan to question his own faith. Yet the makeshift plastic cross protects Mark (who isn't even Catholic) because he doesn't allow doubt to enter his thinking. Whereas religion is a major destructive force in *Carrie*, faith becomes the means of salvation in *'Salem's Lot* and the only way of defeating evil. Since King has expressed his belief in God but has been openly critical of organized religion, this scene effectively articulates this philosophy of personal faith.

One last theme I'd like to discuss is the idea of the "evil place," which crops up in so much of King's fiction and which I will examine in more depth in the chapter on *The Shining*. Suffice it to say that King has personified this idea in the town of Jerusalem's Lot in general and the Marsten House in particular. According to this theme, there are evil places that exist on the earth—these places may have something to do with King's concept of the multiverse, which he presents most clearly in the Dark Tower books and which I will also examine in later chapters. In King's multiverse, there are places where worlds touch, leading to either evil places or portals between the worlds, and some places are magnets for the attraction of evil.

'Salem's Lot serves as another example of a horror novel that reaches well beyond the strict genre of horror. Despite its use of the traditional vampire trope, this novel is about much more than vampires, as it highlights the demons and sins that exist within us all and how simple it is to succumb to our baser desires or have them exploited by an even greater evil.

Evaluation

'Salem's Lot made a major contribution to the horror genre by taking Old World vampires out of Victorian Europe and transporting them into a small American town. The unspoken message is that if this type of evil can exist in a tiny, remote place like the Lot, then it can exist anywhere

and therefore no one is safe. Small towns are notorious for knowing the most intimate details of everyone's lives, and King documents this gossip in the novel. The fact that such a nefarious evil as vampirism could go undetected, spread, and take over the town magnifies the horror. While the novel owes much to the Gothic tradition, it does convey terror directly into the mundane world of the average American citizen, which makes 'Salem's Lot an important book in the weird tale canon.

Interesting Fact

The title of the book was changed from *The Second Coming* because King's wife Tabitha felt that it might be subject to sexual innuendos and *Jerusalem's Lot* contained religious overtones.

Notable Quote

"The town kept its secrets, and the Marsten House brooded over it like a ruined King."

3

Rage

Getting It on in the Schools

Background

Rage is perhaps the least known of all of Stephen King's novels, not only because it was the first book published under the Richard Bachman pen name (1977) but because it was intentionally allowed to go out of print and is the only King book that remains out of print. I happen to own a beat-up Signet paperback version of *The Bachman Books* from the 1986 printing as well as the 1994 French edition *Rage: À l'école de l'enfer* that I keep meaning to read to practice my French foreign-language proficiency, which I had to demonstrate in graduate school before they'd give me those coveted letters *P*, *H*, and *D* after my name. The book, originally titled *Getting It On*, was written in 1966, while King was a senior in high school, and rediscovered and rewritten in 1970–71.

In the preface to *The Bachman Books*, King explains why he adopted the pen name, so I won't rehash his reasoning here. The books written under the pseudonym are different from the typical King novel. They were released as paperback originals ("just plain books," according to King, who wanted his alter ego to "keep a low profile"). The Bachman books are distinctive in their subject and style as well and do not fit within the horror genre that is part of King's brand name. *Rage* is a mainstream psychological crime novel, if one were forced to place it in a category, and both *The Long Walk* and *The Running Man* fit into the science fiction/dystopia category, while *Roadwork* is another psychological study of a man who holds himself hostage to prevent his house from being destroyed to make way for a new highway. In these novels, King was able to explore different genres without damaging his "brand." As paperback originals, these novels were not meant to be taken too seriously. They are much shorter than the massive tomes that King would become famous for, are "grittier," and their themes are more immediately accessible. Each of the Bachman books will be discussed in later chapters of this volume.

The fact that *Rage* is out of print is not a great loss for the literary community by any stretch of the imagination. Although it has been linked with some school shootings, I have no doubt that without the existence of the book, the crimes would have occurred anyway with the shooters using something else as their "inspiration." Still, as an educator myself, I can understand King's point of view, and both he and his publisher have put financial considerations aside and taken direct action to address the problem of violence in the schools.

Because *Rage* is not easily accessible to the Constant Reader and because it is not one of King's best novels, this chapter will be brief. However, there are some things about this book that are worthy of mention.

Summary and Narrative Devices

Rage is the story of Charles Decker, a troubled high school student who loses control and attacks and nearly kills a science teacher; he is allowed to return to school until the completion of his psychiatric report. Then, after more than a week, he is called into the principal's office to face the consequences, which in a "progressive school" include counseling. This is when Charlie "gets it on," storming out of the office, retrieving a pistol from his locker, and returning to his classroom where he shoots and kills his math teacher and a history teacher before holding the class hostage. Charlie then conducts what may be thought of as a "therapy session" in the class before he is finally wounded by the police and eventually sentenced to a mental hospital.

The novel is told from the point of view of a violent and mentally ill narrator and does offer a window into the thinking of a "disturbed" student. It is told in a fairly straightforward style, with Charlie recounting the story after the fact from the psychiatric hospital to which he has been sent. Although the narrator seems to be what English professors call "reliable" (believable) in that he is telling the truth as he sees it, it must be remembered that Charlie's truth, while enlightening from a psychological standpoint, does reflect a warped view on life. Once the story begins, it is told in a chronological manner from the morning of the shooting until the end, with Charlie's flashback memories filling in the backstory of how he arrived at the mental state he is in.

Archetypes

Rage was written before Columbine and before school shootings became a terrible and widespread phenomenon in American culture; however, the deadly shooting at the University of Texas occurred in August

1966, around the time King was writing *Rage*. This tragedy resulted in 18 fatalities. In November of the same year, five students at the Rose-Mar College of Beauty were taken hostage and killed in Mesa, Arizona. These events may have been the real-world archetypes for the novel, which King, then a high school student, rewrote from a fictional perspective.

Themes and Subtexts

Reading *Rage* as an English professor, I tend to look at the book from an educational point of view rather than that of a literary critic. It must be remembered that this novel was originally written while King was still a high school student and far from at the height of his literary prowess. As an educator, however, I find the book to be frightening on a personal level and as an example of how not to deal with mentally disturbed students on a professional level. Charlie's ability to terrorize a high school is enabled in many aspects. First, his father's abuses fuel Charlie's rage and his leaving a gun and ammo in a place where his son can take it directly leads to the violent behavior. When Charlie first attacked a teacher with a pipe wrench, nearly killing him, he should immediately have been isolated as a threat to himself and others. The confrontation with the principal goes terribly wrong; the school's leader is clearly not able to handle the situation, and Charlie is allowed to leave the office and wander back to his locker and to class without any supervision whatsoever. Recognizing his violent state, the school administration, again, should have had him removed from the school grounds.

The first part of the book is, thus, a clinic on what NOT to do with a mentally disturbed and violent student, and that is where I see its major value. The second half, after Charlie takes his class hostage, is far less realistic, as the students settle down and take part in a sort of group therapy session. As we have seen in actual school shootings, students react with panic and chaos, and I don't see them reacting the way they do in this novel, with two dead teachers in the classroom. Although the book does highlight the issues of being a high school student in America (at least in the 1970s), these themes could have been more realistically addressed without the artificial hostage situation. From a Constant Reader's point of view, unless you have read and reread everything else King has published, I wouldn't spend much money or effort tracking down this out-of-print novel.

Human Universals

While "Constant Readers" hopefully would not fully understand what would cause someone to murder innocent people, the novel does reflect the human universal trait of "rage." This emotion, if unchecked, can lead to tragic results and can be triggered by events experienced in the real world. Crimes of passion are just one example. In his book *Why We Snap*, neuroscientist R. Douglas Fields identifies nine triggers that can unleash the rage circuit in the human brain, which he labels LIFEMORTS (life or limb, insult, family, environment or territory, mate, order in society, resources, tribe or society, and stopped). In King's novel, Charlie, mentally ill to begin with, is triggered by insult, a common-enough issue among adolescents.

Evaluation

Modern American literature will not suffer any ill effects because *Rage* is out of print. It is an early work of King's, interesting in that it does show his development and growth as an author from this attempt, which suffers major flaws (especially the second half of the book, where students engage in a lively debate with their kidnapper). And one can argue the merits of King's self-censorship. The novel's value is best realized by scholars: mental health professionals, who can gain some insight into the workings of the teenage mind (King was in high school when he wrote the original draft), and literary scholars who can examine how King's work matured from this early effort to his more mature works.

Interesting Fact

From 1988 to 1997, five school shootings seem to have been "inspired" by *Rage*, including one in 1993 where a student killed his English teacher because he was upset that she had given him a C grade on his essay about King's novel. These incidents caused King and his publisher to allow *Rage* to go out of print.

Notable Quote

"American kids labor under a huge life of violence, both real and make-believe."

4

The Shining
Iconic Horror

Background

When the name "Stephen King" is mentioned, *The Shining* immediately comes to mind. This story of the Overlook Hotel has become enmeshed in popular culture. Originally published in 1977, it was made most famous by Stanley Kubrick's 1980 film (which King has criticized for decades now). It was adapted into a miniseries in 1997, there is a Shining board game, and even coronavirus protective masks created with the pattern from the iconic orange-and-red carpet from the Overlook Hotel in the Kubrick film adaptation.

Personally, *The Shining* was the first King novel that I read when it was released in paperback. I'd read *Nightshift*, his short story collection, and became an immediate "Constant Reader"; I was working in a factory at the time and was five years away from enrolling in graduate school, so I read this book just for fun, and I have to say it is one of the few horror novels that really scared me (the moving animal hedges gave me wonderful nightmares).

Summary and Narrative Devices

The plot of *The Shining* is, of course, very well known, though most of America is more familiar with Kubrick's film adaptation than they are with the book. This is basically a version of the haunted house story, only the house is a secluded hotel in the mountains of Colorado, and the family that lives there for the winter can't leave because of the bad weather and the fact that the main character, Jack Torrance, has been hired to take care of the place until it reopens in the spring. His son, Danny, has a psychic ability called "The Shine" that allows him to see into others' minds and see things that others can't.

The concept of psychic abilities is a common thread in King's books, beginning with *Carrie*, of course, and he uses this as a plot device to explore themes that can't quite be reached by traditional mainstream narrative. As a narrative device, it allows readers to speculate about what-if scenarios. Speculative fiction (horror, science fiction, and fantasy) makes excellent vehicles for authors to investigate ideas that are beyond the scope of "literary fiction" in that they enable authors to place their characters into a laboratory, of sorts, and show what might happen to them. These stories can look at philosophical and psychological issues in a unique way that stretches normal boundaries by tapping into the imagination and making the impossible seem real. Thus, in a story like *The Shining*, we can imagine what it might be like to be able to see into other realms and to experience psychic phenomenon through the character of a young boy.

Perhaps the most important narrative device that King uses in *The Shining* (and in all his books, for that matter) is the development of very realistic characters that are placed in extreme situations. Although King is adamant that in fiction "story is boss," in his nonfiction book *On Writing*, he speaks about the importance of characters being more than just game pieces on a board but as realistic, breathing characters that are changed by the things that happen to them. Unlike the predictable characters in a teenage slasher film who merely play the parts of victims and survivors, King's characters (even many of the minor ones) are individuals whose strengths and flaws play a role in what happens to them and who are what English professors call "dynamic characters"—in other words, characters that change, evolve, and grow throughout the story.

The Shining features the character of Jack Torrance, a man who has a "tragic flaw" that brings about his downfall, and the destruction of his family unit. The tragic flaw is a device that has been used from the very first narratives known to us, from the ancient Mesopotamian tale of Gilgamesh to American classics such as *The Great Gatsby* and *Moby Dick*. From the pride of Oedipus to the indecision of Hamlet, to the stubbornness of Ahab, human flaws have been the cause of characters' misery throughout the worlds of literature.

In the Kubrick film version, Jack Torrance is presented as mentally deranged and inherently violent, the personification of insane evil. The novel, however, depicts a much more human and realistic character (which is one of the reasons that King dislikes the film adaptation). Jack is a flawed individual, but he is far from evil. He suffers from an addictive personality and is especially susceptible to alcohol use disorder (AUD), which is a broad clinical term that describes someone whose alcohol use results in health issues, either mental or physical. Whether Jack is an "alcoholic" or not is irrelevant—his dependency on alcohol directly leads to his emotional and mental problems, including his violence toward his son and a student, which is part of the backstory of the novel. The closed environment of the Overlook Hotel, which Jack had hoped would help with his drinking, only magnifies the problem.

Of course, it is well known that Stephen King suffered from overuse of alcohol and drugs to the point of having his family intervene and make sure he received help. In fact, King has said that Jack Torrance is a reflection of himself during the time he was writing *The Shining*. There is no indication that King experienced any violent or overt psychological effects. (In fact, he attended several different conventions, such as Necon and the World Fantasy Convention during this time, where I observed that he was genial, coherent, and eloquent, though he usually did have a beer in hand.) However, King is perfectly aware of the perils of addiction and takes these dangers to the extreme in creating Jack's character. It is obvious that Jack's alcohol use ultimately led to his downfall, and his addictive personality was the tragic flaw that led to his death, the destruction of the Overlook, and the tragedy of his family.

Another flaw in Jack's personality is his lack of work ethic, and that also contributes greatly to his downfall. As any author will testify, writing demands discipline and dedication and is, frankly, hard work. As Edison is claimed to have said, "Genius is 1 percent inspiration and 99 percent perspiration," and that is true for writing. Jack, even though he may have a talent for stories, lacks the willpower and work ethic to follow up. He has published a few short stories, which brought him notoriety and landed him a job teaching writing, but he does not have the motivation to write a novel, and although he has an idea for a play and does begin writing it, his discipline is not strong enough to finish the work. Instead, he falls into the trap of researching instead of writing and allows the Overlook to highjack whatever productivity he has and turns it into an obsession with the hotel itself. Whereas the film version depicts Torrance endlessly writing—"All work and no play make Jack a dull boy"—the novel shows him turning his attention to writing a history of the hotel, and instead of writing even that, he makes the mistake that many writers make and buries himself in research without actually putting words on the paper.

Archetypes

The Shining represents the Gothic haunted house tradition that has been transplanted to modern America. As such, it finds its roots in Hawthorne's *The House of the Seven Gables* (1851), which noted horror writer H.P. Lovecraft called "New England's greatest contribution to weird literature" in his essay "Supernatural Horror in Literature." The novel was the archetype for several of Lovecraft's works, including "The Case of Charles Dexter Ward." Trapping Jack and his family in the Overlook puts this novel firmly in the "Monster in the House" subgenre, as explained by Jessica Brody in *Save the Cat! Writes a Novel*.

King consistently employs the device of the "evil place" in his fiction, and *The Shining* is a perfect example of this. The evil place tradition has been the basis for much of horror fiction's tropes since Hawthorne, including Shirley Jackson's *Haunting of Hill House*, Daphne du Maurier's *Rebecca*, and Henry James's *The Turn of the Screw*, to name just three examples.

Themes and Subtexts

Two of the subtexts and themes of *The Shining* are derived directly from Jack's tragic flaws: his alcohol use and his poor work ethic. The substance abuse theme fictionally documents the disastrous effects of alcohol and drugs on families. While the novel uses supernatural elements to magnify the consequences, the story accurately depicts many of the effects of addiction in the real world. Domestic violence is often triggered by alcohol and drugs, and Jack is guilty of this long before his involvement with the Overlook. Alcohol often causes problems at work as well, and in Jack's case it leads to his losing his job and results in his failure to be a productive writer. And there is always the dangers of a DUI; Jack and his colleague crash into a bicycle while under the influence and feel fortunate that they hadn't killed a child.

Jack's other tragic flaw, his poor work ethic, also becomes a theme in this novel. Throughout the history of literature, writing (or producing creative work of any kind) equates to life itself. This is most obvious in *The 1001 Nights* stories where Scheherazade must entertain the king with a story every night in order to stay alive. This theme expresses the idea that creativity and storytelling is an important part of the human condition. In fact, evolutionary biologists like Brian Boyd have called the human species "The Storytelling Animal" and have made reasonable claims that the ability to tell stories and create narrative with language has benefited the survival of *Homo sapiens*. Think of the Paleolithic hunting expedition that went wrong, and the survivors' ability to convey what happened so that whatever mistakes were made wouldn't recur.

For Jack, writing also means life. His writing is critical to his ability to obtain and maintain a teaching position. More important perhaps, Jack's writing is key to his mental health. As King has said, "Life isn't a support system for art. It's the other way around." This theme reappears in a number of King's other works. Many of his characters are writers, artists, musicians—in other words, artistic and creative people. In his books with author protagonists, their writing and creative ability often determine their survival, as I will discuss in later chapters (*Misery* is the most obvious example). King believes (as do evolutionary biologists) that creativity is essential to human happiness and survival, and Jack exemplifies what happens when an artist fails to pursue the art. Creativity is important to mental health, and Jack's health suffers greatly when he is unable to write. Our desire to create and leave something behind is the foundation of a human work ethic, whether we are creating engines or epics. Taking work away from people leads to depression, economic hardship, and a feeling of helplessness, which may open the door for what we might think of as "evil." This is one explanation for higher crime rates among impoverished people. As for Jack, his lack of focus on finishing his play results in his being open to assault by the hotel, the "evil place."

The evil place is another theme in *The Shining*, a theme we have already visited in *'Salem's Lot*. According to this idea, there are certain places where evil forces congregate, and although this may be an overused trope for the haunted house story, King handles it creatively in *The Shining*. He makes sure that the protagonists cannot escape the clutches of the hotel by having them isolated from the rest of the world by bad weather and Jack's obsessions. He also makes the terror much more real by using Danny Torrance as a protagonist, a child with a special gift called "The Shine."

As we have seen in *Carrie* and will see in several other novels, psychic abilities are a mainstay of the King universe. Sometimes they are destructive, but in this case Danny's ability ultimately saves him, allowing him to connect with his future self, who tries to warn him, and with Halloran, who rescues him. In the sequel, *Doctor Sleep*, King will return to Danny and once again explore both the benefits and the curse of "The Shine."

Human Universals

Although Jack seems to be the target of the Overlook Hotel, its true intended victim is Danny, a child who has "The Shine." As such, the novel taps into the human universal trait of what the neuroscientist Jaak Panksepp terms "CARE," the desire to care for and protect children. King creates a very lovable character in Danny, a character interesting enough to warrant a sequel (*Doctor Sleep*) and one that is a memorable part of popular culture. The boy's innocence and vulnerability strike a chord with readers who fear for the boy's life and root for him to overcome the horrors presented by both his father and the hotel. In the novel, his mother Wendy is depicted as a strong, resourceful woman who fights bitterly to save herself and her child and who stands up to her husband when it becomes clear he is unhinged (one of King's criticisms of Kubrick's film adaptation is the weakened character of Wendy). This instinct to protect a child represents an evolutionary adaptation of the human species, where offspring are dependent on parents for the first decade of their life and beyond. This makes it easy for the Constant Reader to relate to the situation and develop a genuine fear for Danny's welfare.

Of course, another of Panksepp's human universal emotions, FEAR, forms the basis for most of King's stories and for the horror genre itself. Humans are programmed with fear in their DNA, and thus we are born with an innate terror of the dark, snakes, spiders, heights ... the list goes on. Our primary fear, however, is the unknown in its many forms, and King exploits this in *The Shining*, which is generally considered one of the scariest books ever written. Every room of the hotel has its secret and horrific surprise. Even its garden with attractive hedge animals proves to be a source of terror. The question can be asked, of course, of why anyone would purposely subject themselves to the uncomfortable situation of experiencing something that would terrify them. Although the answer is a bit complicated, there is no doubt that humans love to be frightened, provided the fear is in a controlled setting—hence, the popularity of thrill rides, Halloween haunted houses, and horror fiction and films. Mathias Clausen explores this phenomenon in detail from a psychological perspective in *Why Horror Seduces*, as does S.A. Bradley in *Screaming for Pleasure*. The bottom line, I believe, is that we are preprogrammed to experience adventure and fear, and yet the life of the average American is (thankfully) quite mundane. Despite news reports of violence and bloodshed, the average person is unlikely to experience horror on a daily basis, unlike our ancestors who had to battle Smilodon and other predators. So we exercise our fear muscles, so to speak, with artificial horrors. We can enjoy these fears because we know that they aren't really life threatening. If we become too frightened at a horror movie, we can close our eyes and it will go away, and we know that the roller-coaster ride is a short one that won't end with death. Stephen King has successfully exploited our instinctive fears in his horror novels, and *The Shining* is, according to many Constant Readers, the most successful of them all.

Evaluation

The Shining is generally considered one of the best horror novels of all time, and as an English professor, I concur. The novel does activate

4. The Shining

the human universal emotion of fear in a way that few stories can. Unlike much horror fiction, it realistically gives the characters a legitimate reason to put themselves in an evil place, and the setting ensures that there is no easy means of escape. Furthermore, the characters are richly drawn and believable, memorable enough to have become embedded in popular culture. The Overlook Hotel, itself a "character," has become iconic, a symbol of the complexity of evil in the modern world.

However, I believe *The Shining* transcends the horror genre and has become a classic American novel. I say this because the novel, while exploiting fear, uses the supernatural to reveal larger universal themes that the average Constant Reader can relate to. The book explores the difficult topics of addiction, abuse, and mental health in a subtle but powerful way that reveals truths without hammering them home. It is, I believe, one of King's best books, and even though it's impossible for me to pick a favorite, I would easily rank it in the top five.

Interesting Fact

The blood in the bloody elevator scene was real animal blood, and Kubrick told the Motion Picture Association it was "rusty water." The MPAA believed the lie.

Iconic Moment

From the film version, Jack Nicholson smashing into the hotel room with an axe and shouting, "Here's Johnny!"

Notable Quote

"redrum"

5

The Stand

The Modern Plague

Background

The Stand was first published in 1978, with extensive cuts from the publisher to make the book more palatable to the reading public despite King's objections to the cuts. In 1990, once King had become a true "brand name" with a worldwide readership of millions, the "complete and uncut" edition was released, with the setting moved ahead ten years and the original material restored. As a Constant Reader who read the original version in 1978, I'm placing this chapter before *The Dead Zone*. *The Stand* is considered one of Stephen King's best, both by readers and by critics, and is said by many to have forecast both the AIDS epidemic, and the Covid-19 pandemic. It was filmed as a miniseries for ABC in 1994 and for CBS All-Access in 2020.

Summary and Narrative Devices

For all practical purposes, *The Stand* is a trilogy packed into a single volume and the uncut version could probably have been released as three separate books in a series. King has said that he was looking to write a modern epic in the tradition of Tolkien's *Lord of the Rings* trilogy.

Part 1 of *The Stand* recounts the apocalyptic story of a superflu, Captain Tripps, that wipes out over 99 percent of the world's population. In this section, the Constant Reader is introduced to the complex cast of characters, random survivors of the disease, and how they endure the initial shock and horror to pick up the pieces and rebuild society. For the most part, the survivors are normal, everyday people without any special talents or powers. Stu Redman is the embodiment of "everyman" and Fran Goldstein, "everywoman." Some of the survivors, like Nick Andros,

5. The Stand

a deaf-mute, and Tom Cullen, a lovable mentally challenged individual, are characters who would be considered disabled, yet they become heroes. Some of the survivors are much more sinister, like Lloyd Heinreid, a mass murderer, and a pyromaniac known as "The Trashcan Man."

In the second part of the book, each of the characters receives a "call to action" in their dreams, either music and a vision from the saintlike Mother Abigail or in promises of wealth and power from the demonic Randall Flagg. The characters choose a side and begin their journeys to join one of the sides, either Mother Abigail on the "high ground" of Boulder, Colorado, or Flagg on the "low ground" of Las Vegas, "Sin City." This section traces the hero's journey of each character to their destination and introduces the love triangle between Stu and Fran and the jealous Harold Lauder.

In the last third of the book, the two camps, "good" and "evil," engage in a showdown where only one of the two societies can survive. In one of King's most widely used conventions, evil is destroyed by the purifying element of fire—though the ending indicates that Randall Flagg resurfaces again in a different multiverse.

An entire book could be written on just *The Stand* (and they have; see the section on suggested reading). From an English professor's point of view, this epic novel is a success both in terms of its story and in its richness of meaning. King uses effective plot devices and detailed characterization to move the story forward, and although some may have criticized the ending as being too contrived, it is a satisfying resolution that achieves closure, and the reader is satisfied that justice has prevailed.

The major plot device of the story is the interweaving of the "hero's journey" of several of the major characters, a device described by Joseph Campbell in *The Hero with a Thousand Faces*. This hero's quest archetype has been around since the very first recorded narratives, including the *Epic of Gilgamesh* from ancient Mesopotamia ca. 2000 BCE, and is a mainstay of Hollywood blockbuster films such as the *Star Wars* franchise and world classics such as *The Odyssey*. In his study, Campbell identifies a very distinct formula for the hero's quest story, with the protagonist passing through most or all the steps. The hero's quest follows a three-act structure: separation from his home, entry into a source of power, and regenerating return. The hero passed through a number of steps during these three acts. Larry Underwood, Stu Redman, Fran Goldstein, and the team of Nick and Tom all pass through the stages. I will use the character of Stu Redman to illustrate this idea.

The hero begins his journey by going about his or her various activities and then facing a "call to action" that requires leaving home. For Stu, this occurs when he is taken away to a government facility where he faces another "call to action"—to escape from what he sees as a prison. He passed through the next step, "refusal of the call," and decides to wait to see what will happen, but eventually he acts, with the help of "outside aid" (sometimes supernatural). He "crosses the first threshold" by escaping his cell and finds himself in "the belly of the whale," deep inside the compound.

The second act begins when he escapes from his situation and faces a "road of trials," which eventually brings him to a "meeting with the goddess," Mother Abigail. Often the sequence is repeated, and it reoccurs for Stu when he knows he must go to Las Vegas (another call to action), followed by "woman as temptress" when Fran begs him not to go. He accepts the quest, undergoes another road of trials, and when he is injured badly and can't go on, he finds "atonement with the father" and makes peace with his own death. As a result, he reaches an apotheosis, a deep understanding of life. Finally, he achieves the "ultimate boon" when he witnesses the nuclear explosion that destroys Las Vegas.

Finally, in act 3, when he has resigned himself to his own death (the "refusal of the return"), he experiences the "magic flight," where he is rescued by Tom Cullen with the supernatural aid of Nick Andros. After "crossing the return threshold" (his arduous journey home), he becomes the "master of two worlds" and is granted the "freedom to live" by moving back to Maine.

This hero's quest can also be found in the stories of the other characters, and once you start looking, you will see versions of it in films, books, and drama. As Campbell suggests, it is a staple of narrative and can be seen as the driving source for stories ranging from the legends of King Arthur and *Beowulf* to modern works such as *Star Wars* and the universe of *The Walking Dead*. People enjoy reading about heroes overcoming obstacles, and that pleasure is not about to go away as long as the human race exists.

One of the strengths of *The Stand* is the realism of the characters. Each person exhibits great depth and complexity as King brings us into their backstories and shows how the protagonists all grow into their roles as heroes. Tom Cullen, for example, is more than just a cliché of a mentally challenged individual. His unique character is both endearing (as when he plays with toys that Nick finds for him), memorable ("M-O-O-N" spells everything), and heroic as he risks all for the benefit of his friends. Despite his lack of intellect, he is not fooled into joining Randall Flagg, and he, in fact, outwits the "Walking Dude" to escape and rescue Stan.

As is often the case in the hero's quest, the villains are just as interesting as the heroes (think Darth Vader, Dracula, and the great white shark in *Jaws*, for example). King gets into the mind of the Trashcan Man as he blows up enormous oil tanks, while revealing his unfortunate past of abuse and untreated mental illness. Lloyd is also portrayed as almost sympathetic, though he has a history of murder. Underneath this exterior is a man looking for acceptance. King's "bad guys" are three dimensional and have motivations for doing the things they do.

Finally, Randall Flagg is the ultimate symbol of evil and chaos as he reappears in several of King's novels, including the Dark Tower series. He is the ultimate "trickster" figure, an archetypical character that appears as the serpent in Genesis, the Joker in the Batman series, and of course, Pennywise the Dancing Clown in *It*. Trickster figures have long been a part of narrative and mythology and illustrate both the dark side of human nature and, in some cases, our secret fantasy to live on the dark side, as evidenced by the attraction of dressing up for Halloween, a practice that both children and adults enjoy. Popular adult costumes such as the rogue pirate, the sexy nurse, and the evil demon allow us to play the role of the dark side for one night a year without violating any moral or ethical codes. Flagg embodies many of the trickster figures from mythology in his ability to change his shape, move freely to any place in the world in an instant, and to use deception and violence to attract followers and overcome enemies.

Archetypes

As I discussed in the previous section, King uses the archetype of the hero's journey to structure the story and the trickster figure as the villain. But *The Stand* also owes its inspiration to the long line of apocalyptic fiction that preceded it. Michael Crichton's *The Andromeda Strain* (1969) imagines an alien microorganism that finds its way to earth by piggybacking on a military satellite designed to capture bacteria for possible germ warfare. Las Vegas also plays an important role in Crichton's story.

Themes and Subtexts

The most obvious theme in *The Stand* is King's distrust of the government. As a product of the 1960s, King was involved in protests against the war in Vietnam, the civil rights movement, and the ideas of equal rights and free speech. He also experienced the tarnishing of the office of the president, from the beloved John F. Kennedy to the scandals of Watergate and the Nixon years. This distrust of the government remained with him throughout his career and can also be acknowledged in most of his books, from *The Dead Zone*, where a presidential candidate will destroy the world if not stopped, to his many books depicting "The Shop," a secret government organization that will violate any human right in order to achieve its objectives (*Firestarter, The Golden Years*, etc.).

In *The Stand*, King suggests the very realistic scenario that governments may be engaging in the creation of deadly pathogens to be released as weapons and anticipates what might happen if they were released into the population through accident or negligence (again, a very realistic scenario, especially in light of the Covid-19 pandemic). This novel warns us not only to be mistrustful of governments but is also a cautionary tale of what disaster might result not just from abuse of power but by engaging in research and projects that have inherent risks to humanity at large. King has never kept any secrets about his politics, and his warnings about corrupt or inept governments have become louder than ever. This is a theme that American readers can relate to as evidenced by the continued impact of books such as Orwell's *1984* and *Animal Farm* and Huxley's *Brave New World*.

Another major theme of *The Stand* concerns the fragility of life, a concept that has become even more significant as a result of the Covid-19 pandemic, which has taken hundreds of thousands of American lives and created a new reality in a very short time. King's novel is an exaggerated but not unrealistic version of a worldwide pandemic that symbolizes an event over which we have no control that can end our lives or change them dramatically. The superflu that King creates in his universe is based more on chaos theory than logic in that it seems to kill randomly rather than with a specific purpose. There is no way of preventing it and no cure. It seems to follow no known scientific law in determining who lives or dies, and therefore, there is nothing any of the characters can do to avoid it.

This disease is symbolic of the random acts that we have no control over that influence our lives. As King has said in several of his books, "Life turns on a dime," and *The Stand* illustrates this quite graphically. This book reminds us that there are things beyond our control that just seem to happen. Many of these events are deadly or life changing and we must be aware of these possibilities. Indeed, King's near death after being run over by a minivan in 1999 wound up being such an event. The message, if there is one, is to take nothing for granted and, by extrapolation, to make the most of our lives. The survivors of the superflu continue to live, to strive, and to accept and adapt to the terrible changes that have occurred in their world.

Perhaps the most important subtext of *The Stand* is its denial of social Darwinism. In simple terms, social Darwinism claims that people achieve their success based on the "survival of the fittest" in human society so that those who are stronger, more talented, and genetically "better" outperform the rest of us. This view has provided pseudoscientific support for racism, among other evils, and has been disproved by evolutionary biologists and the human genome project, which shows that all humans share the same genetic makeup in their DNA and that cultural differences in areas of the world are largely based on the randomness of geography during prehistoric times (a concept that is the thesis of Jared Diamond's fascinating book *Guns, Germs, and Steel: The Fates of Human Societies*). No one is exempt from becoming a victim of Captain Tripps: it brings down rich and poor alike and saves both professors and deaf-mutes without any logic. Nature, indeed, does not distinguish between the social classes in this novel.

Human Universals

While showing the fallacy of social Darwinism, *The Stand* does demonstrate the value of cooperation and altruism. The whole idea of why people are altruistic has been the subject of discussion by evolutionary biologists for decades. According to a strict interpretation of Darwin's theory, the strongest individual should rise to the top, yet we find that when people are less selfish and more cooperative, they form groups and cooperate. E.O. Wilson and other evolutionary biologists have therefore concluded that a group of cooperative individuals will outperform a group of selfish individuals every time, a conclusion that has also been demonstrated in game theory. The two groups in *The Stand* represent the extremes of altruism. On the one hand, we have Randall Flagg, who puts his selfish interests first and rules by fear and intimidation; on the other hand, Mother Abigail's group consists of altruistic, cooperative individuals who will work for the common good. In fact, they will—and do—sacrifice their individual lives for the cause. According to science, the cooperative group will win, and in *The Stand*, they do.

Evaluation

Although *The Stand* is a good read and a favorite among Constant Readers, it is much more than just another book about the apocalypse. It resonates with readers on many levels, not only as a good story but also as a complex book that forces us to look at and understand the world in a different way. As an English professor, I believe it to be one of the most compelling and well-crafted books in modern American literature, a book that is worth close reading and in-depth study.

Interesting Fact

In March 2020, near the beginning of the Covid-19 pandemic, Stephen King released a copy of the audio file of chapter 8 of *The Stand*, which graphically describes the way contagious disease can spread throughout society.

Notable Quote

"No one can tell what goes on between the person you were and the person you become."

6

The Long Walk

Dystopian Nightmare

Background

The Long Walk was written in 1966–67 when Stephen King was a first-year student at the University of Maine at Orono. After it was rejected, he filed it away until January 1, 1979, when it was published under the pen name Richard Bachman. Once it was found out that Bachman was in fact Stephen King, the novel was collected in *The Bachman Books* in 1985.

Summary and Narrative Devices

The Long Walk is a dystopian novel set in an alternate world where America lost World War II after suffering from a German air blitz off the East Coast. Much like Suzanne Collins's highly successful *The Hunger Games* (2008), the authoritarian government of this alternate world uses an annual "game" to both entertain the populace and remind them of the ultimate power of the government over life and death. In this game, dubbed "The Long Walk," 100 teenage boys are chosen and assemble at a starting point in northern Maine and walk south on a predetermined route until only one is left standing, and that boy is declared the winner and has all his wishes granted. The catch, of course, is that the losers don't just drop out of the walk but are killed by soldiers who follow along and shoot anyone who doesn't keep up a four-mile-an-hour pace. Two warnings are given, and the third warning is a bullet.

While the novel is narrated in a straightforward chronological way, King does use some interesting plot devices. The outcome of the story is obvious from the beginning since the protagonist must wind up being the winner in order for the story to succeed. Since the outcome is inevitable, the story really revolves around how Garraty will win, how much he will suffer, and whether he will retain his humanity in a grueling walk to the death. King skillfully manages to keep the story moving along, even at the slow pace of four miles an hour, as we watch the contestants drop out and die, one by one. Garraty, the home-town favorite, makes friendships with his competitors and learns about the true nature of The Major as each of the boys is progressively murdered. The novel uses a classic plot structure of movement forward in time to a predetermined end when time will run out. This game, however, has no time limits and will go on until only one boy remains.

Archetypes

The dystopian novel has become a popular archetype, a sort of cautionary tale in the tradition of George Orwell's *1984*. It certainly reflects King's distrust of government and warns against the possibility of America becoming a victim of despotism. Written during the Vietnam War, this novel shows the unthinkable possibility of the time that America might lose a war. The alternate world is shown as being the aftermath of such a loss, with the mention of contemporary personalities and products such as Ron Howard, Robert Mitchum, and Dial soap depicting the world we could be living in if history had turned out differently. This alternate reality connects with King's overall view of the multiverse as outlined in the Dark Tower series and can be seen as one of the URs, or other universes in this infinite cosmic scheme.

The Long Walk also conforms to another classic archetype, that of the "coming of age" story, one of the oldest forms in all of literature and one that King uses in other novels as well. Garraty and the other 99 walkers enter the competition as innocents, unaware of what they are really doing and, like most teenagers, unable to imagine their own deaths. These boys volunteered to be in the walk and were chosen through a selection process that is never revealed, knowing but not really understanding that their chance of surviving was small. As the walk progresses, the boys lose their innocence, one by one, as they take the long walk into maturity, only to be killed for their efforts.

Themes and Subtexts

For a novel written by a college freshman, *The Long Walk* carries some interesting themes beneath its surface. The most obvious one, of course, is fear of government power. This recurrent theme occurs in several King novels, including *The Stand*, *Firestarter*, and *The Institute*, to name just a few. This, again, comes with the times that King lived through: the war in Vietnam, the civil rights movement, and later, Nixon and the Watergate scandal. The dystopian novel is a popular form in Western fiction, and although it doesn't pretend to predict the future, it does attempt to prevent horrific things from happening.

Garraty's thoughts reveal another major theme of the novel—the futility of sacrificing oneself for a government: "The whole Walk seemed nothing but a looming question mark. He told himself that a thing like this must have some deep meaning.... A thing like this must provide an answer to every question." By the end of the novel, Garraty realizes that the walk does not have any great meaning and, in fact, is a meaningless waste of life designed for the whole purpose of amusement and power. Like the Roman gladiators before them, the walkers seek glory but instead find only death and oblivion. They are not memorialized or honored but are shot like animals in the road. Rather than receive a heroic death, they are assassinated.

The walk continues every year without question, simply because it has become part of the prevailing culture. This calls into question why we continue to do certain things, often when they have outlived their usefulness, and as expressed in the Shirley Jackson story "The Lottery." The Long Walk has become a national holiday where people line the streets to watch the contest without even knowing why they are there. This story and *The Running Man*, its companion piece in *The Bachman Books*, forecast the popularity of reality television, which has evolved to the point that some shows, like *Naked and Afraid*, have become about survival rather than just a game show with cash prize. These two Bachman novels also depict America's fascination with and acceptance of violence. One would think that state-sanctioned murder of teenagers would cause outrage; however, the inhabitants of this world treat it as if it were a film or a video game. In fact, some of America's most beloved sports (automobile racing, bull riding, and even football) come with a significant risk of injury or even death.

Last, Stephen King revisits one of the themes that run throughout nearly every one of his novels—the importance of storytelling. Evolutionary psychologists have acknowledged the importance of storytelling to the survival of the human species. Stories are an effective way of transferring knowledge, information, and even codes of morality from one generation to the next. As a result, we share storytelling as a human universal, and much of our entertainment revolves around narrative in one form or another. "Tell us a story that will take our minds off our troubles," Stebbins asks Garraty as the walkers suffer through their ordeal (393). Story still serves the role of entertainment and helps people cope with tragedy and stress.

Human Universals

The Long Walk is more than just a "growing up" story as in a novel like James Joyce's *Portrait of the Artist as a Young Man*; this is a matter of survival, a human universal goal that is the essence of horror, fantasy, and thriller genres. "Walk or die, that's the moral of the story." King allows his Constant Reader to experience this walk with death, and his readers imagine themselves in this situation and can enjoy the misery without actually suffering it. This is one of the most appealing things about popular fiction and explains why King is so successful. Another human universal is the affective emotion of love, and Garraty's thoughts about his girlfriend Jan keep him going. A love plot is almost essential in popular fiction, and King uses this to keep us hoping for Garraty. The boy sees both Jan and his mother somewhere in the middle of the walk when they come out to cheer for him, and that gives him new strength to persevere. This also helps us identify with Garraty's humanity, makes us like him and root for him, while some of the other walkers are not nearly as likable.

Evaluation

It is hard to believe that King wrote this novel as a college freshman. Although it is clearly an "adult" novel, the American Library Association highly recommends it for teen readers. The novel is very readable, yet deceptively complex, a cautionary tale that succeeds without being didactic or heavy-handed. I rank it as the best of the "Bachman books" and a personal favorite that I have returned to several times.

Interesting Fact

In 2000, the American Library Association listed *The Long Walk* as one of the top 100 best novels for teens between 1966 and 2000.

Notable Quote

"Isn't it too bad the great truths are all lies?"

7

The Dead Zone

Everyman Is a Hero

Background

The Dead Zone was first published in 1979 by Viking, an imprint of Doubleday Books, and was the first of King's books to place in the list of top-selling books of the year. It was adapted for film in 1983 with Christopher Walken as Johnny Smith and Martin Sheen as Greg Stillson. It spawned a TV series "based on characters" from the novel that ran from 2002 to 2006 on the USA Network. This was the first novel to be set in Castle Rock, a small Maine town that would become the setting for many King stories and that became the setting for a *Twilight Zone* type of television series titled *Castle Rock*.

Although the novel is rather tame in terms of language and violence, it placed number 82 out of 100 on the American Library Association's list of banned books for 1990–2000 (one more reason it should be read, in this professor's humble opinion!). Members of the ALA speculate that those who demanded it be banned did so just based on it being a Stephen King novel without ever having read the book themselves.

Summary and Plot Devices

Although King has been typecast as a horror writer, *The Dead Zone* is not a horror book but is rather a thriller with a supernatural element. The protagonist, Johnny Smith, is just an average "everyman"—hence his common name—who is involved in a terrible automobile wreck that puts him in a coma for five years. When he wakes up, he discovers that he has somehow gained a psychic ability and is able to see into the future. After shaking hands with a politician, Greg Stillson, Johnny sees that Stillson's election will ultimately result in his becoming president and causing a nuclear war in the future. He is then faced with the dilemma of how to stop this future from occurring.

The Dead Zone is told from the third-person omniscient point of view, which means that the person telling the story is looking in from the outside and is able to get inside everyone's mind and see the world from everyone's point of view. Johnny Smith, the protagonist, is the focus of most of the novel. But this third-person point of view allows the narrator to tell readers things that neither Johnny nor any of the other characters would know. The narrator, like any good storyteller, knows exactly how the story will go and how it will end. The skill comes in leaking that information to the reader in a way that creates the most suspense. King has mastered all of these storytelling techniques, which is a key to his overwhelming success.

One of the ways he creates suspense is in the use of prolepses, which is a fancy way of saying foreshadowing. King sprinkles hints of things to come throughout the narrative, and these little clues keep readers turning the pages. For example, in the prologue alone, King hints that Johnny will have special powers after he falls on the ice while skating, blacks out, and then has "hunches" about things. King also states that was "before the second accident," leaving readers to anxiously await the results of what that accident might be and what will result from it. King also introduces the character of Greg Stillson, portraying him as dishonest, corrupt, and determined to achieve greatness at any cost. Although the hero and the villain don't square off until the end of the novel, they are both introduced early, leaving readers wondering where and how their paths will cross.

One of King's most effective narrative techniques involves ending a chapter or section with a one sentence paragraph that leaves readers hanging, forcing them to keep turning pages to pick up this thread later. One effective example of this occurs at the end of the first section of chapter 2 with the line, "It was four-and-a-half years before she talked to Johnny Smith again." This is part of what English professors call a "hermeneutic code" (critics and professors love to give fancy names to simple things), a narrative method of inserting giant question marks in readers' minds, puzzles that force them to continue reading to find solutions (Why didn't she talk to him for such a long time? What happened?). This type of plot device lies at the core of the detective and mystery novel, and the suspense novel (Who done it? What happens next?). King's mastery of this device undoubtedly sells books.

Archetypes

The Dead Zone is based on a couple of archetypes. First, it is a Rip Van Winkle story of sorts since the main character is in a coma for five years and wakes up to a different world, where he must learn and adapt. The world has moved on without him. Although he remembers his date with his girlfriend Sara as occurring just yesterday, to her it happened five years ago and she has moved on and married another man.

King also explores the what-if archetype that we have probably all thought about—What if you could prevent a tragedy? This scenario forms a part of the science of game theory in the scenario of "the trolley problem," which explores the idea of sacrificing a single person to save many people. In this game, players are asked to imagine they control the switch or a trolley or train that is out of control and heading toward a group of people who will be killed. Players are asked if they would throw the switch to divert the train so that it would kill just one individual. Many different versions can be adapted from this (what if the individual was your child, for example), but it does propose interesting and difficult ethical dilemmas (utilitarianism, moral obligation, and others that are regularly discussed by my colleagues in the philosophy department of the university). *The Dead Zone* is a novelized version of "the trolley game" that the "Constant Reader" plays out with Johnny Smith.

Themes and Subtext

The Dead Zone is the story of an ordinary man ("everyman") who finds himself in a position to make a difference in the world—in this case, to save it—but at great cost to himself. This theme, or subtext of the novel, asks readers to decide for themselves what they would do in a similar circumstance: If you had the chance to travel back in time to 1889 and smother Adolf Hitler in the crib, would you? And if so, what would you be willing to sacrifice? This is essentially the question that Johnny Smith must answer for himself. Because of circumstances far from his control, he must step up and be a hero, must sacrifice himself for the good of others. In Stephen King's world, ordinary people do have the power to do great things, and in so many of his books, they do sacrifice themselves for the better good.

Another theme, that of psychic phenomena, also reoccurs in many of King's books (*Carrie*, *The Shining*, *Firestarter*, and *The Institute*, to name just a few). In the real, mundane world, supernatural phenomena are fantasy despite the claims of psychics who say they can read your future—for a price, of course. (If they are that good, why aren't they guessing tomorrow's lottery number?) And yet, there are times when we all have feelings, hunches, vague premonitions that turn out to be accurate. Psychologists claim that this stems from our uncanny ability to read people; as uniquely social animals, our very survival depends on our "theory of mind" that allows us to empathize with others, imagine what they are thinking, and predict their likely behavior as friend or foe. If it seems that our dogs can read our minds, it is because they also have learned to read the emotions of their human partners through our body language, facial expressions, and even our breathing rate and other subtle signs. Psychic behavior and intuition, then, may not be as far apart as we might think, and it is truly possible that we might get bad vibrations from a truly evil person.

With that being said, there is the question of whether such powers would be a blessing or a curse. Supersensitive people do seem to have a tough time in life. Talent, too, can be a curse as any starving artist or musician can testify. And some of the most talented individuals do seem most prone to depression and mental illness. Vincent van Gogh is an obvious example here.

In *The Dead Zone*, Johnny Smith is given a "gift" that can be used to save lives. However, it becomes his personal curse. And this gift comes with a terminal brain tumor as an unfortunate by-product. This novel does explore the question of whether we would want psychic ability, and despite being able to perhaps predict a lottery number, King suggests that psychic ability is the type of gift that would, in fact, be a curse.

Probably the most obvious subtext is that of the corrupt politician. Published just five years after Nixon's resignation, this book showcases Stephen King's distrust of the government. A political activist while in college, King experienced the tumultuous years of the Vietnam War, the civil rights movement, and the Watergate scandal. Modern presidents, especially Eisenhower and Kennedy, were admired and respected (a theme King explores in *11/22/63*), but that changed in the late 1960s and early 1970s when politicians were seen in a different light. George Wallace, former governor of Alabama and a third-party candidate for president in 1968, was an avowed racist and defender of segregation (and won 13 percent of the popular vote in the election). Lyndon Johnson, although a champion for civil rights, was universally hated because of his escalating American involvement in the war in Vietnam. And Nixon resigned in disgrace in 1974. Against this backdrop, politicians lost respect, and this paved the way for Greg Stillson as a character.

Human Universals

As I've mentioned previously, this novel does deal with the theme of altruism, of an unlikely hero sacrificing himself for the good of others. Evolutionary biologists have long debated why altruism exists in the human species—after all, isn't it supposed to be the survival of the fittest? If so, why would any individual sacrifice their life for others? E.O. Wilson and other evolutionary biologists have made a strong case that altruistic behavior has been an important survival tool for our species, if not necessarily for the individual. Their theory is that yes, one strong, selfish individual will outperform a weaker, selfless individual; however, a group of people who cooperate will outperform a group of selfish individuals who don't cooperate. Thus, over many thousands of years, cooperative groups have flourished, while selfish groups have perished and mostly gone extinct. In fact, altruism and sacrifice are admired by society. Altruistic people are given awards and medals and win the respect and approval of others. They are featured in "feel good" news stories and recognized for their service. Firefighters, the symbol of altruism, are universally admired by society.

One of the reasons that characters like Johnny Smith are so well liked is because they exhibit this altruistic behavior, yet they do so out of a sense of duty and obligation and not to gain fame or notoriety. Most people believe that given the circumstances, they would be as heroic as Johnny Smith (and to be fair, I think that most people would). The average citizen doesn't really have an opportunity to save the world, but they can experience this possibility through fiction. The average person cannot really imagine themselves as a superhero or a James Bond, but Johnny Smith is familiar to them. He is a realistic hero rather than one from a comic book, and he offers the average reader the chance to save the world, too, by imagining that they also would metaphorically kill Hitler in the crib if given the chance.

Another human universal that has been important to the survival of our species is the ability to recall and relive the past. It has often been said that we learn from our mistakes, and that is certainly true. But we also relive positive past experiences and take great pleasure in remembering and retelling them. This idea of nostalgia is, according to neuroscientists, a positive mechanism where we can elevate our mood, relieve stress, and even cope with trauma. Human beings are probably one of the few (perhaps the only?) creatures who reminisce about the past. Does my dog have fond memories of yesterday's walk to the post office? I can only guess. But I can recall it with great pleasure, and most people take delight in remembering such things even years later. We are all attracted to nostalgia (hence, the popularity of cable television networks like MeTV that broadcast old programs that I watched and loved as a child).

King taps into this idea of nostalgia in many of his stories, as we will see in later chapters. In *The Dead Zone*, he re-creates the fairs we all remember as kids, and Sarah reminisces about the fairs she enjoyed as a child. Sometimes these memories are bittersweet, as when we remember times spent with a loved one who is no longer with us. Yet we are almost magnetically drawn to relive some of our best memories and, in fact, work hard to create new ones that we can store away and relive over and over again. The tourism and hospitality industry are based on this idea. People used to keep scrapbooks and now store away their memories on social media sites to share and relive. This is one reason that King uses brand names and specific details that trigger our memories, which for an old professor like me, may launch a host of fond memories.

The Dead Zone is especially interesting because Johnny's memories of Sarah and their date at the fair, though five years old, appear to him as if they are just days old. Although memories fade with time, Johnny's are as vivid as ever and, since Sarah has moved on without him, more bittersweet than most. This brings into sharp focus our longing for the past and the one-way direction of time, which is the major theme of *11/22/63*, a novel where the protagonist actually does get to relive the past.

Evaluation

The Dead Zone is a very effective novel and one that can be enjoyed by those who are not fans of horror fiction. Even though King has been typecast as a horror writer (and avoided by many readers who dislike horror), many of his books can be classified as speculative fiction and enjoyed by a wider audience. The book's strength, I believe, is in its democratization of the hero to the point that any one of us Constant Readers can relate to the protagonist and imagine ourselves faced with this dilemma. The outcome of the book is particularly satisfying as Stillson destroys himself by showing the public what kind of man he really is.

Interesting Fact

The novel is loosely based on the life of Peter Hurkos (1911–1988), a famous "psychic" who claims to have gained his powers after falling off a ladder, hitting his head, and falling into a three-day coma.

Iconic Moment

Greg Stillson sealing his own fate by using a child to shield him from the assassin's bullet—his selfishness is the exact opposite of Johnny Smith's altruism and it puts an abrupt and certain end to his political ambitions.

Notable Quote

"Nobody lives forever ... but everybody tries."

8

Firestarter

Don't Play with Fire

Background

Firestarter was first published by Viking in 1980 just after two excerpts from the book were released in *Omni* magazine in the July and August issues. It was adapted into a film in 1984, and a sequel, *Firestarter: Rekindled*, was filmed in 2002. The novel pays homage to two great authors in the fantasy field—Shirley Jackson, the subject of its dedication, and Ray Bradbury, whose epigraph from *Fahrenheit 451* begins the book: "It was a pleasure to burn." Like *The Dead Zone*, this novel isn't horror but could be better classified as science fiction or, I believe, a thriller with supernatural elements.

Summary and Narrative Devices

Once again, King turns to the idea of an ordinary person having extraordinary psychic abilities. In this case, a child, Charlene McGee, nicknamed "Charlie," was born with the power to ignite fires with her mind, or pyrokinesis. This power is a genetic result of the fact that both her parents participated as volunteers in a government experiment by taking a substance called "Lot 6," a hallucinogenic drug that "The Shop" (King's version of the CIA) was hoping would transmit superpowers to ordinary people, who could then be militarized. The government has been secretly keeping tabs on the McGee family, and when they learn that the child may have some special powers, they are very interested. Andy McGee isn't willing to allow his daughter to become a lab rat, however, and the novel chronicles their attempt to avoid pursuit from government agents who have already killed Charlie's mother in the backstory. Charlie and Andy are eventually captured and hidden away at a secret government facility where they hope to harvest the girl's powers and weaponize them.

Like much popular fiction, the story opens in the middle of the action, what professors call in medias res, which is Latin for—you guessed it—"in the middle." The stakes are life and death as Charlie and her father flee from the DSI (Department of Scientific Intelligence), better known as "The Shop." King shows his readers a glimpse of Charlie's powers as she lights a man's shoes on fire in the airport, and we see a glimpse of Andy's powers as he "pushes" the taxi driver into thinking he was getting a $100 bill. We also learn of the deadly consequences of them getting caught as a flashback shows how The Shop killed Charlie's mother, which also sets up the measures the government will take to achieve its end, including "being sanctioned," their euphemism for murdered.

King skillfully leads readers along with questions that wait to be answered, building suspense the entire time. If, for example, Charlie can nearly incinerate a man by letting her ability get just a little out of control, what is she capable of if she really lets it loose? We are also given a deadline, so to speak, since Andy can use his push sparingly, and each time he does use it, his headaches get worse. It is obvious that using his power will kill him if he is not very careful. Worse than his own death is the fact that his daughter will be completely alone in the world.

Archetypes

In terms of structure, there are two major ways to organize a thriller. The first, as we have seen, is the hero's quest, best demonstrated in *The Stand*, which can be seen as a modern American version of *The Lord of the Rings*. In this type of story, the protagonist is chasing something or trying to achieve something. The alternative story can be thought of as the escape story, where the main character is running away from something. *Firestarter*, like several other novels we will examine, is a story of flight. This hero's quest, if you will, is to gain freedom from pursuit. This device often used by storytellers and is common in *The Fugitive* (both the television series and the film), the film *Alien*, and King's own novel *The Running Man*. Being pursued by a corrupt or authoritarian government is especially frightening and accounts for the popularity of George Orwell's *1984* and Ray Bradbury's *Fahrenheit 451*, which King used as inspiration for this novel.

Escape stories often turn into revenge stories, another very popular motif that readers and audiences love, and *Firestarter* doesn't disappoint as Charlie's pursuers are both destroyed and exposed. It is part of human nature to see justice served; it is the glue that holds civilized society together and discourages and punishes those who violate codes of acceptable behavior. The irony of this novel lies in the fact that those who are supposed to uphold the law, the government, are the ones breaking it. Their destruction is even more satisfying.

King's own novel *Carrie* is really an archetype for this story. Whereas Carrie has many psychic powers, including the ability to start fires, Charlie has but one. Unlike Carrie, she was brought up in a loving household where her powers were acknowledged by her parents, and she has been cautioned to avoid using them. She is a likable girl who, if left alone, would probably lead a normal life despite her strange abilities. However, like Carrie, she is provoked into using her talents to hurt those who are hurting her. The difference, of course, is that the victims of her wrath in *Firestarter* deserve everything they get.

Another possible archetype for this narrative might be a short story by Jerome Bixby, "It's a Good Life" (1953), about a boy with supernatural powers so strong that he is virtually a god. The story was adapted into a *Twilight Zone* episode and was selected for inclusion in *The Science Fiction Hall of Fame* anthology by the Science Fiction Writers of America.

Themes and Subtexts

Although probably not one of the "deepest" and most philosophical of King's novels, *Firestarter* does have some interesting themes and subtexts. Anyone who has lived through the Vietnam era and the Watergate hearings has developed an instinctive distrust of government. As in *The Dead Zone*, this theme is replayed in *Firestarter* and will be revisited in other King novels. Government is shown as not just corrupt but as downright dangerous, willing to willfully violate the civil liberties of its own law-abiding citizens and even innocent children with no thought about the ethics or consequences of such actions. This novel, like *The Dead Zone*, was highly influenced by the civil unrest that resulted from the war in Vietnam, where innocent protesters exercising their First Amendment rights were shot by the National Guard at Kent State University, and the Nixon administration had no qualms about illegally tapping the phones of its political opponents and spying on them. This concern with government overreach continues today, with the ability of the government to hack into computers and the presence of surveillance cameras virtually everywhere. Although many of these measures are necessary to prevent crime and terrorist attacks, King's work does remind us that they also have a more ominous edge. Even though the technology of "The Shop" in 1980 was primitive compared to what is available today, *Firestarter* remains, perhaps more so than ever, a cautionary tale of the consequences of an unchecked government power that can track down and even "sanction" innocents that it considers dangerous.

As in *The Shining*, *The Dead Zone*, and other novels that will be examined in later chapters, *Firestarter* explores the question of innate talent and its effects on the individual possessing it. Charlie's pyrokinetic ability is part of her genetic makeup, not something she has learned or cultivated. Like many "talents," it is not a particularly useful one, except if she is at a wiener roast and no one has a match to start the fire. Unless the ability can be developed into a weapon, the objective of "The Shop," it has little to no practical value and, in fact, takes tremendous effort from Charlie to control. This is evident from the near disasters that occurred when she was an infant and lacked the ability to keep her powers in check.

Charlie's powers can be seen as an analogy for talent in general, which can be useless and perhaps even dangerous if misused. As an avid (and law-abiding) sports shooter, I have seen expert competitive shooters put a neat little hole through a bull's-eye about the size of the head of a pin (these sharpshooters are much more talented than I). These people could also take a human life with the slightest pull of a trigger. Yet being disciplined professionals in full control of their abilities, they do not (by far, the vast majority of gun owners have never even pointed a gun at another person—the number one rule of gun safety—let alone shot someone). Their talents and ability have resulted from years of disciplined practice and training, something that is required of any talent if it is to be mastered. Even the ability to use words, considered by many to be a talent, has the potential to be misused and abused by an Adolf Hitler or a power-hungry politician like Greg Stillson in *The Dead Zone*. Words do matter, as we have all witnessed, and can be used for better or worse. In fact, any talent can be used for good or bad: music can incite patriotism or riots, photographs can inspire sympathy or violence, and even something as innocuous as a soccer game can turn harmless fans into an angry mob.

In *Firestarter*, King shows that what may be considered a talent or an ability can be a curse (something that any struggling writer or actor knows firsthand). Those who have innate abilities and who are aware of them feel compelled to use them. As any creative person will attest, they are not complete unless they are able to create. An artist must create art, a singer must sing, and a writer must write to feel happy and fulfilled. Yet much, if not most, of this art is not marketable, which causes frustration, the curse that accompanies talent. Charlie McGee has a very powerful ability, one that is incredibly dangerous. Once she becomes aware of this, she must hold back and not use her ability, something that is unnatural to her. After all, starting fires does feel good—hence the Bradbury quote at the beginning of the novel, "It was a pleasure to burn." The fact that her powers can cause harm to others is painful to her. Even more so is the knowledge that her power can be weaponized by the government and by selfish individuals for their own purposes.

Another compelling theme in *Firestarter* concerns the power of the human mind. Although psychic phenomena are considered pseudoscience, there is compelling evidence by neuroscientists that the human mind contains untapped powers, powers that might just be science that we don't fully understand yet. The idea of "mind over matter," once considered fiction, has been shown to have validity. Experts in meditation can slow down their heartbeats and control their blood pressure and other bodily functions. Documented cases exist where people have cured their diseases and sicknesses through the power of will, and mindfulness practice has been shown to promote good health and help prevent sickness. Since stress is a common and powerful factor in illness, the ability to control stress through mindfulness activities to promote health has a scientific basis. Using fMRI technology, neurologists have demonstrated that such practices can and do change the very structures in the brain.

Furthermore, much of what we call "intuition" is scientifically based. Humans have evolved to be able to "read minds" in order to function in society. Other creatures, like the family dog, know what you are thinking just by "reading" your facial expression. And as a horse owner and trainer, I can attest that my horse can "read my mind" just by the subtle and unconscious cues I give off with my body. And I am so tuned in to her movements that I can usually tell what she is about to do as well.

In *Firestarter* and other novels, King takes this power of the mind to its limits and speculates on what might be possible, especially through genetic manipulation and with the use of mind-altering drugs. As King says, "The brain is a muscle that can move the world."

Finally, as we have seen, King depicts fire as the ultimate cleansing agent. Carrie White causes a fire that cleans the town of its bullies. Jerusalem's Lot ultimately goes up in flames, as does the Overlook Hotel (at least in the novel). Las Vegas erupts in a nuclear holocaust of flames at the end of *The Stand*. A fiery ending is almost a cliché in King's works. So it is no accident that Charlie McGee's power, that of fire, is also an element that can (and does) destroy evil. In a different, comic book setting, she would be transformed into a superhero, fighting the forces of evil by summoning the cleansing flames at her command. But this is no superhero novel but the tale of an innocent child used as a pawn in a much larger game of chess. This fire, the talent, could be used for good; however, the corrupt government wishes to harness it only for destruction and power. In the end, though, the cleansing power of fire wins once again as Charlie turns her attackers into human french fries and then releases her tragic story to the world.

Human Universals

The fear of being pursued, caught, and trapped is a universal instinct of all animals, an instinct that accounts for their survival. This universal trait of humans fuels a book like *Firestarter*, which opens with a chase scene on the very first page. Whereas we fear being chased for real, we delight in pretend chases. The game of hide-and-seek is one of the first games children learn and enjoy, along with tag, and later, "manhunt." *Firestarter* brings us back into the feeling of being chased, but since it is a fictional world, we can enjoy the game without consequences. Readers find it easy to relate to the characters and can safely share their fear and play out a trial run in case they are ever the subject of a chase. King returns to this theme most notably in *The Running Man*, which will be examined in more detail later.

Another human universal that underlines *Firestarter* is the instinct to care for children, especially one's own. This is most evident in *Pet Sematary*, where a father goes so far as to bring his child back from the dead. Every good father can relate to Andy McGee's quest to save his daughter in *Firestarter*. The book propels readers into a parent's worst nightmare, the idea of terrible harm coming to their child.

Finally, as I have alluded to, there is the idea of revenge, which, in this case, is a dish served hot. The idea of justice comes from the human universal instinct to cooperate, a trait that has allowed humans to work together to become the dominant species on the planet. It has resulted in our unique ability to communicate, experience empathy, and to punish outliers and those who do not follow moral and ethical principles that are so necessary for civilization to prosper. When rules are broken, we want to see the rule breakers punished. This is borne out in research in game theory, where test subjects will punish what they see as unfair treatment. There is no doubt that the McGee family has been treated badly. So when Charlie's "rage" instincts are triggered and the offending parties destroyed, readers feel a great sense of satisfaction. This may be a very old plot device, but it is still very effective in the hands of a skillful writer.

Evaluation

Although *Firestarter* cannot be considered one of Stephen King's best works, it is an entertaining book that does handle some worthwhile themes in an interesting way. It is a quick and easy read, yet it, like all of King's works, can be read on more than one level. Its subtext of an overreaching government is a cautionary tale that unfortunately remains relevant.

8. Firestarter

Interesting Fact

In 2007, an adult Drew Barrymore, who played the role of Charlie McGee in the 1984 film, spoofed her role on *Saturday Night Live* with a fake commercial skit for "Firestarter Brand Smoked Sausages."

Notable Quote

"The brain is a muscle that can move the world."

9

Roadwork

Mental Meltdown

Background

Originally published under the Richard Bachman pen name in 1981, *Roadwork* was collected in *The Bachman Books* in 1985 and is now available in a stand-alone edition under the Stephen King name. King has been ambivalent about this book, but in the introduction to the second edition of *The Bachman Books*, he claims it is his favorite of the early novels. *Roadwork* is not a horror novel but lies somewhere in the realm of psychological thrillers.

Summary and Narrative Devices

Roadwork is the study of the mental breakdown of Barton George Dawes, who has lost a son to cancer and whose home is about to be taken by the government and converted to a bypass under eminent domain law. Although the city offers him what is considered a fair price for his home, he finds himself unable to leave because of the years of memories he had there, particularly memories of his son. His breakdown is slow as he destroys his career, ruins his marriage, vandalizes construction equipment, and finally kills himself in an explosion that destroys his house and opens an investigation into the corruption that surrounds the completion of the bypass.

Although this is an early novel published under the Richard Bachman banner, King masterfully uses narrative devices to make the story highly readable. Most notable is his use of a trick advocated by Anton Chekhov, the Russian playwright, who said that if you introduce a gun into act 1, you'd better fire it by act 5. The very opening of the novel finds Dawes shopping for guns in a gun store. It is obvious that he knows absolutely nothing about firearms, which leaves the reader wondering what he is going to do with them, particularly when he tells the owner a made-up story about buying them for his brother. And sure enough, at the end of the novel, the guns, a rifle and a pistol, reappear when Dawes becomes completely unhinged. *Roadwork* has the tension and tone of watching a car wreck. The reader knows it will get ugly and that there's nothing that can be done to stop it. Still, we're unable to look away.

King also shows his mastery of irony in this novel. Irony can be thought of as a deliberate incongruity between two things, as when one thing is said but another is meant. Irony is an important technique to enhance meaning and readers' pleasure. To cite just one example, the owner of the gun shop says, about his brother, that he was "one of the sweetest men you'd ever want to meet. He could bring down a deer at two hundred yards." It is also ironic, of course, that the "progress" created by the new highway will destroy not only homes but businesses as well.

Another interesting technique occurs late in the book, in a chapter called "Stoptime, January 20, 1974," when King dramatically shifts his point of view from third person to first person stream of consciousness. Stream of consciousness is a literary technique where the author attempts to capture a character's thoughts exactly as they are occurring in real time. In this short chapter, Dawes's thoughts become real, as we think along with him and are given a glimpse into his mind and mental state. It is a brief glimpse, though, as the next chapter returns to the third-person point of view.

Archetypes

Roadwork is reminiscent of *The Hitchhiker's Guide to the Galaxy*, a 1978 British radio comedy by Douglas Adams that was later adapted into a series of novels and into film. Adams pokes fun at government bureaucracy that bulldozes the protagonist's house to create a bypass; Earth is then demolished by an alien race making an intergalactic bypass. King's version of this scenario examines the serious side of this government overreach and how it triggers a seemingly normal, well-adjusted man to completely lose control, blowing up his own house in the end during a shoot-out with police.

Themes and Subtexts

The most obvious subtext of this book is the overreach of government in using "eminent domain" as a legal way of seizing property. As a historical fact, cities often used this law to take the property of poor people and underrepresented groups as a means of gentrification, offering very little money for real estate that would be developed into expensive properties. I have firsthand experience with this since my parents' home was taken by the city to build an industrial complex. I was only five years old at the time, but the experience was a traumatic one for my family, particularly my mother who loved her first home and didn't want to leave. (Incidentally, the industrial complex is now vacant, having sent all its jobs overseas.)

Another theme that runs through *Roadwork* is the difficulty that people have in accepting change. Dawes was not particularly happy, yet he was satisfied with his life until the government announced that it was taking his home. He had become accustomed to his life there, his job, his routine, and the comfort that comes with stability. Once this was challenged, he couldn't handle it, and his mental breakdown began, fueled in part by his inability to really accept the death of his son and now triggered by this second death, the death of his home. His entire life is uprooted; even the laundry he has worked for has to relocate, and Dawes is tasked with the responsibility of finding a new home for the business, a job that he is emotionally unable to do.

Dawes, like most people, is uncomfortable with change. He complains about how new things aren't as good as the old. The Grand, the movie theater he went to when he was young, had marble floors in the lobby, a balcony, and real popcorn. King describes this theater in painstaking detail, while referring to modern theaters as "crackerjack little buildings." Dawes also reminisces about old TV shows, the *Jack Benny Program*, *Rin Tin Tin*, and others, and laments the fact that they're gone. This nostalgia really surfaces when he goes to the attic and finds Charlie's clothes neatly packed away. He touches, smells, and holds the clothing, clinging to the memory of his son. This bittersweet nostalgia is a common human experience as we remember fond times of the past that are long gone and can only be relived in memories.

The new bypass introduces a theme about the price of progress, a price that King skillfully embeds into the gasoline and energy crisis of the 1970s. Although progress may have its perks, it also forces us to become dependent on it, just as the America of the novel's time was dependent on oil, which had suddenly become scarce and expensive due to the oil cartels of the time. The bypass turns out to be unnecessary, which causes a political scandal after Dawes's death. By this time, it has cost him his life and his sanity.

Finally, *Roadwork* directly confronts the theme of mental health during a time when it wasn't fashionable to do so. Much like the previous

Bachman novel *Rage*, the protagonist is suffering from mental illness that goes largely unnoticed and completely untreated. The signs of Dawes's impending breakdown are everywhere, yet no one seems willing to intervene and do anything to help. His wife suggests a therapist but doesn't really press the issue of follow-up. And largely due to the stigma of mental illness, Dawes refuses to seek help on his own. This theme of mental illness reappears in many of King's books and remains an issue even in today's world, which claims to be more enlightened about such things.

Human Universals

Stephen King's fiction is especially good at appealing to what evolutionary psychologists call affective emotion, or, in nonprofessor terms, human nature. His stories home in on and trigger the specific emotions that we are hardwired for and draw readers in by eliciting them. Neuroscientists have demonstrated that reading about something fires up the same brain regions as if we were actually doing what we are reading. World-class athletes and performers use this visualization technique to improve their performance.

One of the most basic human universal emotions is rage, the blind anger that can be triggered by any number of factors. This emotion is hardwired into our psyche as a survival mechanism that enabled our distant ancestors to fight for their lives when necessary (and in Paleolithic times, it was often necessary!). In our modern world, this emotion and its consequential actions is often harmful to us rather than good. But it remains with us just the same and still serves a useful function if we experience a legitimate physical attack.

In *Why We Snap: Understanding the Rage Circuits in Your Brain*, Douglas Fields has identified specific triggers that activate the rage response, and several of these triggers apply to a study of *Roadwork*. One of these, the "stopped" trigger, occurs when someone feels trapped and unable to escape or has no control of a situation. The government's use of the eminent domain law in taking Dawes's home qualifies under this definition. The "order" trigger occurs when we experience a sense of injustice or something not being fair (one example of this is the violence that sometimes breaks out during political protests). Dawes, of course, feels that he has not been treated fairly in being forced to give up his home. Finally, the "resources" trigger activates when someone or something tries to take away our property; that's why it is legal to act against an intruder breaking into your home. To a lesser degree, there is also the "insult" trigger since Dawes feels that he's been insulted by his government. And there is the "family" trigger, an instinctual mechanism whereby we defend our family and loved ones. Dawes sees the confiscation of his home as an attack on his family, particularly the memory of Charlie, his dead son. So, although readers might wonder why Dawes acts in the irrational manner that he does, we do understand his behavior at a visceral level. His rage, though self-destructive, is based on instinctual urges that are hardwired into our brains and, coupled with his repressed emotions about the death of his son, create a powder keg that is set to explode.

Evaluation

Although *Roadwork* is certainly not King's strongest book, it still holds up even though the oil crisis has ended and the world has changed. Governments still do engage in overreach, average citizens are still treated unfairly, and cancer still strikes down young people prematurely. Perhaps more important, this book, like *Rage*, helps shed understanding on why people do snap and engage in violent, irrational behavior.

INTERESTING FACT

The "mangle" machine in the laundry also references a short story called "The Mangler" (1972) reprinted in *Nightshift*. King, who worked in a commercial laundry before becoming a best-selling author, was intimately familiar with such equipment.

NOTABLE QUOTE

"People are only remarkable in books."

10

Cujo

He Tried to Be a Good Dog

Background

Cujo was published in 1981 and written while King was struggling with alcohol addiction. In his nonfiction book *On Writing*, he admits to having no recollection of writing the novel because of his alcohol dependency during that time. King says that the story was inspired, in part, by an incident that happened to him in 1977 when his motorcycle broke down and he was confronted by a large dog that lunged at him at the repair shop. *Cujo* was adapted into a film in 1983.

Summary and Narrative Devices

Set in the iconic fictional town of Castle Rock, Maine, *Cujo* is the story of Donna Trenton and her four-year-old son Tad, who are trapped in their car by a rabid Saint Bernard when Donna drives to a repair shop to have the starter fixed. Unfortunately for her, the mechanic and his family are away and the car won't start, so they are stranded in the middle of nowhere, so to speak, with no way of getting help. As time goes by, the danger worsens as the car heats up and they suffer from hunger and thirst.

Both *Cujo* and King's later novel *Gerald's Game* are about helpless women who are trapped in a deadly situation with no means of escape. In both cases, their "prisons" are mundane (a vehicle and a bedroom), but these everyday settings turn into what we would now think of as "escape rooms," posing the puzzle of how to break out and gain freedom. In both cases, the women show amazing strength and do escape their predicament without the tired cliché of a man coming to their rescue.

What complicates Donna's situation is her son Tad, a child who is totally dependent on his mother. If she had been alone, she would have made a run for it and either fought off the dog or tried to reach safety before he could catch her.

Cujo, like so much of King's fiction, is not a horror story in the traditional sense, yet it depicts a horrible event and evokes a sense of terror in the reader. Cynophobia, or fear of dogs, is experienced by 7–9 percent of the population and is often the result of a frightening incident with a dog. King, of course, plays on these fears by turning a "good dog" into the ultimate canine monster.

Stephen King begins this novel with a reference to Frank Dodd, the serial killer that Johnny Smith helped to stop in *The Dead Zone*, and refers to him as a monster that has invaded Castle Rock and whose evil comes to Tad in a nightmare. King tells us that the monster never dies and has returned to Castle Rock, presumably by entering the mind of Cujo. King's referencing other books in his canon occurs quite frequently as the stories of Castle Rock, Derry, and other King locations reappear throughout his works.

Another plot device that King has used in this book—and has been criticized for by his fans—is allowing the child to die at the end of the book. It is generally considered too horrible to fictionally kill a child who has been an important part of the story, and, in fact, the film adaptation allows Tad to live. King received numerous angry letters from fans about the death of Tad and how it wasn't fair that Donna had fought so hard to save her son, only to have him die anyway. King, of course, responded with the idea that "life's not fair," and that is one of the themes of the novel. From a plot standpoint, though, Tad's death reminds us that no one is safe in the Stephen King multiverse and that we can expect even the most innocent to die at any time and at any place, which happens quite often in King's novels. This device warns us to look elsewhere if we seek a happy ending. Our favorite character might survive and succeed. And then again, he or she may not.

Another interesting note is that King begins the story with the well-known phrase "once upon a time," and goes on to tell the story of Frank Dodd, a monster who came to Castle Rock. This leads the reader to believe that this story is a fairy tale, a harmless fantasy that will end with "and they lived happily ever after." As an English professor, I know—and King knows—that the fairy tales we were told as children are the sanitized versions and that the originals were much darker and grimmer (pardon the pun on the Grimm brothers) than the ones in the kids' picture books or the retelling by the Disney machine. King references this in *Later*, where an English professor gives the young protagonist a copy of the unexpunged version of Grimms' tales. This clever fairy-tale opening, then, is a trick to make the reader expect a happy ending and then turn the story into a tragedy where the mother does live, but her son perishes in the overheated Ford.

Archetypes

In some ways, *Cujo* follows the archetype of King's best-known prison story *Rita Hayworth and the Shawshank Redemption* (as we will discuss in a later chapter), but in this case, the prison is a more mundane one, Donna's Ford Pinto, and her "jailer" isn't a prison guard but a monster, a 200-pound rabid Saint Bernard. Furthermore, she is trapped with her son, someone whose safety she is responsible for. As an English professor, I see a correlative between this story and a section of Homer's *Odyssey* where Ulysses and his sailors are trapped in a cave by Polyphemus, the monstrous giant cyclops who plans to eat them.

Themes and Subtexts

King's fiction examines some of the problems of popular culture, but it also looks at some of the "big questions" of philosophy. One question he probes in several of his books is the debate between those who believe in determinism and those who favor the concept of free will. Of course, no one can answer this question with any degree of certainty, and King himself shows both sides of the issue in various stories in the canon. In *Cujo*, however, he favors the side of fate rather than choice, as the powers of the universe all line up perfectly to bring about the horrors that Donna and Tad experience in the family car. Neither the Trentons nor Cujo could have anticipated or prevented the tragedy unless they had possessed the supernatural powers of looking into the future. Even then, Cujo would not have been able to schedule an appointment to receive a rabies shot even if he had known. As King so accurately says, "Free will was not a factor."

This begs the question of whether King is right or not, yet this novel does show that we are not always in control of what happens to us and that there are forces of either fate or chance that may work to bring about certain events that we cannot expect or prevent. In this context, blame does no good. As King says, Cujo had always tried to be a good dog and obey his masters. But the chance act of him being infected with rabies changed all of that. King often turns to this idea that one tiny, seemingly insignificant event can domino into catastrophe—the "butterfly effect" in chaos theory where the beating of a butterfly's wings in Africa can possibly cause a deadly hurricane in Florida, for example. This theme will be revisited in much more detail in *11/22/63*, where the protagonist attempts to change history.

This idea of "fate" or "randomness" leads to the next important theme in the novel, the idea of fairness. Most people would readily admit, I think, that life isn't always "fair" (in fact, it is usually unfair), and *Cujo* demonstrates this truth in dramatic form. None of the characters in the book are without faults—what human is? And although they do suffer from their flaws, it is the most innocent, those without faults, that suffer the most. The obvious example is Tad, the four-year-old boy who hasn't lived long enough to have developed the vices of adulthood that so often bring about self-destruction. He is the victim, and his life is taken before it has really had a chance to begin. Tad does nothing wrong, has no tragic flaw that leads to his death, and is too young to make even the most basic decisions for himself. He is merely propelled along by the universe and comes into a collision course with Cujo, another innocent victim of fate.

Cujo, a "good dog," is infected by rabies through no fault of his own. Yes, his owners were negligent in not getting him a rabies shot, but the dog had no say in that matter. Saint Bernards are known for their affectionate demeanor, and Cujo is not the least bit mean or vicious until he contracts the disease that reshapes his brain. Yet despite his innocence, he is the one who suffers the most, enduring a slow and painful death caused by a virus that turns him from a lovable family pet into a monster. At the end of the novel, Cujo is no longer himself but has been transformed into a vicious beast who has no control over his actions.

King's readers recognized that the book wasn't "fair" and wrote letters complaining that Tad should have lived. The film adaptation of the novel did end with Tad surviving, but the reason King killed the little boy in the book was precisely to show that no, life isn't fair. This is a difficult and painful truth that every person learns, but that doesn't make it easier to accept.

The final theme I will discuss is the role of the two wives in the book, Donna Trenton and Charity Camber. At first look, these two women seem to be complete opposites. Donna, a former librarian, is educated, has a professional background, and seems to be in charge of her own life. Charity, on the other hand, lacks education, has never had a career, and is completely controlled by her husband. But in truth, both these women succumb to their husbands' will. Donna gives up her career and her former life to follow her husband's path and finds that she has become "the fabled American housewife, taking care of the house and feeding the kid." Although her husband is not abusive, she feels trapped in a marriage that she no longer cares about and has an affair purely out of boredom, an affair that does become abusive. Charity is also the stereotyped housewife and is also trapped in a marriage that is abusive and that allows her no freedom. Her only escape is the death of her husband. At the conclusion of the novel, she gains her freedom, while Donna decides to return to her husband and try to pick up the pieces. In these two characters King shows the issues that women face in American society, where they are often forced to choose between family and career in a no-win situation.

Human Universals

In their study of neuroevolutionary origins of human emotions, Jaak Panksepp and Lucy Biven have identified CARE as one of the seven fundamental emotions of our species. The CARE system accounts for nurturing love, particularly the love that parents have for their children. This basic emotion, maternal and paternal love, has proven essential to the survival of the human species since children (unlike other animals, such as fish) need more than a decade of care before they are able to survive on their own. Born helpless and totally dependent on his or her mother, the newborn elicits the CARE response immediately, which explains why parents will put themselves at great risk or even die in an attempt to save their child from harm. This simple but essential human emotion is the foundation on which *Cujo* is built.

Any parent who reads this novel immediately channels the emotions of Donna, putting themselves in her place and imagining what they would do to save themselves and their child from the rabid dog. The empathy we feel toward Donna gives the book its power, especially because it is not just her own life at stake but also the life of her helpless child. The powerful grip of this elemental force of human nature drives the dramatic tension of the novel and helps account for its popular success since the CARE emotion forms a common thread that joins all people. We experience it with our own children, and we understand it when we see parents experiencing it with their children. Donna's dilemma of how to reach safety with Tad becomes the reader's dilemma, and this creates the tension and conflict in the novel that makes it a page-turner.

Interesting Fact

The name "Cujo" was based on the media's misspelling of the alias of Willie Wolfe, a member of the Symbionese Liberation Army, a terrorist organization in the 1970s that was involved in the kidnapping of Patty Hearst and other crimes.

Notable Quote

"Free will was not a factor."

11

The Running Man

Reality TV on Steroids

Background

The Running Man was written under the Richard Bachman pen name and published in paperback in 1982. It was collected in *The Bachman Books* in 1985 after it became known that Bachman was, in fact, Stephen King. The novel was adapted into a film starring Arnold Schwarzenegger in 1987. Although the film was entertaining, it deviated greatly from the book. The production of a new, more faithful version was announced in February 2021.

According to King, he wrote the novel in a single week.

Summary and Narrative Devices

Set in the dystopian world of 2025, *The Running Man* is a fictional version of the kids' game "hide-and-seek," which was renamed "manhunt" by older kids when I was young. In King's version, the world economy is nearly destroyed, the planet is overpopulated and polluted, and the protagonist Ben Richards lives in a totalitarian society. One of the few ways to survive is by being chosen to appear on government-sponsored game shows of which "The Running Man" is the most popular and the most violent. In this game, the contestant is named an enemy of the state and released with a 12-hour head start to then be chased down and captured by hunters hired to kill him. The contestant earns money for every hour he is able to stay alive and for every hunter he is able to kill. The grand prize, $1 billion, is awarded if he survives for 30 days.

Unlike the Schwarzenegger character of the film version, the Ben Richards of the novel is depicted as skinny and weak and volunteers to be on the television show out of desperation. Rather than being a superhero,

11. The Running Man

the novel's protagonist is an average man fighting for his life so that he can feed his family.

The Running Man consists of 101 chapters that "count down" from "Minus 100" to the last chapter, "Minus 000 … and counting." This technique was successfully used by Ray Bradbury in a short story titled "Zero Hour," which was part of *The Illustrated Man*. Bradbury's story is a countdown to an alien invasion and uses the convention of the countdown to the launching of a rocket into space. King's novel also implies that something tremendous is going to occur when the countdown hits zero, and it does, as Richards steers a jetliner into the skyscraper containing the government-run television production company, inadvertently foreshadowing the events of 9–11 that occurred decades after *The Running Man* was published.

In this novel, King makes special use of extremely short chapters, averaging about four pages each. This, combined with the countdown technique, makes for a compelling reading experience.

Archetypes

The archetype for *The Running Man* is the dystopian novel, the first of which was "invented" by the Russian author Yevgeny Zamyatin in 1924. This novel, *We*, was published in England in 1924 and banned in Russia until 1988. Inhabitants of this dystopia were forced by the state to undergo an operation that destroyed the part of their brain responsible for creativity and imagination. Other dystopian novels followed, the best known of which is probably Orwell's *1984*. The genre has been extremely popular and successful since then and includes notable books such as Huxley's *Brave New World*, Bradbury's *Fahrenheit 451*, and Suzanne Collins's *The Hunger Games*, to name just a few. The premise for this type of novel is for the author to take an issue, such as censorship in *Fahrenheit 451*, and carry it to the extreme where, in this case, *all* books are banned and burned.

The Running Man uses this motif in relation to television game shows and, in effect, predicted the reality TV craze long before it became a real part of popular culture. Reality television shows such as the extreme survival show *Naked and Afraid* have put contestants in danger, much like King's novel predicted.

Themes and Subtexts

The dystopian novel is a very effective vehicle for criticizing governments and for warning about possible issues and their consequences in the future. Orwell warned about "Big Brother," Bradbury about censorship, and Jeff VanderMeer (*Hummingbird Salamander*) and other contemporary authors are depicting the possible effects of climate change in their novels. *The Running Man* is a cautionary tale about the dangers of tyranny. On a more personal level, though, the book shows how games and entertainment can distract us from paying attention to the important issues in the world. It is the Roman Empire of "bread and circuses" to entertain the masses while the emperor engages in debauchery. Only in the Ben Richards world, there is no bread, just violent and decadent reality television to amuse the populace and make them forget about what a horrible world they are living in.

When *The Running Man* was written, reality television hadn't been invented. The closest thing was traditional game shows that offered prizes for luck (*Card Sharks*), skill (*Jeopardy*), or a combination of both. As Richard Bachman, King took the game show concept to its limits with outlandish prizes should one actually win and punishment and death for the losers. This prediction of the dangers of "reality TV" has foreshadowed increasingly dangerous "games," beginning with *Survivor* and continuing with even more risk in shows such as *Naked and Afraid*, where survivalists are dropped into a hostile environment with nothing except a personal tool of their choosing, such as a machete or a roll of duct tape. It has become routine for participants in this show to "tap out" for medical emergencies. In King's game, of course, there is no option to "tap out," and contestants can and do die on the show, much to the delight of the home audience.

This theme forces us to look into the mirror and understand how, on a visceral level, we are fascinated by the suffering of others. It is more fully played out on television shows like *Cops* and, even more disturbing, in the constant playing and replaying of video footage from police shootings, like the George Floyd case, where the public was repeatedly shown the murder of a Black man on network news. While airing this video was not necessarily a bad thing (it has forced Americans to become aware of racial inequality and the overuse of force by law enforcement), it does say something about our species when we are unable to look away and, in some cases, seek out such horrible videos, as in the case of terrorist beheadings, which were posted on the internet and viewed by millions of people.

Human Universals

The Running Man appeals to human universals in several ways. In the novel, Ben Richards is an average man, not physically strong and not particularly noteworthy (unlike the persona of Schwarzenegger, who plays the character in the film), and rather than being drafted into the game (the movie version), he willingly volunteers. His family is impoverished, his daughter needs medical help, and he has no prospects for employment. In short, he is desperate and unable to care for his family. This affective emotion of CARE has been ingrained into human nature over eons of evolution, and we will do whatever is necessary to care for those we love. Parents will sacrifice their own happiness for their children, will work as many jobs as necessary to put food on the table and provide health care, and people often make the ultimate sacrifice for a loved one, shielding them from danger at the cost of their own lives, as has happened during mass shootings.

It is no surprise, then, that Ben Richards is willing to take part in a suicidal game with the belief that it may save his family's lives. He is willing to become a tool of the government and put himself hopelessly at risk for the opportunity to earn enough money to get medical help and food for his family. The reader easily accepts this insane proposition since most readers would do the same under these dire circumstances. We "run" with Ben Richards because it is the most human thing to do. As the book says, "In 2025, the best men don't run for president, they run for their lives."

Once Ben learns that it is too late to save his family, Ben's CARE instincts turn into RAGE. As has been discussed in previous chapters, RAGE is a universal human emotion that can be triggered by numerous factors and doesn't only belong in the province of violent people or killers. Anyone can be provoked into rage if the right triggers are pulled.

In the case of Ben Richards, rage becomes a survival mechanism brought on by the instincts of what R. Douglas Fields terms "life or limb" and "stopped." Even a cornered mouse will fight back against the tomcat when cornered in the classic fight-or-flight response when flight is no longer an option. And so Richards turns from an average meek individual into a warrior capable of killing others to fight for his survival. This is an instinct we can all understand, and the Constant Reader easily adopts this position in the story, rooting for Ben to do whatever it takes to survive. This is a rather classic storyline—the average person becomes a fighter when necessary—and average people commonly adopt this position, though usually by use of the courts, protecting an injustice, or in self-defense of their person or property. In fact, attorneys and politicians routinely market themselves as professionals who will adopt the warrior role for you and "fight" for you and your rights.

The RAGE circuits of our brain are also triggered by threats to our mate or our family, so when Ben Richards's wife and child are threatened, he becomes enraged. The "resources" trigger also plays into this since wild creatures will fight for food. This is particularly evident in *The Running Man* where the state forces its people to violently compete for limited resources. Once again, even the average American couch potato will experience rage when faced with the challenges that are put forth in this novel, and we easily identify with and figuratively take part in the plight of Ben Richards, even when he commits what would be considered a terrorist act—crashing a jetliner into a government building. This revenge theme is a common but very effective trope in fiction, and we feel no remorse for the occupants of the government-run television station when it is destroyed. The revenge theme is even clearer in the film version, when "Arnold" becomes the superhero who confronts Killian and (as is appropriate to his name) kills him directly in a final scene that satisfies the audience's need for justice.

Stephen King also invokes the PLAY response in his Constant Readers. While all mammals seem to enjoy playing (even as I'm writing this, my little dog is running around with a toy), humans have taken play to new extremes. Play is an evolutionary instinct that helps us learn about the world, try out new things in a safe environment, and stimulate the senses. Once our basic survival needs are met, we turn to play and entertainment to amuse ourselves, and those of us who are fortunate enough to have leisure time are constantly searching for the next form of entertainment.

The Running Man utilizes games directly to elicit the PLAY response in its readers. "Hide-and-seek" and "tag" are among the first games that children learn, an evolutionary holdover from the prey/predator days of prehistoric humans, no doubt. Despite its complex rules and technology, the game of The Running Man is really just a sophisticated version of these childhood games, with the readers as participants in the fictional persona of Ben Richards. In this novel, the Constant Reader is able to replay childhood games on an adult level and in the safe environment of a book. It is no wonder that *The Running Man* was successful even under the Bachman pen name and was chosen for a film adaptation even though the producer had no idea that it was a Stephen King property.

Interesting Fact

When producer Rob Cohen bought the rights to film *The Running Man*, he didn't know that Richard Bachman was really Stephen King.

11. *The Running Man*

Iconic Moment

Ben Richards foreshadows 9-11 by flying a jet aircraft into an iconic government building.

Notable Quote

"Say your name over two hundred times and discover you are no one."

12

Rita Hayworth and the Shawshank Redemption

Hope Springs Eternal

Background

Rita Hayworth and the Shawshank Redemption is probably best known in popular culture as just "The Shawshank Redemption" because of the very successful film adaptation. Most non–Stephen King fans aren't even aware that the film is based on a King novella that was originally published in *Different Seasons*, a collection of four short novels that was released in 1982. Although I have chosen to concentrate only on full novels in this study rather than stories or novellas in a larger collection, both *Shawshank* and *The Body* have become such iconic parts of King's work (mostly because of the highly successful film adaptations) that I felt they deserved their own chapters.

Summary and Narrative Devices

Rita Hayworth and the Shawshank Redemption is a story about an innocent man being sentenced to prison and then escaping to regain his freedom. The story is narrated by "Red," the guy who can "get it for you" in prison, as he relates the story of Andy Dufresne and his quest for justice in the Shawshank State Prison, a setting that has become iconic in the Stephen King universe. Not your typical action-packed prison escape story, this short novel is mostly a character study of two prison inmates—Andy and Red. Even though the story is about Andy, it is also about Red, as the narrator says at the end of the book. Listed under the chapter heading "Hope springs eternal," this is a story about never giving up, no matter how remote the odds.

12. *Rita Hayworth and the Shawshank Redemption*

Written as a mainstream novel rather than as a horror story, *Shawshank* succeeds as a mystery story waiting to be solved. As such, King's narrator sprinkles clues throughout the tale that come together in the end that solve the mystery of how Andy was able to escape. The geology hammer, the pin-up posters, the repeated mention of rocks, and other clues all add up to reveal Andy's multidecade quest to break out. The "rocks" are the clues to what is happening and also reference "The Rock," the iconic Alcatraz prison and setting for a real miraculous escape in June 1962. Throughout the story, Andy is shown handling rocks and stones, which might lead to the idea that he is digging a tunnel. And there is the hammer, which Red obtains for him and then doesn't see again until it is worn down after 19 years of use. The hammer, like the loaded gun in a Chekhov play, is introduced early and its use is revealed in the last act of the book. Mention is also made of a "bad draft in his cell" and how for all but eight months of his incarceration, Andy was the sole occupant of that cell.

Andy is also shown as being very tenacious and very patient, and Red drops numerous hints about this trait. He endures the abuse of "the sisters," but in good time he exacts his revenge. He writes repeated letters to the state to obtain funds for the prison library, even when told that the idea was hopeless, and is finally rewarded with money after years of effort. As Red says, "Think about what a man can do, if he has time enough and the will to use it, a drop at a time."

Archetypes

Rita Hayworth and the Shawshank Redemption is listed among the top ten pieces of escape fiction by *The Guardian*. The prison break or escape story has been around forever—Shakespeare's romance play *The Tempest* fits into this category, as Prospero escapes his deserted island "prison" and exacts revenge on his evil brother who put him there. This archetype relies on our human sense of justice, which is disturbed when innocent people are punished. As a result, escape stories remain very popular and include classics such as *The Bridge Over the River Kwai*, *Prison Break* (a television series that originally aired in 2004), and *The Great Escape*, to name just a few.

Shawshank, however, best fits the archetype of the classic novel *The Count of Monte Cristo* by Alexandre Dumas. This tale has both the "impossible" escape and the revenge plots going for it, which is why it has been modernized into several successful film versions. In *Shawshank*, Andy does pull off the impossible escape and humiliates the corrupt warden and the prison in the process, forcing him to resign. As part of the outcome, justice is served.

Themes and Subtexts

Stephen King examines several important themes and subtexts in *Shawshank*. The most obvious, of course, is the failure of the prison system. Shawshank Prison is designed to punish rather than rehabilitate, and it is managed in a way that leaves it open for corruption. The hypocritical Bible-carrying warden is far more concerned with his own financial gain than he is with justice. Even when he learns that Andy is innocent, he refuses to even investigate, let alone see justice served. He has no problem keeping an innocent man in prison if it serves his purposes. He goes so far as to bury any evidence of Andy's innocence since Andy is useful to him in committing his crimes.

As for rehabilitation, Red expressed the idea best: rehabilitation is a "politician's word." The prison budget funds guards and guns, not the prison library or any other programs that would enable prisoners to transform their lives and perhaps become productive citizens. And the punishment is harsh: beatings, midnight burials, and extended solitary confinement for minor infractions of the rules. Gang rape is allowed, and probably encouraged, as Red graphically describes in a very unsettling paragraph.

On the positive side, *Shawshank* does explore the theme of hope, as evidenced by this chapter's subtitle "Hope Springs Eternal." Although most people would give up hope completely and fall into depression and perhaps even suicide, Andy remains determined and always hopeful, even in the direst circumstances. As Red says, Andy "carried around a kind of inner light." Andy is emblematic of what a person can accomplish "if he has enough time, and the will to use it." Andy is willing to plug away at his escape tunnel for years and then decades, even though his project seems hopeless. He tears a hole through the prison wall one pebble at a time, refusing to give up or lose hope. This trait serves as a powerful symbol of human willpower to accomplish what seems impossible: the building of the Great Pyramid, landing humans on the moon, and medical advances toward the cure for cancer. If Andy, a single educated but average man, can accomplish such a long-term and grueling task, then there is hope for each of us and for humanity as a species to overcome whatever challenges may face us.

Human Universals

Human nature is once again tapped into in this short novel, as King pulls the strings of universal emotions and fears. Most notable, this story triggers our fear of being trapped and imprisoned, a basic fear that mammals have evolved as a survival mechanism. A cornered animal has the

12. Rita Hayworth and the Shawshank Redemption

urge to fight back once flight is no longer an option. Andy does fight back after being imprisoned, but he does this using his wits rather than physical strength. It is this urge for freedom that drives him, an urge that drives human beings to accomplish incredible things, including the overthrow of oppressive governments. This is the urge that drove enslaved people to flee from their masters despite the risk of beatings or death. Freedom is a basic human desire that all people share, and when freedom is taken away unjustly, we try to make things right—and we root for characters like Andy who work to escape from their oppressors.

Justice is another human universal that humans crave, as has been previously mentioned. In this case, justice is achieved through perseverance and hope, but it comes at a high price since Andy has lost decades of his life at Shawshank Prison. Still, this novel shows that there are things in life worth waiting for, worth fighting for, and worth sacrificing for. This message of hope in the face of adversity makes this book and its film adaptation a beloved story that has endured the test of time.

Evaluation

Although not a typical horror story, *Rita Hayworth and the Shawshank Redemption* is among the very best pieces of King's fiction. The book has a universal appeal to general audiences as well as King fans and is a brilliant metaphor for hope and determination.

Interesting Fact

Stephen King sold the film rights for $5,000 but never cashed the check. He later had it framed and sent back to director Frank Darabont with a note, "In case you ever need bail money. Love, Steve."

Iconic Moment

Red and the prisoners drinking beer on the roof of the license plate building as Andy watches.

Notable Quote

"Things come in three major degrees in the human experience. There's good, bad, and terrible. And as you go down into progressive darkness towards terrible, it gets harder and harder to make subdivisions."

13

The Body

The Birth of a Writer

Background

The Body is a short novel that was also collected in *Different Seasons* under the chapter title "Fall from Innocence," which articulates the major theme of the book: the loss of our childhood innocence when we become adults. Like the other novellas in this collection, this story could be considered mainstream fiction. This story is best known by the 1986 film adaptation *Stand by Me* directed by Rob Reiner.

Summary and Narrative Devices

The Body relates the adventures of four 12-year-old boys who go off on a hiking trip to try to find the body of another boy who was reported to have been hit by a train but whose remains were not recovered. The narrator, Gordie Lachance, is an adult looking back on his childhood and telling the story as a reminiscence. Gordie is now a successful novelist, and this "memoir" helps explain how he became a writer.

In English professor terms, *The Body* is a bildungsroman, which is a fancy name for a coming-of-age novel. This type of story has proven to be highly successful in literature. Some of the best-known novels fit into this category, including *The Catcher in the Rye*, *To Kill a Mockingbird*, and *Jane Eyre*.

King uses an interesting point of view in this short novel. The narrator, an adult, retells the story of this important event that occurred in his childhood. The story is accurately told, but the narrator now has the benefit of age and maturity to look back on the events from an adult perspective and explain their importance to him, an importance that he did not understand at the time when the story was happening.

13. *The Body*

The structure of the story fits the heroic epic of the hero's journey. There is the call to action, the refusal, and then the acceptance of the quest, as the four boys make plans and set off. They cross the first threshold by escaping from "Chopper," the junkyard dog, and enter "the belly of the whale" when they traverse a railroad trestle and are nearly killed by a train. Gordie's encounter with a deer can be seen as a meeting with the goddess, and the train tracks represent the path they follow on their road of trials. Gordie receives enlightenment (apotheosis) when the boys do find the body, and he comes to understand death and, specifically, the death of his older brother, which has been an ongoing source of grief for his parents. He returns home with the ultimate boon, a sense of pride and self-worth that will fuel his continued journey as a writer.

The writer as protagonist is common in Stephen King's stories— these writer-characters range from total failures (the narrator of *UR*, who remains an unpublished wannabe in every one of the millions of universes in King's multiverse) to the highly successful author protagonist of *Lisey's Story*. Gordie, emblematic of Stephen King himself, is one of the more successful writers in King's world, with several books to his credit, which have been adapted into films. Gordie displays the traits necessary to become a popular writer: a sense of curiosity, a talent with words, and the drive and perseverance that often sets apart talented "wannabes" from professional authors.

King also employs an interesting technique of putting stories within the story. He revisits this technique often, most notably in *The Wind through the Keyhole*, part of the Dark Tower series, which not only contains stories within the book but which is itself a story told within the gunslinger universe. In *The Body*, Gordie the storyteller recites his fictional pieces to his friends. These stories are, in fact, stories written by King himself as a youth.

Archetypes

The Body, as we have seen, fits into the archetype of the bildungsroman, the coming-of-age story, a story that has been told for centuries beginning, in English at least, with *Beowulf*, the medieval tale of a hero discovering his heroicness (a story that also fits into the hero's journey archetype). Specifically, King's short novel bears close resemblance to James Joyce's *A Portrait of the Artist as a Young Man*, at least in theme but definitely not in style. *The Body* is the story of the creation of an artist— in this case, Gordie, who would go on to become a successful writer of fiction. Joyce's story also shows the maturation of a writer but in a style that relies on interior monologue, stream of consciousness, and where, frankly, nothing much happens in terms of plot.

As we have examined in the section on subtext, *The Body* is derived from the archetype of "the hero's journey" as outlined by Joseph Campbell in *The Hero with a Thousand Faces*. This type of story is one of the oldest, best-known, and popular stories and probably comes closest to Campbell's idea of a "monomyth," a single story that is the model for all stories. It includes ancient classics such as Homer's *Odyssey*, *Beowulf*, the Arthurian legends, as well as modern renditions such as *Star Wars*, *The Lord of the Rings*, and even modern literary fiction interpretations such as James Joyce's *Ulysses* (a book that only English professors read).

Themes and Subtexts

The chapter title for this story, "Fall from Innocence," articulates the major theme of the book: the loss of our childhood innocence when we become adults. This subtext is usually an important component of the coming-of-age story as adults look back on a simpler, more innocent time in their lives and relate how innocence turned into maturity by way of experience. It is an interesting facet of life that, as children, we want to grow up and "get big." Then, as adults, we look back with nostalgia to those years and wish to relive them. This novel captures this idea best when it speaks of the friendships we had as kids: how the best friends he ever had were when he was 12. He then addresses the reader directly—"How about you?"

Bullying is another subtext that forms an important part of this novel and reoccurs throughout the King multiverse beginning with *Carrie*. In this book, the younger boys are bullied by older boys who take great delight in tormenting them. The adults aren't much better. The owner of the junkyard sends a vicious dog after them; Teddy's father, a victim of PTSD during the war, held his eight-year-old son's face down on a hot plate and burned off his ears; and Chris also has an abusive father. Gordie's parents aren't abusive to him, but since the loss of their oldest son in a jeep accident, they are absentee parents. Once again in a King novel, we see the tragedy of losing a child. In this case, though, the result is the neglect of the remaining child.

Finally, there is the theme of writing and what it takes for a writer to be successful. This, again, involves a certain loss of innocence. This becomes apparent when the adult Gordie says that his wife, kids, and friends all envy his imagination. But as Gordie says, imagination also has "teeth" and every now and then it bites you like a cannibal. Writers like Gordie—and Stephen King—see the harsh reality of the world and express it in their stories. Or as King has said, "Fiction is the truth within the lie."

Human Universals

One of the most basic of human affective emotions is the SEEKING response described by Jaak Panksepp. In non-neuroscience, non–English professor terms, this aspect of human nature is just our curiosity, our desire for knowledge. This is the result of Adam and Eve's eating the forbidden fruit (the fruit of knowledge), according to the Christian Bible, and the result of Pandora opening that infamous box in Greek mythology. It is the impulse behind the voyages of the starship *Enterprise* ("to seek out new worlds"), and it is the reason that people go on vacations and adventures and desire to learn. It is also the motivation for the boys in this Stephen King novel to go searching for the body of a missing dead boy.

H.P. Lovecraft (1890–1937), one of the pioneers of the modern horror and the "weird tale," employed this concept in his fiction, the search for "forbidden knowledge," even if obtaining that knowledge leads to misery. Thus, once the atomic bomb was invented, it can't be "uninvented." And on a smaller scale, this explains why people slow down to look at the aftermath of a car wreck on the highway, even though what they see might be highly disturbing. We have a fascination with the unknown, and death, the great unknown, is perhaps the most fascinating subject of all, especially since talking about it is "taboo" in modern American society.

The initial call to adventure, then, is this quest to find the body and see what death looks like face-to-face. Even though the boys instinctively know that this "forbidden knowledge" will be unnerving, they set out on the quest anyway and lose some of their innocence in the process. This is the essential dilemma of human existence, that "growing up" means facing difficult things and learning difficult truths. It is the driving force of the coming-of-age story and the reason this story continues to be so appealing to audiences. Death is both terribly frightening and intimately fascinating, and this paradox fuels horror stories in general and explains so much of Stephen King's popular success as a storyteller. *The Body* is just one of the many examples of his ability to tap into this part of human nature.

Nostalgia is another shared human emotion and has led to the need for storytelling. People enjoy reminiscing about the past, reliving the good times and using the difficult ones as both therapy and as cautionary tales. Brian Boyd, one of the literary critics who uses Darwin's ideas to analyze narratives, has labeled *Homo sapiens* "the storytelling animal." Although other species may communicate with their fellow creatures, humans are the only living beings on the planet who have developed both language and imagination to the point that we can tell long, complex, and multilayered stories. According to Boyd and evolutionary psychologists, this ability to tell stories (and now even preserve them in writing) has resulted in our becoming the dominant species on earth. Storytelling allows us to pass on knowledge from one generation to the next, including survival strategies, and allows us to build new knowledge based on what has come before.

Gordie represents the storyteller, the individual who can not only share his past experiences but who can also command an audience who will listen. Storytelling is a common motif in the Stephen King multiverse. As a successful novelist, King understands the power of narrative and the value that is placed on a good story. In fact, people find it almost impossible *not* to tell stories whenever they get together. Although most narrators aren't as talented as King or his stand-in Gordie, there is something about a good story that grabs our attention, no matter who is telling it. In *The Body* and other novels, King picks on this thread by immediately introducing Gordie as a storyteller anxious to relate his adventure. The Constant Reader complies, metaphorically pulling up a chair and sitting down to listen.

Evaluation

The Body succeeds in accurately capturing the lives of teenagers and the process of growing from boyhood to manhood. As a man and a writer, I can immediately relate to the story, yet unlike the more "literary" story by James Joyce, it provides plenty of excitement to keep the plot moving forward. Most people who claim that King is a "hack writer" are surprised to learn that he is the author of both *Shawshank* and the novella that was adapted into *Stand by Me*. Both of these novellas place King firmly in the role of a major American writer of our times, in my opinion.

Interesting Fact

After watching the adaptation of his story into the film version, Stephen King "was moved to tears, because it was so autobiographical."

Iconic Moment

The boys cross the railroad bridge with the train bearing down on them.

Notable Quote

"The most important things are the hardest to say."

14

Christine

America Loves Its Wheels

Background

Christine was first published in 1983 and was adapted into a film that same year, directed by John Carpenter. The book is a dramatic story of America's love with cars, especially by teenage boys.

Summary and Narrative Devices

The plot of *Christine* is pretty simple and, if one were to pitch it to an editor or producer, almost silly—a haunted car seduces a teenage boy into buying "her." Yet King was able to take this plot and turn it into a memorable best-selling novel that was also adapted into a major Hollywood film. The story even turned the name of the car into a cultural icon, the epitome of an evil vehicle.

The story begins when Arnie Cunningham, the proverbial high school nerd, drives past a beat-up red-and-white 1958 Plymouth Fury in an old man's yard and, despite the advice of his best friend Dennis, buys the car for $250. Dennis has a bad feeling about the car and his instincts are correct: it turns out that "Christine" is demonically possessed, and once Arnie rehabs her, bad things begin to happen.

Christine is emblematic of a classic supernatural horror plot: something weird is going on, let's find out what it is, and then let's destroy it. Arnie falls in love with the car, and so it is Dennis, the voice of reason, who takes on the role of Van Helsing, the "vampire hunter," who solves the mystery, gathers his forces, and destroys Christine. This plot device is successful because of Arnie's infatuation with the car. As soon as he lays his eyes on the Plymouth, he loses all his reason and becomes obsessed with the vehicle, even to the point of addressing it by name. He remains blissfully

77

unaware of the car's evils even after Dennis and the reader have figured the whole thing out. Normally, we would ridicule the character that "makes poor decisions in a horror movie," to paraphrase a Geico insurance advertisement, but despite his foolish and irrational behavior, Arnie remains a very sympathetic character who illustrates how love—even for an inanimate object—can cloud someone's judgment. And as the former owner of a powder-blue 1966 Mustang convertible with wire-rimmed wheels, I can attest to the fact that teenagers can fall in love with a car, even if mine did clock more miles on the back of a tow truck than it ever did on the highway. The suspense is created by Arnie's *not* knowing and in our fear of how far this will go before it is resolved. Christine takes lives in this novel, so the stakes are high.

Fiction writers are advised to choose a point of view and stick with it throughout the story; however, King successfully breaks this cardinal rule in *Christine*. He divides the book into three distinct sections, each focusing on a specific character's point of view. He begins the book from a first-person point of view looking out at the world directly through the eyes of Dennis. This first section, "Teenage Car Songs," casts Dennis as the viewpoint character. Dennis is in a unique position to watch the actions of his friend and to chronicle his increasing infatuation with Christine and his irrational behavior. As the only friend that Arnie has, Dennis can observe and comment about the situation and make reasonable conclusions since he has no attachment to the car and genuinely cares about his friend's welfare and worries about the path he is taking. And since Arnie confides in him, Dennis can glean the truth while Arnie deceives his parents and others in the community. Dennis laments the changes that happen to his friend, changes that Arnie himself is not even aware of, such as him taking on some of the persona and traits of Christine's former owner, LeBay.

If Dennis had been able to intervene, things might not have escalated to the point that they did. But King was able to avoid that plot pitfall and maintain the suspense and the danger by taking Dennis out of the story in part 2, "Teen-age Love Songs," when he suffers a near fatal injury while playing football and is hospitalized for over a month. The point of view switches to an omniscient one in the middle section of the book with more of a focus on Arnie, and Dennis is left out of the main narrative entirely. This allows King to adopt a different perspective, with the omniscient point of view showing the actions of the possessed car in a detached, factual way, not clouded by the suspicions of Dennis. In this section, bad things happen directly, and we can see them unfolding in real time, so to speak. Christine kills several of the town bullies and even repairs herself by returning to the garage where Arnie restored her. We truly understand that Christine is possessed and that all the supernatural fears about her are true.

The final section, "Teen-age Death Songs," returns us to Dennis's point of view. This is where Christine becomes the hunted, and Dennis and Leigh become the hunters. This change in point of view is also effective because it puts the reader directly into the action. Since it's written in the first person, we are reasonably sure that Dennis will survive, but the suspense remains about the fate of Arnie and Leigh. And even though they defeat Christine, there is a cost, and the epilogue opens the possibility that the possessed car is still out there somewhere and gunning for Dennis.

Archetypes

As an English professor, I can identify several archetypes that King would be aware of and, either consciously or unconsciously, would have influenced *Christine*. In terms of structure, classic horror novels such as *Dracula* provide the narrative structure of the story, the "something strange is going on here" supernatural mystery that has become a basic formula for much weird fiction. It has been used by Edgar Allan Poe, Bram Stoker, H.P. Lovecraft, and too many more to name and continues to be a staple in the genre. The reader suspends disbelief and takes the ride to find out what is causing the weirdness and how to stop it.

The demonic possession idea is straight out of the Bible, from the initial encounter with the serpent in Genesis to the legions of demons in the New Testament. This idea was clearly adapted into humans being possessed in *The Exorcist* and other novels and films, and on more than one occasion King has embodied inanimate objects with demonic powers, as in the short story "The Monkey," the infrastructure of the Overlook Hotel, and even, to a certain extent, the rabid dog Cujo. Whether readers actually believe in demons and the devil is irrelevant. These malevolent religious icons make for an exciting story of good versus evil and still enjoy popularity even in our world of science and technology.

Themes and Subtexts

The most obvious and important theme of *Christine* is America's irrational love with the automobile, especially by teenage boys who equate cars with manhood. In the setting of Christine, whoever has the coolest car gets the girl, and even the nerd-like Arnie lands the pretty girl once he refurbishes the 1958 Plymouth. And although this teen love of cars and pretty girls may seem innocent enough at face value, it does have a more sinister side.

The invention of the automobile has changed American culture in dramatic ways, fostering the creation of the suburbs, travel and tourism (as the car ad from the 1960s said, "See the USA in your Chevrolet"), the invention of motels, creating a private space where teens could explore their sexuality, and wildly popular sporting events such as NASCAR. The downside to this is that the automobile also led to plenty of cases of what would now be considered "date rape," deadly car wrecks, and the slow but steady pollution of the environment and a reliance on fossil fuels. This culture of the car disdains public transportation; Americans, myself included, are not about to give up a convenient means of transportation and will, in fact, spend extra money for automobiles that look good and have the latest technology. Most households, according to the latest census reports, own two vehicles, and 93.1 percent of eligible drivers have at least one automobile. (As a sidenote, if we still relied on horses for work and transportation, that would create major problems with the environment as well, both from the methane gas they discharge and from the issue of solid waste disposal. As the owner of two horses, I can attest to that!) The evil possession of Christine, therefore, could be looked at as a symbol of the "evils" caused by automobiles in general.

Another theme involves the way we think about automobiles and other inanimate objects, almost as if we consider them to be living beings with motivations (I don't think I'm the only one who believes that, on some days at least, my computer is out to get me!). We become enamored of things and sometimes pay more attention to them than we do living people. This is the case with Arnie, who spends more time with Christine than he does with his friends and family. This is one of the prices we pay for technology as people spend more time with video games, cell phones (a subject King addresses directly in *Cell*), and computers at the expense of "face time" with loved ones.

Music forms a huge part of *Christine*, providing both an organizing strategy for the book (Teenage Car Songs, Teenage Love Songs, and Teenage Death Songs) and as a major thematic element. Music seems to be a human universal since it is enjoyed by every culture and every race of people on the planet in one form or another. In creating this novel, King spent a small fortune in obtaining permission to include song lyrics in each of the 50-plus chapter headings in the book. Getting them was, as King admits in the author's note, "hard work," so he must have had a good reason for including them. In my view, this collection of lyrics having to do with cars supports the teenage love of cars theme previously discussed. But on another level, the lyrics help to transport the Constant Reader into the story. King even goes so far as to provide a playlist of songs to enhance enjoyment of the book. The novel, as fantasy, supports an escape into an alternate reality where automobiles really do take on a life of their own, and the accompanying music adds a layer of subtext to this idea, creating a musical backdrop for what happens in the novel. This all comes together to make the unreal events of the novel more real and more believable.

Human Universals

As the horror master H.P. Lovecraft wrote in *Supernatural Horror in Literature*, fear is "the oldest and strongest emotion of mankind," and *Christine* appeals to this human universal that inhabits the deepest reaches of our brain, the parts that we share with all other creatures from the insect that scuttles into the cracks of the wall when a light is turned on to the mouse that trembles in fear when it smells the presence of a house cat. Although most people do not enjoy "real" fear, we do seem to be attracted to the artificial variety in the form of roller coasters, video games, and horror fiction and films. There are a number of theories on why this is so (I'd refer you to *Why Horror Seduces*, an outstanding study by Mathias Clasen), but there can be no doubt that most people enjoy being afraid, so long as the threat is make-believe and there is no real risk involved. King's exploitation of this fear reflex is one of the reasons he has been so successful—and one of the reasons that his fan base criticizes him when his work deviates from horror into a different genre.

Nostalgia seems to be another human universal, and King exploits this emotion in *Christine* as well, inviting all of his male readers (and probably a good percentage of his female readers as well) to fondly recall their very first car (in my case, it was that 1966 Mustang convertible, and although I can't remember all of the vehicles I've owned in my life, this first one is a permanent part of my memory). Many Americans grew up in an automobile, where they experienced their first kiss, their first real sense of independence, and the comradery of riding with friends and listening to music on the radio. All this forms part of the fabric of *Christine*, which remains a popular novel and which is considered a cult classic as a film.

Evaluation

Christine is definitely a fun novel to read, but in terms of the King canon, I'd place it somewhere in the middle. Technically, it is well written and interesting, but I wouldn't rank it as one of King's best novels.

Interesting Fact

The 1956–58 models of the Plymouth Fury were only available as two-door, not four-door, sedans, like the one described in King's novel.

Iconic Moment

Leigh choking on a burger from McDonald's.

Notable Quote

"People are only rational on the surface."

15

Pet Sematary
Sometimes Dead Is Better

Background

Pet Sematary was published in 1983 as the last novel required to fulfill King's contract with Doubleday before changing publishers. Originally written while he was a writer in residence at the University of Maine and living near the university, the book was based on the real-life tragedy of the family cat being killed and then buried at a nearby cemetery for pets. King was reluctant to tell his daughter about the cat's death and wondered what would happen if it were possible to reanimate the feline. A short time later, his two-year-old son ran toward the busy road while playing and King just managed to catch him before he ran into the path of an oncoming truck. In the introduction to the 2020 edition, King explains how this what-if turned into the novel.

At the time, King thought the book was too horrible to publish, but with encouragement from his wife and friends, he decided to use it to finish up his contractual obligations. He did little to publicize the book despite Doubleday's massive publicity campaign, and King still claims the book is his scariest. *Pet Sematary* was adapted into a film in 1989, and a remake was released in 2019. A sequel based on the premise was also made in 1992.

Summary and Narrative Devices

The protagonist of *Pet Sematary*, Louis Creed, is a medical doctor who moves to rural Maine and takes a position running the medical clinic of the nearby university. He and his family are very happy with the new place but do have some concerns about a busy highway that runs past the house and where huge trucks regularly speed by. Louis is warned by his neighbor Jud Crandall that the highway has killed lots of pets, so many, in fact, that the local children have constructed a "pet sematary" deep in the woods behind the Creed home. Louis neuters the family cat, Church, to try to keep him from wandering into the road, but the pet is killed by a passing vehicle anyway while his wife and the children are out of town on a family visit. Jud then shows Louis the *real* "pet sematary" which is much deeper in the wilderness. Pets that are buried here come back, but like the child in "The Monkey's Paw," the well-known Jacobs story, they are not quite right. Unwilling to tell his daughter the truth about the cat, Louis does bury it in the secret pet sematary, and it returns, zombielike, aggressive, and foul smelling. No one except Louis and Jud know what has happened, of course, but everyone instinctively stays away from the cat after its return. Of course, the inevitable happens and three-year-old Gage runs into the road and is killed by a truck. Louis ends up burying him in the secret place, too, with horrible consequences.

In terms of narrative devices, this story is "frontloaded" with detail that anticipates what will happen, and the horrible conclusion occurs rather quickly in narrative time. While the usual horror story has a three-part structure (something weird is happening, we figure out what it is, and then we destroy it), this story is more of a "we know what's going to happen—don't do it!" type of tale. The story is thick with foreshadowing, beginning just eight pages into the novel when Jud warns the Creed family about the big trucks on the road. The novel is, in many ways, suspense more than horror as the reader senses the danger and is unable to prevent it. This is a familiar enough situation for anyone who has watched someone head down a destructive path and has been unable to stop them. From an English professor's perspective, this technique is called "narrative determinism," and from a reader's point of view, it is like watching a train speeding toward a car stuck on the tracks. The inevitable will happen, and it is part of human nature to watch. So first the reader is thinking that Louis should build a fence to keep his kids safe, and then later, as Louis considers bringing his child back to life, the reader thinks, "Don't do it!" all the while knowing that he will. This creates suspense in the story, even though we know the outcome will not be pretty.

Archetypes

Pet Sematary is based on the archetypical story of "be careful what you wish for," which has been told in many times and in many places, from fairy tales "The Frog Prince" and "The Midas Touch" to more modern but classic retellings like Mary Shelley's "The Mortal Immortal" and Oscar

Wilde's *The Picture of Dorian Gray*, both of which involve a character who wishes to live forever. King admits inspiration for his novel came from the W.W. Jacobs story "The Monkey's Paw," where a dead child is returned to life and things don't go well. This story, though old, resonates with readers because everyone has wished for things, and sometimes when these wishes do come true, the results aren't what we had hoped for. We might land a job we coveted, for example, only to find out that we now have more stress in our lives than we need. Of course, we all know that wishes are simply that—fantasy—yet that doesn't stop us from wondering "what if...." In *Pet Sematary*, King builds this wish fulfillment into a narrative reality. After all, even the impossible can and does happen in the Stephen King universe.

Another archetype of this story is the Native American legend of the wendigo, fictionalized by Algernon Blackwood's short story of the same title. The Native American legend originated in the Northeastern United States and the Great Lakes region and describes a cannibalistic type of zombielike creature with insatiable hunger. The legend seems to have been linked to instances of cannibalism among the Native population due to food shortages and also serves as a metaphor for the insatiable hunger of the European settlers who displaced the Native tribes (see an interview with a Native American about this topic in a book titled *The Science of Stephen King*).

This wendigo archetype is also part of the mythology of sacred and sometimes haunted Native American burial grounds, which has become a trope in horror fiction. Some critics have suggested that this idea may be part of America's collective unconscious about repressed guilt for owning land that originally belonged to Indigenous people and in its pollution and destruction by a capitalist society.

Themes and Subtext

By its very nature, horror fiction and fantasy allow readers to imagine the impossible, and by doing so, it provides a gateway to themes that would be impossible to explore using more traditional genres. The very idea of bringing the dead back to life is beyond the scope of both science and literary fiction. However, once the thing becomes possible in the fictional world of horror, we can enter the realm of what-if and see what the consequences might be. And although a discussion of the medical ethics of reanimation might be thought provoking, the average reader isn't very interested in reading essays or scholarly articles on philosophy. That is where Stephen King comes in.

Pet Sematary deals directly with a theme that most Americans would rather not think about—death. The subject is taboo in our society as is evidenced by all the euphemisms we have to describe it ("passed on," "gone to a better place," is "no longer with us," etc.). Although death is part of the natural order of things—all forms of life are genetically programmed to die—we have a difficult time imagining our own death or thinking about the loss of a loved one. But in *Pet Sematary*, King forces us to do exactly that. This is the reason that King considers this novel to be his scariest, and although the novel is entertaining, it is also highly disturbing, especially for parents whose worst nightmare is the death of a child. The story forces readers to confront their fears, stare down the possibility of death, and ask whether they would do the same thing that Louis Creed did were they in his situation. The answer is uncomfortable at best and not easy.

In choosing to reanimate both Church the cat and his son Gage, Louis shows that bringing the dead back to life is a selfish action done for those left behind and not for the dead who, for all we know, may indeed be in "a better place." This leads to the question of why we keep terminally ill patients alive even when they are leading a life of misery with no hope of recovery. Sometimes people refuse to euthanize a suffering pet because they can't let go. And medical ethics and most laws forbid taking the life of a suffering patient. Victims of terminal illness, like Rachel's sister Zelda, are doomed to endure unending agony since physician-assisted suicide is illegal in all but a handful of states in America even though the majority of Americans favor a person's right to die. As King says in the novel, "Sometimes dead is better."

Pet Sematary also contains a subtext of secrets and how people keep things from one another. The obvious example is Louis not telling his family about the death of the cat and then secretly planning to bring his son back to life. Even Jud and his wife kept secrets from each other, secrets that were only revealed when Gage was brought back to life.

The greatest secret, though, is the existence of the *real* pet sematary, hidden far behind the one that the children built. To me, the interesting thing is not that the place is kept secret but that the secret is shared at all. It seems to be part of human nature to share the things we should not. In fact, tabloid newspapers thrive on people's hunger for gossip and sensational stories. Although Jud keeps the secret of the magical cemetery, in the end, he shares it with Louis, fully knowing that his friend will use the power of the place to bring his daughter's pet back to life. It is the sharing of this secret that ultimately brings about so much death and destruction to the Creed family.

Human Universals

Much of Stephen King's success, in my opinion, comes from his ability to tap into human universal emotions, things that are genetically programmed into our DNA as a survival mechanism for the human species. This is most evident in *Pet Sematary*, which hinges on the human universal trait of caring for their children at all costs. Unlike fish, which might spawn millions of offspring, humans generally have just one child at a time. And unlike fish that can swim as soon as they hatch, human newborns are completely helpless and dependent on their parents for survival. It takes decades for a child to become mentally and physically strong enough to live an independent life. Since the "superpower" of the human species is intelligence rather than speed or strength or stealth, evolution has adapted us to a lifetime of gradual growth and learning rather than the hit-the-ground-running strategy of, say, horses. For this to work, however, human parents must care for, nurture, and educate their offspring for a long, long time compared with every other species on the planet. Thus, we are all hardwired to value children greatly and spend an enormous amount of time and energy on ensuring that they both thrive and survive. It is for this reason, evolutionary biologists say, that the death of a child is so traumatic.

King exploits this trait of human nature in *Pet Sematary* by allowing his readers to experience the death of a child, an event that is heartbreaking even when we don't know the child personally. But King takes this one step further in this novel by forcing his readers to imagine the death of their own child, or of another loved one, and forcing them to consider the lengths they would go to to stop it. Most parents would risk their own lives to save the life of their child. They will shield them with their own bodies during a mass shooting and will run into burning buildings to rescue them.

As I mentioned in the section on theme, King also capitalizes on the human fear of death in general. As far as we know, *Homo sapiens* is the only species on earth that understands its own mortality. Although other creatures certainly have an instinctive fear of anything that might harm them, humans are the only ones who know that they will die. It is why we have created funeral homes, life insurance, and even religion. While all horror stories rely on our fear of dying, *Pet Sematary* makes it agonizingly real.

Evaluation

I would rank *Pet Sematary* as one of the most successful stories ever written in the horror genre in general and one of King's best novels. While many if not most horror stories make the reader question the actions of the protagonists (remember the Geico commercial that says characters in horror movies make poor decisions), this King novel shows Louis doing what any of us might do under the circumstances. It is easy to sit in the recliner and predict that this isn't going to end well, but given the opportunity to resurrect a loved one, especially a child, who wouldn't at least consider going ahead with it? King has, in my opinion, used the horror motif to tap into the collective subconscious, which places *Pet Sematary* firmly among the best of contemporary novels.

Interesting Fact

The Ramones produced a hit song, "Pet Sematary," for the 1989 version of the film. It became a top ten hit and was part of their repertoire in the 1990s.

Iconic Moment

Louis Creed returning to his son's grave and digging up the little boy's body.

Notable Quote

"Sometimes dead is better."

16

Eyes of the Dragon
Genre-Bending Fantasy

Background

Stephen King wrote *Eyes of the Dragon*, originally titled "The Napkin," as a fantasy tale for his daughter and published it in a limited edition in 1984. Viking released it as a mass market edition in 1987.

By the time *Eyes of the Dragon* was published, King had established himself as a "brand name" in the horror field, and his Constant Readers expected a steady dose of ghosts, vampires, madness, and mayhem. Many fans dismissed the novel as merely a children's book and expressed displeasure and even anger that he had penned an epic fantasy novel. This, of course, was partially responsible for his writing *Misery*, the iconic novel about an author's "number one fan" who forces him to write the kind of book she wants and is used to.

The critics responded favorably to *Eyes of the Dragon*; it is undoubtedly poetic in its style and has a completely different tone from King's previous novels. And as any King aficionado knows, it is rich in references to what would become King's Dark Tower series, with a "dark tower" of its own where the protagonist is imprisoned by Flagg, another incarnation of "The Man in Black" in the gunslinger multiverse.

Summary and Narrative Devices

Eyes of the Dragon is an epic fantasy reminiscent of the European fairy tale and set in a medieval-type world with wizards, magic, dragons, and even the handsome prince. It is a classic tale of good and evil, with Peter playing the role of the good prince and Flagg taking the part of the satanic villain who engages in evil merely for evil's sake. Flagg's immortal mission is to create chaos, havoc, pain, and destruction in any world or universe he might inhabit. In this story, he works himself into the role of trusted adviser to a weak king who has a worthy heir and another weak son as a backup. Flagg arranges the king's death and frames Peter as the murderer so that Thomas becomes the heir and Flagg can control him as well. It is an often-told story of sibling rivalry, yet portrays Thomas as a sympathetic character, weak and easily manipulated by Flagg. Peter, imprisoned in the tower for years, manages a "Shawshank Redemption" type of escape by collecting threads from his napkins and tying them together to painstakingly build a rope from which to descend from the tower. In the end, of course (spoiler alert), all is corrected, and Peter resumes his rightful place on the throne.

King uses most of the traditional narrative devices in this story—foreshadowing, ending chapters with a cliffhanger, and typical King, ending a section with a single pithy sentence—for example, at the end of section 31, "It was the last word he ever spoke." These techniques keep the pages turning, make readers stay up past their bedtimes with a book, and make them forget about doing mundane tasks like dishes, laundry, and feeding the dog (until the dog reminds us, of course!). If there were a formula for creating suspense, King would own the patent.

In *The Eyes of the Dragon*, though, he also uses a different and clever technique by making the narrator a distinct character, "The Storyteller." Children love to be told stories, and this novel does just that with its "once upon a time"-style opening. This is probably why so many readers mistook this novel for a children's book when it is deceptively sophisticated, especially in the use of poetic and figurative language, the kind of language one would expect from a professional spinner of tales. On more than one occasion, the storyteller's persona emerges, usually to remind us of his own inadequacies in being able to tell the story. This irony (since the storyteller is quite adept at his craft) places the reader in the position of an attentive listener enjoying an exciting bedtime story being read by a beloved adult. The reader, in a sense, becomes a child and can ask for just one more chapter, please, a request that turns into two or three or more. So, in one way, it is a children's story and a brilliant one at that so long as the "Constant Reader" agrees to adopt the role of a child listening to a fairy tale—and honestly, who wouldn't enjoy that role once in a while in this modern, hectic world?

Archetypes

As an English professor, I understand that mythology forms the basis of so many of the world's stories. Every culture has its creation story, its apocalypse story, and its hero's quest. Every culture also has another interesting character in its mythology, one whom Claude Lévi-Strauss and other structuralist critics have termed "the trickster." The trickster is the rule breaker, the one who upsets the status quo, the one who brings chaos and disorder into society. Examples of tricksters include the serpent in the Old Testament book of Genesis; Prometheus, the Greek god who upset Zeus by giving fire to mortal humans; and Loki, the god of Norse legends who was constantly causing trouble. Native American and African cultures have their own tricksters, which include Raven and Anansi, respectively. Some have even proposed that former president Donald Trump is a contemporary example of an American trickster, but since my aim is not to delve into politics, I will leave that for readers to decide (though I believe Stephen King would agree with that assessment).

Flagg fits the description of the trickster perfectly, both in *The Eyes of the Dragon* and in the Dark Tower series. His only agenda is to cause discord, work against all rules of ethics and human decency, and create suffering. And as critics have observed of tricksters, he does inadvertently create a new world from the ashes of the old as Peter rids the domain of Flagg and rebuilds the kingdom. In the guise of The Man in Black and The Dark Man, Flagg will repeat this cycle again in other multiverses.

Another archetype that King employs is the fairy tale itself, as he patterns himself as a modern-day Brothers Grimm. Fantasy authors have often used fairy tales as a storytelling method (one of my personal favorites is Tanith Lee in her short story collection *Red as Blood: Tales from the Sisters Grimmer*). The opening, "Once, in a kingdom called Delain," immediately invokes the fairy-tale motif and transports us into a world of make-believe. This type of story, perhaps one of the oldest forms of narrative, is a part of every culture on earth and is reminiscent of ancient peoples huddled around a fire to listen to the storyteller spin a yarn about faraway places and magical worlds. This story technique, old as it is, never gets old.

I believe that *The Eyes of the Dragon* can also be thought of as a modified version of Shakespeare's last play, *The Tempest*. Both stories revolve around the plot of two brothers, one exiled so the other could assume power, and the quest for the wronged brother to put things right. Shakespeare's Prospero, the protagonist, is the wizard in his play, but Peter performs some wizardry of his own with his mother's dollhouse and loom where he fashions an escape rope from threads from his cloth napkins. Although it is not supernatural magic, this spinning of a yarn (pun perhaps intended—only Stephen King would know) does remind us of the craft, skill, and patience of Shakespeare's magician who also escapes from his island of exile.

Themes and Subtexts

The narrative technique of storytelling also leads to the theme of storytelling, as so many of King's novels do. As he has said in his nonfiction guide *On Writing*, "the story is boss." So many of King's narrators and protagonists are writers, and in this case, the narrator is a self-proclaimed storyteller who dares us to believe the story and often, in true critical thinking fashion, even asks us to decide the truth for ourselves. This feeds the idea of the importance of stories in our lives and is a reminder that storytelling is an innate human ability, one that, to the best of our scientific knowledge, separates man from all other living creatures on the planet. Storytelling is not merely part of our culture but has proven an important tool for our survival. As the literary Darwinists remind us, the prehistoric tribe who had a storyteller who could recount the successes and failures of a hunting trip was more likely to learn how to repeat good technique and avoid lethal mistakes and would thus outperform tribes who lacked this skill. All other things being equal, natural selection rewarded the storytellers and weeded out those who were unable to spin a convincing yarn. Even today, in our modern world of technology and whizbang gadgets, we still love to tell, and to listen to, a good story. *The Eyes of the Dragon* reminds us of this fact.

As we have seen in *Rita Hayworth and the Shawshank Redemption*, justice is a recurring theme in King's fiction. In both novels, an innocent man is falsely imprisoned and, over decades, manufactures his escape and the delicate balance of justice is restored in the finale (or what we English professors call the "denouement"). This sense of fairness and justice runs deep in the human spirit, and readers experience intense satisfaction when the "good guy" wins and the villain is vanquished.

Human Universals

Although we have discussed storytelling already, I'd like to return to it as a human universal, a vital part of human nature, if you will. It is without question that every human being on the planet enjoys a good story. Just the multibillion-dollar film industry is proof enough of that. And what kid doesn't want a bedtime story read before the lights get turned out? Go into any social gathering and what do you hear? People telling stories. In fact, according to Roger Schank (*Tell Me a Story*), our storytelling ability is a better measure of our intelligence than our IQ, and the world's best storytellers (like Stephen King) are rewarded handsomely for their efforts.

As I've said, storytelling has been an important survival method for our species. It is how we have passed on knowledge, created shared cultures, warned each other of danger, and taught each other how to build civilizations. Without the ability to tell stories, our kind would have most likely gone extinct during the last ice age, if not before. *The Eyes of the Dragon*, therefore, works on two different levels. First, our desire to hear a good story, our attraction to "once upon a time." Second, this novel does elevate the storyteller himself to a mythical status by including him as a character. King takes this idea to even more complex levels in the Dark Tower series, where King himself becomes a character in his own story, and the storyteller, as creator of imaginary worlds, becomes a god to these imaginary characters.

Finally, this novel, like much of King's fiction, appeals to the human desire for justice and fairness. This human universal has developed more through cultural evolution than biological evolution according to the experts and is a direct result of a sense of altruism and fair play that holds a society together. Although there may be the occasional outlier, the general idea behind group selection theory, as suggested by David Sloan Wilson and others, states that groups who cooperate outperform those who don't, which results in cooperating becoming a part of the human condition most of the time. Consequently, society has little tolerance for cheaters and other "tricksters" who obtain rewards for themselves at the expense of others. This condition has resulted in the invention and implementation of codes of law that force fair play on outliers and punish those who don't play by the rules. This is not to say that there won't be injustices (there are plenty to choose from in a typical day's news cycle); however, when an injustice is perceived, we have a strong desire to see it corrected. This is the sort of thing that leads to punishment for one's crimes (a good thing) and sometimes horrific wars, acts of terror, and even mob violence (a bad thing), when an injustice either is not resolved or continues to occur. When a story results in justice and closure, readers experience great satisfaction, as is the case with *The Eyes of the Dragon*.

Evaluation

The Eyes of the Dragon is, in my opinion, one of the most underrated of King's novels. It is one of the books I recommend to parents who want to introduce their kids to King without traumatizing them with horror.

Interesting Fact

King began writing *The Eyes of the Dragon* on a yellow legal pad during a blizzard.

Notable Quote

"All questions seem simple if you know the answers, and most horribly difficult if you don't."

17

Thinner

The Book That Outed Bachman

Background

Thinner was the novel that officially "outed" Richard Bachman as the pen name of Stephen King when his name was uncovered on a copyright form at the Library of Congress by an enterprising bookstore clerk. *Thinner* sold 28,000 copies under the Bachman name in 1984, then hundreds of thousands of copies once the pseudonym was exposed. It was adapted for film in 1996.

King claims the idea came to him when his doctor ordered him to quit smoking and lose weight, and he wondered what would happen to someone if they couldn't stop losing weight.

Summary and Narrative Devices

While the Gypsy curse is probably no longer considered politically correct, it has long been a part of folklore. In *Thinner*, the protagonist Billy Halleck runs down and kills an old Gypsy woman who emerges from between two parked cars. Although it was technically an accident, Halleck was somewhat preoccupied and otherwise would have been able to stop in time to avoid the incident. A prominent attorney and Halleck's friendship with the judge, police chief, and other officials ensure that no questions are asked, and he is cleared of all charges. As he emerges from the courthouse, however, the 100-plus-year-old Gypsy patriarch touches his face and curses him with the word "thinner." From that moment on, the obese Halleck begins to steadily lose weight from 246 pounds in chapter 1 to 122 pounds by chapter 25, regardless of how much he eats. This results in a monstrous appearance and, in the later chapters, heart arrythmia which, if the curse isn't lifted, will result in his death.

Thinner uses an interesting plot device in its organization as it includes Halleck's weight in most chapter headings, and these weight numbers steadily count down toward what would presumably be zero if Halleck could survive long enough to waste away to literally nothing. It quickly becomes apparent that he would die before this zero goal was reached, but since neither the reader nor Halleck himself know what the fatal number might be, this countdown creates additional suspense. This is heightened even further once Halleck's condition becomes so critical that it is difficult for him to be seen in public and for him to even attempt to physically confront his tormentors. It is also unclear exactly how much suffering he will have to endure before he succumbs to the curse. Two other men involved in the case were also cursed: one suffered an agonizing death in the intensive care unit of a hospital as his entire body became encased in scales, and the other took his own life before a different but equally horrific skin condition destroyed him.

Putting a deadline on a character's success or failure is an ancient but time-honored technique that attracts readers. In addition to the countdown of Halleck's weight, King also has him declared mentally unstable by his wife and doctor, who attempt to catch him and return him to a hospital where he will undergo useless treatments. Halleck knows that the only way he can survive is by forcing the Gypsy to lift the curse. Since neither his doctor nor his wife believes in curses, he is completely on his own until he calls on a former underworld client to help him in more unorthodox ways.

Archetypes

Thinner is based on the archetypical legends of Gypsy curses collected both formally and informally throughout history. Francis Hindes Groome's stories of Gypsy folklore from 1899 include stories of cannibalism, savagery, and the belief in the "evil eye." There are plenty of urban legends of curses, both Gypsy and otherwise, including one about the town of Lafayette, Oregon, which has supposedly been cursed since the 1800s when an alleged witch cursed the town when she was hanged. Apparently, curses are considered "real" by some people: an internet search turns up several sites explaining how to either cast a curse or how to remove one.

Curses in general have been an important part of literature since the ancient Greeks. Cassandra, one of the heroines in Homer's *The Iliad*, for example, is cursed with the "gift" of prophecy, with the downside that no one will ever believe her. Other notorious curses appear in Hawthorne's *The House of the Seven Gables* and in stories of the curse of Tutankhamen, or "King Tut's curse."

Themes and Subtexts

The major theme of *Thinner* revolves around the idea of guilt. Unless one is a sociopath, guilt is a normal human emotion, probably not an instinctual one so much as a culturally learned one. Taking the life of another would evoke the most guilt of all, even if the death was the result of an accident. And even though Halleck did kill the old Gypsy woman by accident, he still feels responsible, especially because he was being distracted by his wife when it occurred. In fact, the doctors blame his weight loss on mental stress caused by his feelings of guilt in what they call psychological anorexia.

Most neuroscientists do put credence in the theory of mind over matter to a certain extent. Studies have shown that people can modulate their blood pressure and other bodily function through meditation, and stress has been proven to be a leading cause of sickness and death since it does result in the overproduction of neurotransmitters that affect metabolism. Whether the Gypsy's curse is real or not is almost irrelevant—had Halleck not felt guilty about killing the old woman, it is doubtful that the curse would have been effective. *Thinner* demonstrates how guilt can, in this case quite literally, eat away at a person.

As in many King novels, the theme of justice is also evident in *Thinner*. In this case, Halleck is the "guilty" party but enjoys the benefits of race and class privilege to escape punishment. Of course, since the victim did emerge onto the street from between two parked cars without looking, it is questionable whether Halleck would have faced legal consequences even if he wasn't friends with the judge and the police chief. But his privilege ensured that no questions would be asked, questions that might have resulted in embarrassment at the very least and possibly criminal or civil charges at worst. Without an investigation, justice was circumvented; thus, the old Gypsy felt compelled to take justice into his own hands and place hideous curses on the parties involved. This induced karma was overkill and in the long run caused tremendous collateral damage (especially, we are led to believe, after the book has ended). Whereas true justice failed, the vigilante justice of the Gypsies proved to be even worse; after all, the old woman did have some culpability by recklessly crossing the street, and for the victims of the curse, the punishment far exceeded the crime.

Finally, *Thinner* calls into question the ideas of fate, cause and effect, and predestiny. Again and again, Halleck questions why, of all nights, his wife chose this time to masturbate him in the car, something she had never done before. As King writes in *The Institution*, "great events turn on small hinges," and this anomaly in Heidi's behavior had huge consequences, a "butterfly effect" of sorts that cost people their lives. Halleck plays the what-if game and wonders what might have happened had things been different. Who, indeed, hasn't wished to change the past or get a mulligan, a do-over for a past mistake? In *Thinner*, Halleck isn't given another chance. King returns to this theme often, most notably in *11/22/63*, when a time traveler tries to change the past and prevent John Kennedy's assassination. In King's multiverse, fate is not easy to change and often results in a worse future than if things had been left alone.

Human Universals

The most fundamental trait of all living things is to survive. *Thinner* is the ultimate story of survival as we slowly count down the pounds until the protagonist can no longer survive. And even though Halleck has some unlikable characteristics (he is, after all, a lawyer whose clients aren't Boy Scouts by any means), he is sympathetic. He feels remorse for what he has done and wishes he could make it right. He is not solely at fault for the woman's death—his wife and the victim herself share some of the blame. And the love he has for Linda, his daughter, is without question. It is easy, then, for the reader to join him, first to share his fear and horror at what is happening to him and then to root for his survival. Despite what he has done, we want him to succeed, to have the curse lifted and return to his normal life.

Another universal trait is the desire for people to form groups, beginning with prehistoric tribes all the way to the patriotic identity that goes along with being a citizen of a country in our modern world. This idea explains why fans rabidly follow sports teams, even associating themselves with college teams belonging to schools they never attended. It explains why wars are fought and why people in a church group band together to help one of their members who is going through tough times. Religion, nationalism, and cults are all by-products of this group behavior, a behavior that was vital to the survival of our species in prehistoric times, where it took teamwork and cooperation to bring down a mammoth to feed a tribe. Even in our modern world, cooperation is a positive thing. The downside of all this, of course, is an evolutionary artifact that pits groups against one another. This might be quite harmless in a rivalry between two football teams, but it has also resulted in horrendous acts, including the Crusades, the Holocaust, genocide, and racism, which still pervades even our so-called enlightened society.

Thinner exploits this tendency of people to belong to an "in-group" and to dislike and perhaps even hate those in the "out-group." From Halleck's point of view, the Gypsies are the "out-group," which is subject to persecution and bigotry. Had the woman he had struck down with his vehicle been a privileged white woman, things probably would have gone quite differently. If nothing else, Halleck would have been faced with a civil suit by a victim's family who had access to a good lawyer. The Gypsies, members of the out-group, are not given the benefit of even an attempt at justice.

Likewise, the Gypsies themselves are an in-group and consider everyone else outsiders. They, therefore, feel that it is OK to take the law into their own hands and exact a vengeance that far exceeds the crimes they perceive that were committed against them. This group conflict that we all recognize and even relate to in some ways is a part of human nature, a disturbing part of ourselves that we would rather not look at or acknowledge. This novel, however, forces us to examine it whether we want to or not. The result is not pretty.

Evaluation

Thinner, although certainly not one of King's best novels, is a good read, and coming in at under 300 pages, its thinness (pardon the pun) makes it easy and enjoyable.

Interesting Fact

When *Thinner* was released under the Bachman pen name, a review in *The Literary Guild* praised the novel as "what Stephen King would write like if Stephen King could really write."

Iconic Moment

Houston, Halleck's doctor, accuses his patient of sounding "like a Stephen King novel" when he tells him he has been cursed.

Notable Quote

"If you don't have someone to run out of town once in a while, how are you going to know you yourself belong there?"

18

It

We All Float Down Here

Background

It was published in 1986 and, according to *Publisher's Weekly*, was the best-selling hard-cover book of that year. King conceived the idea for the novel while walking over a bridge in Colorado and wondering if a troll lived under the bridge. The novel, a whopping 1,000-plus pages, took him five years to write, interspersed with other books he was working on, including *Cujo*. The book was adapted into a miniseries in 1990, then remade and released as two separate films, part 1 in 2017 and part 2 in 2019. This novel is considered a fan favorite, and its villain, Pennywise the Clown, is one of the most recognizable in popular culture.

It could easily be the subject of an entire book, and, in fact, an entire collection of essays titled *The Many Lives of* It: *Essays on the Stephen King Franchise* was edited by Ron Riekki and published in 2020.

Summary and Narrative Devices

It is really two books in one, and the 2017 and 2019 film versions were released in that way. The first book is about seven kids who are called upon to fight a horrible presence that has infected the town of Derry, Maine, in 1957–58. The second part calls the "Losers' Club" back together in 1984 when "It" reappears, and as adults they must vanquish the monster once and for all.

The story begins with the iconic scene of George losing his paper boat in the sewer and Pennywise, the evil clown, luring him closer and then dragging him down into the sewers of Derry. This beginning sets the stage for a horror that kills children and lets the reader know that the forces of evil in Derry will know no bounds.

The narrative then diverges into two parallel lines that alternate between the 1950s and the 1980s. The novel is divided into five distinct parts that alternate back and forth between 1957 and 1958 and 1984–85. Part 1, the introduction, begins with a brief account of George's disappearance and opens with a "teaser" that informs the reader that the "terror" will not end for another 28 years (if it ever does end). The narrative then jumps ahead in time to 1984, when it begins anew, and then the first part sets up the reconnecting of the Losers' Club to return to Derry and face an unnamed evil once again.

The hero's journey forms the book's internal structure, complete with the descent into the underworld to confront the personification of evil in the form of Hades, Satan, or, in this case, It. In this novel, the hero is really a group, the "Losers' Club," rather than a single individual, and this group travels through all the steps of the hero's journey twice, first as children and then later as adults. In both cases, they leave the safe confines of home, face terrible obstacles, descend into the "belly of the whale," and emerge victorious and very much changed by the experience. The children's portion of the tale is a bildungsroman, a coming-of-age story; the return trip as adults is, in some ways, even more frightening since the protagonists have lost their innocence and now fully understand what they are getting into—so much so that one of them takes his own life rather than face this trial again. In both cases, the story is suspenseful and frightening and demonstrates both the courage and the resilience of the human spirit.

Archetypes

Stephen King recounts how the idea for the story occurred to him as he was walking across a bridge and thought of the idea of "Three Billy Goats Gruff" and wondered, What if a troll were hiding under this bridge? He later transported this idea to his fictional town of Derry, Maine, and recast the river as a sewer. This old Grimm brothers' fairy tale, then, can be considered an archetype for this story. The idea of scary things living in creeks, rivers, and sewers is an old one, and despite modern far-fetched urban legends of alligators living in the sewer systems to emerge through a bathroom toilet, this ancient fear is based on reality. Ancient waterways were filled with a host of dangerous and deadly creatures, and there are still cases of people being attacked by alligators and crocodiles, hippopotami, and, even in America, the poisonous cottonmouth, better known as the water moccasin, which I know from personal experience can be quite aggressive. So, mysterious and dangerous horrors living in waterways beneath us have been part of our collective unconsciousness since at least the time when the ancient Greeks invented the river Styx that coursed through the underworld.

Themes and Subtexts

One of the reasons that *It* has such great appeal is its theme of the victory of the underdog. "The Losers' Club" has become a cultural icon in America and can be found on T-shirts, coffee mugs, and other collectible items. The United States itself can be thought of as a nation founded by "losers" in the strict European definition, men and women who didn't fit in for any number of reasons: religion, poverty, lack of a title or social status, refusal to follow rules.... Yet these pioneering people were able to carve out a nation that has become a world power through their hard work, wit, determination, and, in some cases, just plain stubbornness. One might debate the ethics of the treatment of Native Americans and slaves, but there can be no doubt that America was founded and built by those who were considered "throwaways," a diverse group that included enslaved people, immigrants from nearly every country in the world who often arrived on the shores penniless, and those who were able to risk everything for a chance at a better life, sometimes to escape persecution in their homeland and sometimes to escape famine. King's "Losers' Club" is in many ways a representation of our heritage, a diverse group of children who are outcasts among their peers.

In sports and in life, it is an American tradition to root for the underdog. The 2004 Boston Red Sox (the subject, incidentally, of King's nonfiction work *The Faithful* written with O'Nan), the 1968 New York Jets, and the victory of the American ice hockey team over the dominant Russians in the 1980 Olympics (dubbed the "Miracle on Ice") are all part of underdog legend. The "rags to riches" story forms an integral part of the American dream. So it is no accident that American culture has appropriated King's Losers' Club as an example of how the power of courage and determination can prevail over the greatest odds.

The Losers' Club, of course, is not composed of "losers" at all but of kids that don't fit in with their peers. One interesting facet of American culture is that the "brainy" kids in middle and high school are not considered the "cool" kids. In the United States, adolescents revere the athletes and the cheerleaders rather than the members of the chess club or the math team. These "nerds" are often bullied and persecuted relentlessly, as is someone who doesn't fit in. This theme also runs through much of King's fiction. Of course, the follow-up is that the "jocks" seldom become successful in King's fiction, while the "nerds" often go on to enjoy successful careers (which, I believe, is also true in real life). This is the case in *It* where the protagonists all pursue lucrative careers while the bullies become the losers. It is interesting to note that beginning in 2005, nerds became portrayed as heroes in television shows such as *Numbers* and *Bones*, where mathematicians and scientists solved crimes. This trend has continued even into the comedy genre where the lovable nerds of *The Big Bang Theory* are considered "cool."

Accompanying the theme of the underdog, of course, is the exploration of "bullying," which is especially prevalent in teenagers and is a core element in so many of King's books, beginning with *Carrie* and continuing through the Hodges trilogy and into *Elevation*, where even adult characters are threatened and bullied because of their sexual orientation. While *It*, written in the 1980s, deals with traditional bullying, this issue continues into the present with bullying and threats on social media as well as usual harassment. King's fiction points out the disastrous effects this persecution can have on children and adults.

While *It* creates a rich tapestry of themes and subtexts, the final one I will consider here is its relationship to King's macrocosmic world, the multiverse that connects all his works into a single worldview that is best seen in the Dark Tower series. *It* goes beyond the traditional horror of ghosts, werewolves, and vampires—and even creepy clowns—to create a cosmic horror in the vein of H.P. Lovecraft, the master of that genre. In the climactic scenes of *It*, the heroes are thrown into the middle of this all-encompassing world where they confront the elemental forces of universe itself. Although they are victorious, we realize that they have won just one tiny battle in an immense cosmic struggle that is far beyond their understanding. This level of horror underscores the idea of human insignificance in the universe at large. Yet this insignificance is tempered with the realization that although our species might be mere specks in a cosmic sense, each individual can make a powerful difference within the realms of his or her own small world and may, on occasion, even stand up to the cosmos itself.

Human Universals

A fan favorite, *It* is ranked as Stephen King's second-best novel by both Barnes & Noble and Goodreads, which for me as an English professor means that he has successfully appealed to readers on a human level. In fact, *It* does touch several nerves on both a visceral and emotional level, enough so that it is not only a fan favorite despite being written over 40 years ago but also resulted in successful film adaptations.

Typecast as a horror writer, Stephen King's greatest tool is the ability to evoke fear, which, as Lovecraft has stated, is "the oldest human emotion." *It* is a masterpiece of terror. There are many reasons why modern readers enjoy being terrified. For the most part, these reasons come down to the level of neuroscience, but suffice it to say that fear is a basic human instinct that our modern culture has turned into entertainment. In *It*, King brings out all of the things that we are instinctively afraid of—dark places, spiders, squishy things, rotting things (the sewers)—and combines them with fears that come from modern culture—parental abuse, being picked on by stronger kids, people wearing scary war paint on their faces (clowns), old, abandoned buildings, creatures from horror films ... and the list goes on. This novel has touched such a strong a nerve that clowns, once funny and beloved, have become the subjects for scary Halloween costumes.

It also taps into the human universal emotion of GRIEF from the very beginning with Georgie's disappearance. Grief is, of course, bad enough under normal circumstances but is compounded here since Georgie's body is not found and closure is impossible. Bill also suffers from the guilt of not having been with his little brother when he disappeared, which triggers the SEEKING response, to find his brother, learn what happened, and reach closure. Although Georgie is only a character at the very beginning of the novel, his spirit runs throughout the book, unseen but omnipresent.

Finally, *It*, like other King novels, explores the idea of kinship and the whole being stronger than the sum of its parts. This concept, perhaps best expressed in the Dark Tower books as *ka-tet*, explores the strength in unity and the power of a strong, tightly bonded group to accomplish nearly impossible things. This goes back to Wilson's theory of altruism that states that the moral group is stronger than the immoral individual, a cultural evolutionary trait that has allowed humans to become the dominant species on the planet. It is true that this in-group and out-group belief can lead to hatred and horrible atrocities—wars, genocide, and racism—but when channeled properly and more inclusively, it has also led to amazing accomplishments, such as international efforts to fight the Covid-19 virus. *It* is about a heroic group, a *ka-tet*, rather than a single individual hero. Only the strength, courage, and multiple talents of the group allow them to overcome the evil that resides in the sewers of Derry.

Evaluation

As a Constant Reader, I see *It* as one of the most frightening horror novels ever penned; after reading it, I have never regarded a clown the same way again! As an English professor, I see an epic-length book that explores human fears at a deep and profound level, a book that forces me to think about what really does scare me the most and why. This goes beyond the superficial fear of things that go bump in the night and forces the reader to really look at his or her place in the cosmos and realize that for all our bluster, we are not the center of the universe. Life is fragile, and even the survival of our species and our planet is tentative at best. *It* helps us to put this notion in perspective, and although we understand that we can achieve great things by working together, we are reminded that these achievements come with much effort and sacrifice, often at great cost, and are not guaranteed to be successful.

Interesting Fact

The infamous scene in which each of the members of the Losers' Club have sex with Beverly was considered too controversial to include in any of the film adaptations. King saw the scene as a symbolic rite of passage into adulthood and has said in interviews that times were different when the book was written, and it was not intended to be provocative.

Iconic Moment

Pennywise handing Georgie a balloon.

Notable Quote

"We all float down here."

19

Misery
The Price of Fame

Background

Misery was published by Viking in 1987 and adapted into a highly successful film in 1990 for which Kathy Bates won an Oscar for her harrowing portrayal of Annie Wilkes, every writer's worst nightmare come to life. Partly autobiographical, the novel was King's answer to some of his rabid fans who expressed disappointment and outright anger that some of his work had deviated from the horror genre that they expected. By this time, King had also achieved celebrity status and was hounded by fans for autographs and by tourists showing up outside the gates of his home in Bangor, Maine. In one instance, a fan even broke into his house and waited for his return. Although he has been accused of disparaging his "Constant Readers" in this novel, King sees the book as a way of expressing his independence as a writer; with his fame and notoriety came the wealth to be unbeholden to the marketing demands of either his readers or his publishers, thus enabling him to write the stories that he wanted to write.

Summary and Narrative Devices

Misery is not a horror story in the traditional sense (ghosts, vampires, werewolves), but it does contain all of the elements of horror that King identified in *Danse Macabre*: terror, horror, and the gross-out. Once again, the protagonist is a writer, a theme that is especially important in the stories he wrote during this time (*The Dark Half* and "Secret Window, Secret Garden"), where he seems to have exorcised his own writing demons in print. In these narratives we are treated to some of the paranoia that successful writers have, the loss of privacy, the fear of being accused of plagiarism, and the whole issue of pen names and being typecast in specific genres.

19. *Misery*

Paul Sheldon, the protagonist in *Misery*, is a very successful novelist who writes what might be termed bodice rippers, Victorian-type romances that are mostly read by women and that have little to no literary merit. His real dream is to write books that have artistic value, and so he fictionally "kills" Misery, his heroine, and writes what he considers a meaningful book. Unfortunately, on his way to deliver the manuscript to his publisher, he crashes his car into a ditch beside a remote road and is saved from certain death by Annie Wilkes, his "number one fan." Once Annie, a psychopathic ex-nurse, learns of his new novel and the death of Misery, she forces him to burn his new manuscript (he has violated the author's number one rule of not having kept a backup copy) and forces him to resurrect Misery and write a new novel about her. She accomplishes this goal using torture, the threat of withholding his needed painkillers, and by keeping him locked up so that he can't escape.

The story begins in medias res with the protagonist slipping in and out of consciousness. We don't learn the man's name until page six but just sense his pain, which fluctuates between levels, and in his first real experience is being brought back to life through mouth-to-mouth resuscitation from a woman he doesn't know. The reader, like Paul Sheldon, struggles to understand what has happened and remembers the situation with him as he slowly becomes aware. This interesting plot device has the reader discovering Paul Sheldon's backstory even as he remembers it and as Annie fills in the details of his car crash.

On page eight of the novel, the great truth is revealed: "Annie Wilkes was dangerously crazy." As the story progresses, we learn just how dangerous she is. Herein lies the plot of the novel and the central question—How is Paul going to escape from this woman and this place? The stakes increase as Annie reveals the true extent of her insanity, and Paul discovers that she has killed in the past and will kill him once he finishes his new Misery novel for her. So, this story, much like *Shawshank*, is an escape story where Paul must use all of his wits to break out from what amounts to death row before it is too late.

While *Misery* uses many of the same techniques we have already discussed to build its suspense, this novel introduces another tool that King uses to great advantage: fiction within fiction. This concept was used within *The Body*, where the protagonist re-created some short narratives he had written as a boy. But in *Misery*, this technique is used with great skill to show the concrete style differences between Paul Sheldon's romance novels, which are in sharp contrast to King's style, and, presumably, that of Sheldon's "literary" novel, *Fast Cars*.

It is apparent from the excerpt of "Misery Returns" that the genre-specific bodice ripper books that Paul Sheldon writes are simple, with a strictly linear chronological plot, whereas "Fast Cars" uses many of the literary techniques that English professors isolate and analyze. Annie doesn't like the novel for many reasons, including its tendency to jump around in time. This technique of playing with time, or course, is central to much of King's writing: as I have discussed in the chapter on *It*, that book relies on two parallel time structures that flip back and forth, a technique that adds to the book's suspense and effectiveness.

The straightforward, simplistic narrative of the "Misery" book offers a direct contrast to what "good" writing should be in its use of weak verbs and lots of empty-air types of description. The faulty keys of the typewriter also highlight the faulty writing that separates King's work from the typical contrived novel, be it romance or horror.

Archetypes

The major conflict in *Misery* involves Paul's being forced to write to entertain the person who controls his life (or death). This hails to Scheherazade and *The 1001 Nights* where the heroine must tell stories to stay alive. Once the story ends, the heroine knows she will be put to death, so she must continue making up new stories night after night. In Paul's case, he also knows his death is imminent once his story is finished. The fact that he writes novels—stories with a distinct beginning, middle, and end, complicates his predicament since he has a finite number of pages to fill, and the story must reach an end.

This idea of equating writing (or storytelling, or any other art form) with life is prevalent in King's books; King admits that he is "addicted to writing" and cannot stop, even though he no longer needs the income that his work produces. To him, and many other creative people, writing and art are important components of the meaning of life. This is articulated quite eloquently in *The Arabian Nights* and *Misery*.

Themes and Subtexts

Creativity and the arts, as symbolized by fiction writing, establishes a compelling theme in *Misery*. Storytelling, as a human universal, resonates with all people; humans have a strong desire to tell their own individual stories and, most important, have them heard. Annie's refusal to accept Paul's new novel and her forcing him to write something he doesn't want to create produces a sense of frustration in readers, who also wish to follow their own creative urges in whatever discipline they may choose. Paul's being forced to write a book he dislikes mirrors the plight of so many people who are forced to work in jobs they hate and/or create things that audiences demand rather than follow their own passions.

Human beings are also the only creatures on the planet that want to leave something behind after they are gone (besides offspring). We all wish to make a difference, change the world in some small way, and leave a legacy. This accounts for funeral customs and explains why people spend thousands of dollars on headstones and monuments. It also explains why writers, artists, and musicians want to have their work survive after they have died. Paul Sheldon is quite aware that his "Misery" books are the publishing equivalent of junk food. He is hoping that he can leave behind a more meaningful work. Readers, of course, understand that quite well and relate to this theme.

Finally, in *Misery*, King introduces the theme of the rabid fan, which is probably a by-product of the age of mass media. Although celebrity status certainly has its perks, it has also resulted in a loss of privacy and, much worse, cases of stalking and violence. The murder of John Lennon is probably the best-known tragic example, but other celebrities have been stalked as well. Even though this is unusual for writers who have a less visible profile, King has been a victim as well, with one fan accusing him of stealing her book idea and another actually breaking into his Bangor home and waiting for him to return. As a result, King is no longer able to attend horror conventions, makes very few public appearances, and no longer signs autographs. While some might say that this is simply the price one pays for success, *Misery* graphically depicts how fandom can be taken to the extreme. In fact, King has often complained that his fans demand that he write only certain types of books and send him angry letters when he publishes anything different. Due to his celebrity status, he now has an office assistant who handles his public affairs and correspondence and a website that promotes his latest work and has a FAQ section (no, Stephen will not read your manuscript and send you a critique!).

Human Universals

Darwin's theory of natural selection states that each species has developed certain "superpowers" that have allowed it to survive, thrive, and evolve. A hummingbird, for example, has developed a needlelike beak and the ability to hover in place so that it can extract nectar from flowers. The cheetah can outrun any creature on the planet. And *Homo sapiens*, humans, tell stories.

Although storytelling might not seem like a superpower or even a survival mechanism at first glance, evolutionary biologists believe that language in general and our ability to tell stories in particular are major factors in why humans have become the dominant species on the planet. By telling stories, our ancestors passed on knowledge, warned of dangers (don't swim in that pond; just last week, I was there and I saw an alligator eat a boy who was walking along the shore), and, yes, seduced mates (which might explain the preponderance of love poetry and love songs from the most ancient times to the modern).

Storytelling is a human universal trait. When we gather for social events, we do two things: feast and tell stories. Whenever two or more people get together, they begin exchanging stories, which is why, according to Roger Schank (*Tell Me a Story: A New Look at Real and Artificial Memory*), we are smarter, more cleaver, and more creative than computers, even though they might be able to "calculate" faster than we do. We are, as Brian Boyd says, "addicted to story."

Misery (and other King stories that feature writer protagonists) exploits this human universal trait. While the average Constant Reader might not be a writer, everyone feels Paul's "misery" as he is forced to burn the only copy of his beloved manuscript. For someone to devalue and destroy your story is a painful experience, as any student writer can testify when receiving a returned paper covered with corrections and cross-outs in red ink. Annie not only maims Paul physically, but she forces him to "kill" his own story, and as writers well know, their stories are like their children. This universal pain is felt by readers who are not writers since nearly everyone has experienced the pain of having someone try to destroy a cherished dream. This shared experience makes *Misery* a very powerful novel.

Evaluation

Misery is, and will remain, a King classic, and Annie Wilkes has become the iconic example of the rabid fan. While the novel is especially poignant for writers and artists, it touches on themes that are an important part of modern culture and is one of King's best novels in my opinion.

Interesting Fact

Stephen King came up with the idea for *Misery* while on a plane and the passenger next to him claimed to be his "number one fan."

19. *Misery*

Iconic Moment

Annie Wilkes hobbling Paul Sheldon.

Notable Quote

"I'm your number one fan."

20

The Tommyknockers
Mechanized Aliens

Background

The Tommyknockers was published in 1987 by Viking. King hatched the idea for the novel when he was in college and imagined a man stumbling over a flying saucer. He put it aside until the 1980s and wrote it during a time when he was abusing alcohol and drugs.

Full disclosure: *The Tommyknockers* is my least favorite Stephen King novel. Hey, there has to be one, right? Just like there has to be a favorite, except I have more than one favorite. Anyway, when it came time to write this chapter, I was anxious to get it over with and move on to novels I'd enjoyed more. But after reading *The Tommyknockers* again (I hadn't read it since it was first published all the way back in 1987), I realized that (1) it wasn't as bad as I'd thought, and (2) I'd give almost anything if my best fiction was as good as King's worst. So now, with that out of the way, let me read *The Tommyknockers* like an English professor.

Summary and Narrative Devices

First, let's be honest, the plot is rather lame—a writer of Western novels digs up a crashed flying saucer in the acreage in her backyard. Gardner, one of the main characters, articulates this thought: "No self-respecting science-fiction writer would put one [a flying saucer] in his story, and if he did, no self-respecting editor would touch it with a ten-foot pole." Except King *does* put a flying saucer into his novel and makes the story work despite the fact that most of it was written, according to King, while he was bingeing on alcohol and drugs (which is a major theme of this novel). The saucer, buried for millions of earth years, emits a pulse or radiation that infects the locals, causing them to dig it up, and as they do, they become endowed with supernatural intelligence, including the ability to communicate telepathically and to create amazing technology from common household items. (My personal favorite is the robot Coke machine that acts as a sentry and kills intruders by smashing them with its refrigerator-sized body.) The locals slowly transform to become aliens themselves, beings that Paul Gardner, the protagonist, labels as "Tommyknockers." The townspeople become so obsessed with the spaceship and their newfound intelligence that they ignore everything else, sealing the small town off from the rest of the world to complete the task the saucer ship has set for them.

Archetypes

The Tommyknockers is strongly influenced by a 1954 science fiction novel, *Brain Wave*, by Poul Anderson, which accounts for Bobby Anderson's last name (no, King didn't name her after me) and a direct reference to the novel in King's narrative. *Brain Wave* postulates a scenario where the earth enters a portion of space containing an electromagnetic pulse of sorts that changes the laws of physics, allowing neurons to fire faster than light. All that is a fancy way of saying that all earth creatures with a central nervous system suddenly become much smarter and almost every human being becomes a genius. The downside of this utopia is that they lose much of their humanity and become builders rather than thinkers—just like the "Tommyknockers" that King has created.

The novel is also based on the H.P. Lovecraft short story "The Colour out of Space," where an alien artifact crashes in a New England town and begins to change the locals, and not for the better. This artifact, much like the alien ship, has a profound effect on the main character, totally dehumanizing him.

Themes and Subtexts

Stephen King was suffering from drug and alcohol addiction while writing *The Tommyknockers*, which not only weakened the strength of the novel but served as a major subtext of the work. The crashed alien ship symbolizes the power that addiction has over people, forcing them to abandon everything they care about to feed their craving. The desire for the drug becomes an obsession and transforms human beings into almost robotic creatures in search of the next high. The drug—in this case, the poisoned air from the alien vessel—takes away their ability to think for themselves. They become mindless drones doing what the ship has programmed them to do. The "drugged" characters abandon all their moral principles and transform into beings that are no longer human. Bobbi Anderson, who once loved Gardner both as a lover and then as a friend, is willing to murder him to prevent him from stopping her from achieving the goals of the spacecraft. She even turns her beloved dog into a brain vessel of fuel for the craft. Gardner finds her treatment of her pet to be the most disturbing and inhumane act of all.

Through the character of Gardner, King creates an accurate and believable picture of what alcoholism is like. This is particularly poignant in the beginning of the novel when Gardner is introduced. A recovering alcoholic, he knows what drinking will do to him. Despite his best efforts, however, he cannot control himself. His drinking is self-destructive as he ruins his career and stands at the verge of taking his own life rather than face the consequences. Ironically, he turns to Bobbi for help, only to discover that her addiction to the Tommyknockers is even more powerful and destructive than his addiction to alcohol.

Perhaps the most interesting theme of the novel is the concept of building and the opposition of creativity versus merely building something from a predetermined design. The aliens might be master builders, but their building is robotic, without creativity or thought. They simply follow a blueprint, put together the pieces, and build whatever was in the design. They have no room for either creativity or thinking in their world or for emotion. Like artificial intelligence programs that attempt to replicate human art and writing, the result is formulaic and merely functional, with no artistic merit.

Although these aliens might be master builders, they have no arts or culture and no ability to think critically or make decisions that are not preprogrammed. While the closest we come to seeing the aliens is in their takeover of humans, they are reminiscent of the Vogons in Douglas Adams's *The Hitchhiker's Guide to the Galaxy*, who are noted to be the second worst poets in the universe and mindlessly follow ridiculous orders without emotion or question. Despite their amazing technology and building skills, the Tommyknockers are a pretty pathetic species. Without emotions, art, and culture, sentient life really isn't very admirable or interesting.

King also makes mention of "The Shop," the supersecret government agency that exists in several novels of the King multiverse. Although "The Shop" doesn't play a role in this book, its reference does symbolize the overreach of government and how it would eliminate any civil rights to develop weapons. Gardner has the legitimate fear that government and/or big business would cover up and/or destroy inventions that might hurt them or else use these technologies for nefarious purposes.

Human Universals

There have been centuries of debate over what it means to be human. Philosophers, poets, sociologists, psychologists, and biologists have all tackled this question with no definitive answer. And although *The Tommyknockers* certainly doesn't definitively answer this question either, the book does provide some fictional insight into the problem.

One of the basic human universals, according to Jaak Panksepp and other evolutionary biologists, is the affective emotion of PLAY. While this seems to be evident in most mammals (just watch a group of kittens), it has become highly developed in humans and has been significant in our evolutionary success. The PLAY emotion is the driving force behind virtually all human entertainment (films, sports, video games, music, the visual arts, poetry ... the list is almost endless). This PLAY emotion has developed into imagination, the ability to dream of something that doesn't exist, and then create it. This imaginative creation is a polar opposite of the building skills of the Tommyknockers, who are just working on a paint-by-numbers kit rather than creating original art. King shows how bankrupt our species would be if we ever lost our imagination, our artistic desires, and our culture.

To be human also involves having empathy and the ability to love and care for others. The Tommyknockers lack this basic human trait and, instead, have become slaves to technology. They seem to be a violent species, willing to kill without remorse, and willing to program other species in the universe to be just like them. This destruction of humanity within the residents of the town is emblematic of what life would be like without empathy, altruism, and love. It is a hopeless world with a life that isn't worth living.

Their lack of imagination ultimately destroys the Tommyknockers' plans for earth. Gardner, a wild card, puts an end to their grand scheme. He accomplishes this because of his empathy for others—he is highly motivated to bring back the boy from the planet where he's been mistakenly sent, and to free the dog from its inhumane prison—and by his imagination. Gardner can think for himself, to imagine different possibilities, and to carry out a plan that the "genius" Tommyknockers never see coming. As the only real human left in town, it is his inventiveness and thinking that rule the day in the long run.

Evaluation

As I've said, *The Tommyknockers* is my least favorite of King's novels. Admittedly, it was written while King was indulging in alcohol and drugs, which certainly weakens the book. King himself admits it would work better at half its length—the middle section, in particular, seems to plod along without going much of anywhere. Finally, the premise, while it could be interesting, suffers from a lack of verisimilitude.

Interesting Fact

Stephen King admits that the novel, written while he was suffering from substance abuse, isn't very good. In a *Rolling Stone* interview, he said, "*The Tommyknockers* is an awful book. That was the last one I wrote before I cleaned up my act."

Notable Quote

"You had to wonder how loving a God could be when He made men and women smart enough to land on the moon but stupid enough to learn there was no such thing as forever over and over again."

21

The Dark Half

Attack of the Pseudonym

Background

The Dark Half, published in 1989, is another novel with an author protagonist and, like *Misery*, reflects some of Stephen King's deepest thoughts on writing. The book was released after the news of the Bachman pen name became public. The lead character, Thad Beaumont, mirrors King in that he also uses a pen name to write books, only in this case his alter ego, George Stark, is more successful than his real-life creator. *The Dark Half* was adapted into a feature film in 1993 directed by George Romero and starring Timothy Hutton.

Summary and Narrative Devices

The novel opens with Thad Beaumont symbolically "killing" the persona of George Stark, his pseudonym, and admitting publicly that he was the real author of the gritty thrillers that he'd attributed to his alter ego. Soon afterward, strange things begin to happen, people get killed, and Thad realizes that the fictitious Stark has come to life. The novel becomes a test of wills between the two versions of the author as Stark attempts to kill Beaumont and take over the author's life. Once Beaumont realizes that his alter ego has transformed from the make-believe into reality, he knows he must kill him or else he will be taken over by the pseudonym.

The Dark Half has a theme of duplicity and the narrative structure reflects this idea, dividing the plot into "twin" parallel narratives that converge in strategic places when Beaumont and Stark cross paths. As a result of this structure, the reader is privy to things that neither of the pair can know about each other. The novel is essentially "two-faced" with the reader living with each character in turn. When Stark kills two police officers, for example, it is shown through his viewpoint in vivid detail. Beaumont, 500 miles away, is only aware of the violence that his twin is committing through vague, unremembered dreams.

Much of the suspense of the story comes from knowing that these two parallel storylines will eventually intersect and clash as the book reaches its climax. The question of which of the twins will prevail is never certain until the very end; if an innocent child can be killed in *Cujo*, then Beaumont's survival lies on tenuous ground. And, of course, even though Stark and his evil is purged in fire at the end of the novel (a common King tactic), Stark's words and his novels will still exist as long as the pseudonym's works remain in print.

The twin plot device also allows the words of both men to be in print within the pages of *The Dark Half*. Excerpts of Stark's fiction are peppered throughout the book. Most notably, though, the novel does conclude with Beaumont's words leading off the epilogue with a sensitive and poetic passage from *The Sudden Dancers*, one of the surviving author's creations—a passage that clearly contrasts with Stark's no-nonsense prose.

Archetypes

The use of twins as characters in literature has a long history dating back to Shakespeare's *The Comedy of Errors*, where the comedic value of mistaken identity was explored. The idea of the doppelgänger, the look-alike, appeared in Poe's William Wilson, first published in 1839, with horrific effects (King also acknowledged "William Wilson" as the inspiration behind his 2018 novel, *The Outsider*). Poe's story perpetuated the superstition that meeting your double would portend your death.

The novel also uses Robert Louis Stevenson's *The Strange Case of Dr. Jekyll and Mr. Hyde* as a correlative, where the "nice" professor is taken over by the evil Mr. Hyde, a vicious killer. Harlan Ellison's 1975 short story "Shatterday" (later made into an episode for the new *Twilight Zone* series) depicts the creation of an "evil twin" who takes over and absorbs the protagonist.

Themes and Subtexts

The Dark Half forms part of the series of books that King wrote that specifically relate to the craft of writing. Like *Misery*, this novel explores, among other things, the concepts of literary writing versus popular writing. Thad, the "literary" author, publishes meaningful books that are read by only a few people, but the accolades of the critics do allow him to enjoy the comfortable life of a college professor. His pseudonym Stark, on the other hand, writes popular novels in anonymity, creating stories that, although entertaining, have little artistic or cultural value. King sets up an either-or situation in this book, separating authors into two distinct camps—those whom the critics adore and those who people read. And for most successful novelists, this dichotomy holds true: writers tend to be either read or admired. Very few have managed to conquer both worlds. And for most of his career, King was securely in the popular author camp. Only recently has he been acknowledged as being worthy of serious study.

Literary writing represents culture and society, the things that are "good" for us and good for humanity. Popular writing appeals to our baser instincts—the pure adrenaline rush of a good, unadorned story. King intentionally blurs the lines between literary and commercial fiction, however.

The truth is revealed in the lie of fiction. In King's world, the fantastic is the only element that can successfully tell the unpleasant truth that literary fiction is not very marketable. By contrast, genre fiction has a large and captive audience that leads to commercial success. The irony is that this genre fiction carries universal truths while also being of literary quality. This is evident in the two faces of *The Dark Half*—the brutal realism of Stark and the elegant prose of King.

The major theme of the novel concerns the binary nature of man—the civilized intellectual and the savage within. In Freudian terms, the twins represent the ego and the id. Beaumont has a respectable job, writes respectable novels, and lives a quiet, suburban life. Stark, on the other hand, metaphorically only comes out at night and writes violent visceral books with memorable villains. The names even characterize this difference. Beaumont derives from a fancy French word ("beautiful mountain") while "Stark" is a word of old English origin ("unyielding" or "severe") that is often associated with the phrase "stark raving mad." It seems that we have both types of individuals within us, and Beaumont's struggle is the personification of the human struggle at large, to keep the primitive urges in check while elevating our more civilized traits.

Human Universals

The theme of the duality of the human species is reflective of Darwin's theory of natural selection, the survival of the fittest, if you will, coupled with Richard Dawkins's concept of "the selfish gene." There are two Thad Beaumonts, genetically related, since one of them manifested itself from a vestigial twin, and only one of them can live to write another day. The original Thad is the mild-mannered academic, the thinker who uses his brains and intellect to create stories. The upstart, George Stark, is composed of pure emotion. He writes by the seat of his pants, creating action stories that appeal to man's basic needs (and these stories are geared toward a male audience). Even as his character comes to life, Stark shows himself to be a man of action, taking matters into his own hands to ensure his survival and forcing Thad to play defense. And even as *Homo sapiens*, the species has thrived through intellect, developing culture, and working as a group; so does Thad prevail over his alter ego, using his powers of reasoning and his social connections with others to his advantage.

Evaluation

As a writer, I found *The Dark Half* to be disturbing, to say the least. But as a professor, I wouldn't rank the novel as one of King's best. It is rich in what Roland Barthes terms "textual code" (or metalanguage, to use the postmodern term), a technique where writing speaks about writing, and that brings interest to the book. But it does, in my opinion, fall short of King's best efforts that explore the larger human condition.

Interesting Fact

The pen names "George Stark" and Richard Bachman were inspired by mystery writer Donald E. Westlake (1933–2008) who used "Richard Stark" as a pseudonym to write 30 books in addition to writing more than 50 books and some screenplays under his own name.

Notable Quote

"What good is it, writing a thing, if no one wants to read it?"

22

Needful Things

The Downside of a Consumer Society

Background

Needful Things was originally published in 1991 and, according to King, was meant as a satire about the 1980s, dubbed the "decade of greed" due to the financial scandals, leveraged buyouts, junk bonds, and insider trading that characterized that period, made famous by the line, "Greed ... is good" from the movie *Wall Street*. The book was adapted into a film in 1993 directed by Fraser C. Heston, Charlton Heston's son. The novel is set in Castle Rock, Maine, the setting for *The Body, Cujo, The Dead Zone, The Dark Half*, and a number of shorter pieces. Although originally billed as "the last Castle Rock novel," King returned to the town again in the short novel *Elevation*, published in 2018, and the popular television series *Castle Rock* had the town as its title.

Summary and Narrative Devices

Needful Things resembles *'Salem's Lot* since both novels are, essentially, the invasion and destruction of a small town by an outside evil character. This time, instead of vampires, the villain is the devil himself in the form of a curiosity shop proprietor named Leland Gaunt.

Gaunt's shop, Needful Things, has something for everyone, and the shop owner's powerful influence makes his customers see the one thing that they think they can't live without, even though that item is a worthless piece of junk or downright dangerous. Brian Rusk, the first victim, believes a worthless baseball card is a rare Sandy Koufax card, signed and made out to him. The prices of the objects are ridiculously affordable, but like the axiom "If it looks too good to be true, it probably is," the objects come with a hefty price that involves doing seemingly harmless deeds that will ultimately destroy the town and will cost the buyer a soul.

King uses many traditional narrative devices to create suspense. With a large cast of characters, he often ends a section with one character immersed in deep trouble, then changes the scene to another character, forcing the reader to wait for the resolution of the first conflict. This panoramic view of Castle Rock allows King to kill off some of the favorite characters, such as Brian Rusk, the innocent boy who is tormented after purchasing the Sandy Koufax baseball card. This raises the stakes for all the heroes in the story and alerts the reader that no one is safe.

King uses some obvious foreshadowing from the very beginning with the warning that "trouble is on the way" and the question about the shop's name: "Needful Things: what, exactly did that mean?" Using the same technique as he's employed in *'Salem's Lot* with the Marsten House, rumors about the shop appear before it even opens. This sets the stage for the shop and its proprietor to emerge as the central character of the novel.

Perhaps the most interesting technique King employs in this novel is the use of his narrator in the prologue and epilogue. This narrator is a homespun resident of the town who addresses the reader directly as a long-lost friend with the reminder that "you've been here before." This is King, of course, speaking directly to his "Constant Reader" who, by reading King's books, *has* been here before, both in Castle Rock and in other small towns in Maine. The novel is very reminiscent of *'Salem's Lot*, a book that all Constant Readers are familiar with, and the reader knows and understands that trouble is on the way and is prepared to enjoy the ride, wherever it might go. This technique of inviting the reader into the story allows us to become involved on a deeper level, imagining ourselves as residents of Castle Rock and observing the action directly rather than from the sidelines of a novel. Since we have become a participant in the story, we also can imagine what Gaunt might tempt us with were we to enter his shop. (What would this English professor do for a signed first edition of *Carrie*? Don't tempt me!)

The epilogue mirrors the opening lines, reminding us that Gaunt and our "needful things" (which have now morphed into "answered prayers") are still very much with us and will reappear over and over in a never-ending chain of wants and needs. The desire for things, then, is not just a product of one small town but is universal. The story ends with the warning that the temptation of greed may be visiting our neighborhood next and that we must be ever vigilant in keeping our priorities right.

Archetypes

The archetype for *Needful Things* is the Faustian bargain from German folklore, where a necromancer trades his soul for worldly knowledge. A historical Faust lived in the 1500s and claimed the devil as his supporter. The legend was popularized in literature by Christopher Marlowe's play *The Tragical History of the Life and Death of Doctor Faustus* (1604) and by Goethe's early 19th-century play *Faust* (in two parts) where the protagonist makes a wager with the devil. The deal with the devil motif has become a trope in the horror field, though in the traditional story, those who bargain for their souls do it willingly. In *Needful Things*, they don't know what they've done until it is too late.

Themes and Subtexts

As Stephen King himself has noted, *Needful Things* was written as a satire on greed with a slightly humorous intent to poke fun at capitalism gone wild, and he was rather surprised that it was taken so seriously. Whether read as horror or as satire, this theme is obvious in the novel. The obsession with acquisition permeates the story as people buy things that they "need," things that are rather useless in themselves (like Elvis's sunglasses) and are later exposed to be even more useless once Gaunt's veneer has worn off and the items are shown for the worthless pieces of junk that they are.

As is often the case, the things we think we need are wants rather than necessities and are often nothing but a status symbol of something that the owner has that someone else doesn't. This snob appeal is a cornerstone of free enterprise, which explains the concept of limited editions and rare collectables, not to mention items like diamonds and precious metals, which have little real intrinsic value in and of themselves. The idea of designer clothing, luxury automobiles, and expensive art (which is often ugly, if not downright silly) are all examples of a manufactured "need," the "need" to own something that no one else has. Perhaps King's satire was lost on his readers because real-life examples such as a banana taped to a wall at a Miami art show that sold for $120,000 in 2014 are so much more ridiculous than anything that even King's creative genius could imagine.

Interestingly enough, King notes that we are unwilling to even use many of our acquisitions once we have them and sometimes guard them so fiercely that they can't be used. Book collectors, for example, keep their prizes in shrink-wrap and hesitate to read the editions they collect for fear of them losing their value. Vintage automobiles are not driven, luxury writing instruments are not used for writing, antique chairs are not sat in, and trading cards are encased in protective plastic. Many treasures are locked away in safes where they can't be enjoyed, and we dare not advertise our cherished items to the world for fear of being robbed. The inhabitants of Castle Rock hide away their purchases. This, of course, plays into Gaunt's hands since others can't see the items for the worthless pieces of junk that they are. As he says, "Perhaps all the really special things I sell aren't what they appear to be. Perhaps they are actually gray things with only one remarkable property—the ability to take the shapes of those things which haunt the dreams of men and women" (346).

While those who collect things might be guilty of a certain kind of greed, King is also working with the theme of greed in a larger sense. "Buster" Keeton, the town alderman, is a perfect example of this. Keeton wins a bet at the racetrack and then becomes obsessed with money and gambling to the point where he steals from the Castle Rock treasury to support his habit. Keeton personifies the day traders and bankers of the 1980s who used their clients' money for risky ventures that ultimately failed and brought on a massive financial crisis. For many of these so-called financial experts, no matter how much wealth they amassed, it was never enough. Even in King's small Maine town, the wealthy and powerful abused their positions of trust to take advantage of the average citizen.

Human Universals

In his book *Why We Snap*, R. Douglas Fields lists nine triggers that activate the rage circuits in the human brain. Resources, one of these triggers, is activated when something threatens our possessions. Humans are hardwired to jealously guard their resources and will use violence to get and keep food, property, and other things that are valuable for survival. In the modern world, money and things of monetary value are stand-ins for the survival items we need since money is the commodity that secures them. Instead of hoarding food, we hoard possessions that might theoretically be traded for essentials. Gaunt uses this human trait against the residents of Castle Rock when he instigates the residents to engage in vandalism (throwing mud on bedsheets, breaking windows), which, in turn, triggers a rage response that leads to fights and murders.

Insult, with its resulting loss of pride, is another rage trigger that destabilizes the town and results in violence. "Buster" Keeton reacts violently to his nickname, for example, as does Hugh Priest when he is cut off at the bar. People who are disrespected are prone to rage, and Gaunt also uses this trait to achieve his purposes.

22. Needful Things

Evaluation

Although *Needful Things* is one of my personal favorites just because of the satire and fun it evokes, I wouldn't consider it one of King's best novels from a literary standpoint. Its homespun point of view is probably its strongest feature, in my opinion, but the characters are a bit stereotyped—although that is to be expected, I suppose, in satire.

Interesting Fact

Originally billed as "the last Castle Rock novel," King returned to the fictional town in 2018 with the publication of *Elevation*.

Notable Quote

"What's the one thing in all the world, the one useless thing that you want so badly that you get it mixed up with needing it?"

23

Gerald's Game

Escape Room

Background

Gerald's Game was published in 1992; both it and the companion novel *Dolores Claiborne* are set during a solar eclipse. Gerald's game refers to Dolores several times. Although considered "unfilmable" (because of its single setting and character), *Gerald's Game* was adapted into a Netflix movie in 2017 directed by Mike Flanagan. King developed the idea from a dream he had while on an airline flight about a woman being chained to a bed.

Summary and Narrative Devices

Gerald's Game, while not a "horror novel" in the traditional sense, does deal with a situation that involves horror and terror. The story is based on the weekend getaway of Jessie and Gerald Burlingame, who are attempting to spice up their sex life with bondage games. Whereas this fetish seems to be a huge turn-on for Gerald, his wife is more the reluctant partner. When Jessie is handcuffed to the bed, she changes her mind and realizes she doesn't want to play this role anymore. Her husband either isn't listening or doesn't want to listen; Jessie attempts to fight him off and he has a fatal heart attack. Unfortunately, Jessie can't reach the keys to free herself. To complicate matters, they are at their vacation cabin in a very rural area of Maine, far from the nearest neighbor, and no one expects them to be back in town for several days. Jessie is chained to the bed without hope of rescue. She must use her ingenuity and resolve to free herself or she will die of hunger and thirst.

Similar to *Cujo*, this is a novel of entrapment. Unlike the book about the rabid dog, however, in *Gerald's Game*, King confines his point of view to that of a single character, Jessie, who is trapped in the bed, resulting in a very limited setting in which to place the story. King's task, then, is to keep the story interesting within the confines of this microcosmic setting.

King also uses dreams and flashbacks to provide a change of scene to keep readers engaged in the story. *Gerald's Game* is not just about a woman chained to a bedpost; it delves into her search for her past and to a childhood event of sexual abuse involving her father when she was just entering puberty. These flashbacks revolve around the solar eclipse on July 20, 1963. The events of that day are revealed slowly, as the traumatic events of the narrative present dig up the repressed memories of the past. The reader learns that something happened during the eclipse. The mystery of what that event was parallels the question of whether Jessie will escape. This entwining narrative holds the suspense of the story and then is compounded by an intruder, who turns out to be a serial killer. These techniques allow King to introduce other characters and settings, while enhancing the theme of sexual abuse from several different angles, that of a wife, a child, and fear of being a victim of an intruder in her home.

Finally, King carries the narrative forward by creating multiple personalities and voices in Jessie's head. Regardless of whether they are hallucinations or memories, these voices do allow King to write realistic dialogue while presenting different perspectives on both the present situation and the past. These multiple personas and the interaction between them hold the narrative together and effectively move it forward. This technique also shows the different personalities that make up Jessie Burlingame and personify the internal conflicts that populate the human mind.

Archetypes

Although *Gerald's Game* doesn't have any direct correlatives, it is an example of a story about being trapped, similar to Edgar Allan Poe's "The Premature Burial" or Ray Bradbury's "Kaleidoscope" (where several astronauts float in space without hope of rescue after their spacecraft is destroyed). The novel lends itself to the "survival" genre (*Robinson Crusoe*, Stephen Crane's "The Open Boat," and King's own short story "Survivor Type"). And, of course, the story is also reminiscent of *Cujo*. These types of stories force readers to put themselves in the place of the characters and try to figure out an escape but without the actual threat of being in danger themselves. Readers wonder how they would react in such a situation, how they would handle the fear and the stress, and how they might devise an escape.

Another possible archetype is the story where a character finds out something about the past and comes to grips with it. This is more of a literary archetype (as in *The House of the Seven Gables*) than one from genre stories, though H.P. Lovecraft did adapt this plotline into some of his horror tales, where a protagonist (such as Charles Dexter Ward) finds out about a crime committed by his ancestor and comes to terms with it. In the case of *Gerald's Game*, Jessie recalls disturbing events that have happened to her as she enters a near-hypnotic state while enduring sensory deprivation. Although this idea of recalling deeply buried memories under hypnosis to exorcise mental demons was once the rage in psychology, this practice is now considered dubious at best. However, as a fictional narrative, I believe it is acceptable to take Jessie's memories of her abuse seriously despite some of the debunking of the value of repressed memories.

Subtext and Themes

The most obvious theme of *Gerald's Game* is the power of the human urge for survival. Individuals will do almost anything to stay alive, even in hopeless situations. King's short story "Survivor Type" is an extreme example of this, as a castaway cannibalizes himself to survive. Cases have been documented of people enduring horrible pain and even amputating their own limbs to free themselves from entrapment, so this idea is not just fiction. Jessie's scheme to cut her wrist to free herself is entirely plausible and horrible at the same time.

In this novel, King adopts a feminist perspective that examines a woman's right to say no. Gerald becomes increasingly interested in bondage games to revive his failing libido, and Jessie goes along with the program, at least at first. She soon tires of it, however, and then begins to feel demeaned as her husband treats her more like an object than a person (hence the raunchy "pussy" joke that is repeated throughout the novel). Once she is handcuffed to the bed, Jessie decides that she's had enough and demands that her husband stop the game, as is her right. He ignores her, though, either thinking that her refusal is part of the game or, as is more likely, pretending to think she is playacting. She does fight back; unfortunately, her attack on Gerald triggers a fatal heart attack and puts her in a dire predicament. This struggle is a symbol of the trouble a wife can get into if she refuses her husband's advances. Although Jessie avoids the impending rape by her spouse, she, like many victims of abuse, wonders if she should have just gone along with it and suffered the unwanted sex. This dilemma is not uncommon for victims of domestic abuse who live in a no-win situation.

King also invokes the incest taboo in this novel, a taboo that is universal among all peoples and cultures. This taboo, which may be viewed as an evolutionary adaptation to keep the human gene pool healthy, brings about feelings of revulsion in all societies and is forbidden through both laws and moral codes. Even though Jessie's father doesn't have actual intercourse with his daughter, his actions do invoke feelings of disgust in readers. King's detailed description of the event is repulsive and downright creepy. It is no wonder that Jessie buried the memory deep within her subconscious mind.

The father's behavior also accurately illustrates the tactics of sexual predators who make their victims feel like they are the guilty party. Jessie is ashamed by the situation, and her father threatens to tell her mother what happened. Predators insist that it is the girl's or woman's fault and not their own, and sadly, many elements of society still blame the victim rather than the assailant. This story does accurately depict what happens in many child molestation cases and serves as a warning to our society.

Human Universals

Gerald's Game addresses several universal emotions, most of them revolving around the affective emotion of fear. The most basic fear, of course, is concern for what Douglas Fields terms "life and limb," the basic concern for our own survival. Once Jessie realizes she is trapped by her restraints in a secluded house, it doesn't take her long to realize that she will die handcuffed to the bedpost unless she can engineer an escape. The reader identifies with Jessie and can easily imagine the terror of her situation, which invokes the fear response that King is looking for. This reaction is the staple of all horror, thriller, and adventure fiction and forms the backbone of all King's novels.

The idea of being restrained, imprisoned, or held against our will is another basic human fear. Prisons and jails employ this concept as a form of punishment and deterrent. And being imprisoned alone is one of the worst forms of punishment that one can endure. The Southern Poverty Law Center (SPLC) and other organizations have declared solitary confinement to be inhumane, and many studies have documented its harmful effects, both mental and physical. Jessie's confinement is further exacerbated by the fact that it is essentially a death sentence if she cannot free herself. The mental effects of this experience cannot be imagined, and yet, King does force his Constant Reader to imagine them. It is only natural that Jessie seems to be losing her mind and imagining multiple voices in her head. According to the SPLC, people in solitary confinement may experience hallucinations and incoherence of thought, which is exactly what happens to Jessie as King's art imitates life. And the reader, again, is forced to experience these horrors along with the protagonist, making this novel particularly disturbing.

Evaluation

Gerald's Game is a disturbing book on many levels, and although I wouldn't rank it at the top of the King canon, it is a remarkably successful novel. King is able to create a believable female character in this story and, I think, does an admirable job of highlighting abuse in a time before the #MeToo movement and showing the long-term effects of child molestation.

Interesting Fact

In 1982 in an essay in *Fear Itself: The Early Works of Stephen King*, Chelsea Quinn Yarbro criticized King by saying that it was "disheartening when a writer with so much talent and strength and vision is not able to develop a believable woman character between the ages of seventeen and sixty." This motivated King to write several novels featuring female protagonists, including *Gerald's Game*.

Notable Quote

"Sometimes it takes heart to write about a thing, doesn't it? To let that thing out of the room way in the back of your mind and put it up there on the screen."

24

Dolores Claiborne
Justice Served

Background

Dolores Claiborne was published in 1993 by Viking and can be considered a "companion book" to *Gerald's Game* since both novels center on the total eclipse of the sun that was seen in Maine on July 20, 1963. Both novels also explored themes of domestic abuse, and both main characters experience a psychic connection with each other in the respective novels. The film adaptation, starring Kathy Bates, was released in 1995.

Summary and Narrative Devices

The novel features a 65-year-old woman, Dolores Claiborne, as the narrator/protagonist. Accused of the murder of her employer, she dictates her story to the police and a stenographer (and to the reader) to prove her innocence. She does, however, admit to killing her abusive husband some 30 years earlier by tricking him into falling down an empty well shaft in the overgrown backyard and leaving him to die from his injuries. She planned the murder to occur on the day of the solar eclipse in Maine when the residents were distracted by the event. Although there were rumors and much speculation, her husband's death was ruled an accident and Dolores was not charged with the crime. After hearing Dolores's story of spousal abuse, she is cleared of the murder of her employer and not charged with her husband's death in 1993 either.

In *Dolores Claiborne*, King uses the technique of having the first-person narrator address the audience directly by speaking to the police, the stenographer, and by implication, the reader. Dolores addresses each of the listeners by name, revealing their secrets, asking about their lives, and even requesting drinks. This gives the story a sense of immediacy, much like the narrator in *Needful Things* who addresses the reader directly. This technique is not merely a prologue, however, but continues through the entire novel, making Dolores's narrative an extended monologue that was permanently captured by the stenographer.

In addition to giving the story a sense of urgency, this technique also allows Dolores to speak for herself and reveal the depths of her character. The voice is homespun and realistic, complete with the dialect and metaphors that would be attributed to a housewife from rural Maine. This voice depicts her as very intelligent, though not formally educated, and wise in the ways of the world. It also offers a very real insight into the perspective of a battered woman from this time and of a hardworking, moral woman who is trying desperately to care for her children.

Finally, this point of view successfully eliminates any authorial intrusion, biases, or editorializing and allows the reader to make conclusions solely on what Dolores says. The reader, then, becomes a member of the jury, so to speak, who would decide Dolores's innocence or guilt were she to stand trial for either the murder of her employer or her husband. Rather than King declaring her innocence, the reader is forced to come to that conclusion independently. Dolores, though technically a murderer, is the hero of this narrative and the reader applauds her actions. The husband, a wife beater and child molester, is the obvious guilty party here, and Dolores has done what was necessary to protect both herself and her daughter. Justice is served.

Unlike King's typical fiction which is broken up into many short chapters, the novel is one long, continuous narrative without chapter breaks or any breaks at all, for that matter. The only time the narrative pauses is when Dolores stops to address the audience and ask for a drink, tell a story about one of the police officers, or ask the stenographer if she is keeping up with the story and to ask if she can be heard. This is a sly way of inserting some breaks into the story without stopping the narrative. Dolores freely admits that she's telling a long story and taking a long time to tell it, resulting in an extended monologue. She justifies this method as being the only way she can convey her story with the truth and detail that it deserves. This gives more veracity to her confession since despite its length and complexity, the narrative is straightforward and without contradictions or elements that don't ring true.

King does slip some metafiction into the story—fiction that talks about fiction or storytelling—as is typical of his novels. One interesting example of this is when Dolores claims she doesn't know whether to begin at the beginning or at the end, so, like most accomplished storytellers, she says she will "start in the middle." This does create suspense in the story and allows for both foreshadowing and flashback.

Archetypes

The archetype for *Dolores Claiborne* is the "confession" story as practiced by Edgar Allan Poe. In this story, the narrator/protagonist confesses a crime directly to an authority figure and therefore indirectly to the reader. The narrators of "The Tell-Tale Heart" and "The Black Cat" are confessing to the police and "unburdening the soul" of the crime they have been found guilty of, while the narrator of "A Cask of Amontillado" has gotten away with murder, so to speak, and is confessing to his priest now that he is an old man facing death. Like the narrator of "Cask," Dolores has also gotten away with murder and is only now confessing to killing her husband because she is accused of another murder, which she did not commit. Dolores, like Poe's narrators, is very believable in her telling of the story. Yet even though they attempt to justify the unjustifiable, Dolores really does evoke sympathy. As a long-suffering victim of domestic abuse, her crime is justified, and the reader understands why she did what she did. Unlike Poe's narrators who are vindictive, insane, or both, Dolores is a likable character, and the reader is made to see how her husband deserved the fate he received at her hands.

Themes and Subtexts

As in *Gerald's Game*, the theme of domestic abuse pervades *Dolores Claiborne*. Again, responding to criticism that his female characters are weak and not believable, King set out to create a realistic and credible woman and use her to highlight feminist themes. Dolores Claiborne is, in fact, a convincing character. King's technique of giving her a distinct voice that is not contaminated by a narrator creates an authentic character who is quite capable of expressing the issues that women face in rural American society and, by analogy, in society in general.

Dolores's major problem is her marriage to an abusive husband. He strongly believes it is his right to do with his wife as he pleases, and he does so until Dolores stands up to him physically. Even then, he is in control of the family. His drunkenness rules the house, and he is a poor provider and a terrible role model for his children. He takes things to the next level by making sexual advances toward his teenage daughter.

The problem is compounded, however, by the view that this rural society has on marriage, where it is generally agreed that a husband has not only the right but also the duty to keep his wife in line. Women in this world do not have the opportunity to seek help from the law or from society, for that matter. Women are viewed as the property of their husbands, and that is just the way things are. If Dolores had killed Joe based on only his abusive behavior, she would, no doubt, have been charged with and convicted of murder, especially if there were men on the jury. Joe's incestuous behavior toward his daughter is what saves Dolores from being charged. Whereas spousal abuse may be tolerated and even encouraged, incest definitely crosses a moral bridge and will not be tolerated.

Justice is a reoccurring theme in King's fiction, and the "master of the macabre" often portrays vigilante justice in a positive light. Indeed, the revenge story represents an archetype that has always been extremely popular. *Dolores Claiborne*, although not exactly a revenge story (Dolores takes no delight in her husband's death), does portray vigilante justice. Knowing that the law would be of no help to her or her daughter (until it was too late perhaps), Dolores takes justice into her own hands and removes her criminal husband from society. Her justice is not to punish Joe so much as it is to prevent him from committing a crime against his children. By taking the law into her own hands, she saves her children from terrible consequences and delivers justice in a way that would have been impossible were she to have followed the legal process. This justice is satisfying to the reader, who secretly wishes it could be meted out in the "real" world as well.

Human Universals

One of the most obvious human universals is the CARE emotion when it comes to children, and perhaps the strongest version of this is the maternal instinct. I have already discussed this in *Cujo*, where a mother is willing to risk her life for her child; in *Dolores Claiborne*, the protagonist is willing to risk everything to protect her daughter from an incestuous father. As Dolores clearly states, she would be willing to endure her husband's abuse if it were only her life at stake. But when her husband begins making perverted advances to their daughter, the game is seriously changed. Furthermore, there are other children who may be subject to his advances as they enter puberty.

While she temporarily solves the problem by confronting her husband and obtaining the truth from her daughter, Dolores knows that this is merely a short-term resolution. She realizes that her husband's actions will eventually reappear and get worse and that her children are in terrible danger.

This issue highlights another human universal: the need for order in society. The human species has become the dominant life-form on earth because humans have adopted a social model of living where there are specific rules, moral codes, and ways of behaving. Incest is one of those moral codes that exists in all cultures in all parts of the world. Inbreeding, of course, can result in genetic defects and diseases, and although early humans may not have known the science behind this, they obviously recognized the results and codified the incest taboo into law. This places Dolores's husband outside the protection of society and relieves Dolores of the responsibility of his death. Thus, her confession that she killed him is not used to charge her with a crime, and all is forgiven. According to moral codes, she is innocent of any wrongdoing and her protection of her children from an incestuous father is understood. Joe's punishment fits the crime, and no one will show remorse or blame her for his death.

Evaluation

Dolores is one of the most interesting and realistic characters in King's fiction, and the way she tells her story directly to the audience is compelling. The novel, though not in my top ten list, is one of King's better narratives.

Interesting Fact

After meeting Kathy Bates on the set of *Misery*, King wrote *Dolores Claiborne* with the actress in mind as the leading character; it became her favorite movie role.

Notable Quote

"The inside and outside of a marriage aren't usually much alike."

25

Rose Madder

The Fury of a Woman Scorned

Background

Rose Madder was published by Viking in 1995 and is considered by both fans and King himself as one of his weakest novels. Following *Gerald's Game* and *Dolores Claiborne*, it is the third book that directly confronts domestic violence (sometimes called the "abused wife trilogy" by King fans). In this novel, violence is presented in the most graphic and intense manner imaginable. The idea for the story came by way of a news story about a woman who was shot by her husband despite having a protection order filed against him.

Summary and Narrative Devices

Rose Madder, as I see it, is a two-part novel. The first half is a mainstream story of the realistic horror of domestic violence as the protagonist, Rose, escapes from her violent husband and relocates to a different city to begin a new life. The second half of the book involves Rose's discovery of a magic painting that acts as a portal into an alternate world. Rose enters this alternate world to save a baby and, ultimately, lure her murderous husband into the painting as well, where he is destroyed by her alter ego, Rose Madder.

The novel begins with one of the most violent and disturbing scenes in the Stephen King universe, where Rose's husband Norman beats her mercilessly for reading a Paul Sheldon novel, causing her to suffer a miscarriage. This scene of domestic horror introduces the character of Norman Daniels and shows just what kinds of brutality he is capable of and demonstrates his complete lack of remorse. It then transitions nine years into the future when a minor event—Rose seeing a spot of her blood on the sheets—prompts her to take the dramatic and courageous step of fleeing from her husband, stealing his credit card and taking the bus to another city where she is referred to a women's shelter. In this new life, she finds friendship and safety, lands a job as an audiobook narrator, gets her own apartment, falls in love, and obtains the magic painting.

Unfortunately for her, Norman, a police detective, is able to track her to the new city and creates a trail of terror and murder before locating Rose and assaulting her and her new boyfriend. Rose escapes into the painting and lures her husband in after her, where he is torn apart by Rose Madder, who turns into a giant spider.

King uses an omniscient point of view in this novel, which allows the reader access into the sadistic mind of Norman Daniels, who has absolutely no redeeming qualities whatsoever. He is racist, homophobic, misogynistic, and psychopathic. He kills without remorse and prefers biting his victims before murdering them. Norman's stream-of-consciousness thoughts are rendered in italics, and his mental breakdown becomes worse as the novel progresses. While he is a believable villain at first, his character does degenerate into the stereotyped personality of the "bad cop." King attempts to explain Norman's behavior by alluding to his abusive childhood, but unlike most of his villains, Daniels is completely one-sided and totally unsympathetic. And while abusers deserve no sympathy, his lack of any good qualities make him more of a caricature than a character. His destruction is a foregone conclusion.

Archetypes

The alternate universe that exists inside Rose's painting is a distorted depiction of Theseus and the Minotaur from Greek mythology. The Minotaur, an offspring of a human female and a bull, is imprisoned in a labyrinth in Crete where humans are sacrificed and devoured by the monster. The Greek hero Theseus slays the Minotaur and absolves Crete from being forced to sacrifice young men and women to the bull.

When Rose first enters the magical painting, she is tasked with saving a baby from the Minotaur by entering the labyrinth and rescuing the infant. Once she has accomplished this task, Rose Madder, the woman in the painting, promises to repay her. Norman Daniels, of course, becomes the Minotaur, fusing his human self with a rubber bull's mask to become the personification of the legendary beast. Rose Madder herself is based on the Greek myth of the Erinyes, more commonly known as the Furies, deities of vengeance on men who have sworn a false oath. Disavowing his marriage vows makes Rose's husband a target for this female vengeance.

Another archetype is King's own multiverse, where portals exist to connect the various worlds in the Dark Tower universe. References are made to the city of Lud from the Dark Tower books as well as to *ka* and the great wheel that connects all things.

Themes and Subtexts

Rose Madder realistically depicts the plight of the abused spouse and the difficulty that women have in leaving a violent situation. Rose initially suffers from the psychological issues with leaving her husband, especially fear that he will find her and make her pay, and her belief that she is not a "good enough" wife and that the abuse he heaps on her is her own fault. Once she does find the motivation to leave, not only does this fear remain, but it is augmented by financial and practical issues: where will she live, how will she support herself, how will she remain safe, and so forth. King dramatizes these issues very effectively, creating a background of dread and anxiety that permeates the novel. Even when Rose feels safest, trepidation lurks in the background. The excursions into Norman Daniels's mind only enhance this sense of apprehension.

Vengeance and fury create another subtext to the novel. The longer she is away from her husband, the "madder" Rose becomes. Although her sense of dread never really diminishes, she becomes angry at what her husband has done to her as she slowly discovers her self-worth and becomes stronger, both mentally and physically. She finds friends who appreciate her, a job that gives her meaning and fulfillment, a sense of independence, and even a kind man who falls in love with her. Her anger is channeled against her husband, allowing her to stand up to him and fight back once he finds her and tries to kill her. Rose Madder, her alter ego in the painting, personifies her fury of the woman scorned as a vengeful goddess who takes retribution on her tormenter. When Rose symbolically saves the child from the bull in the temple's maze, she releases this fury: "We repay."

Memory forms another theme in *Rose Madder*. Rose is given the option to forget everything that has happened—an attractive proposition—but chooses not to. She feels the need to hang on to the memories of the terrible things that have happened to her because she feels that those who forget the past are destined to relive it, and she vows never to allow herself to fall into such a horrible situation again. On a deeper level, though, Rose understands that her past experiences, as awful as they were, have contributed to her growth and have resulted in her becoming a strong and independent woman. And for the vast majority of victims of domestic violence, forgetting is not an option. Survivors carry scars with them for the rest of their lives, often suffering from PTSD, low self-esteem, and other mental health issues.

Human Universals

Rose Madder directly touches on several human universal emotions that engage readers. The most obvious, of course, is FEAR, that basic instinct that is shared by all living things and that, in some form or another, is necessary for the survival of any species. Fear is a primeval emotion that neuroscientists agree resides in the most primitive part of the brain. In most animals, fear is created by a specific situation (seeing a large, black, hairy spider does it for this English professor!). Humans, however (and perhaps some other mammals), have developed a sense of the future, which transforms basic and immediate fear into anxiety about imagined fears in the future—about what may happen, in other words. This causes worry, stress, and all sorts of related physical problems that humans are plagued with. This fear may be irrational and based on unlikely events or, in the case of Rose, may be perfectly logical and justified. In any event, her dread of her husband is real and can be felt by any intuitive reader as a disturbing sensation that permeates the novel. Rose's goal, then, is to be rid of this fear, and the Constant Reader takes this journey with her, hoping for the Norman Daniels threat to be resolved.

RAGE is also a human universal emotion, according to Jaak Panksepp, and, according to R. Douglas Fields, can be set off by any one or more of nine triggers. These triggers are really part of the evolutionary mechanism we have inherited that contributes to our survival, both as individuals and as a species.

In the case of Rose, she experiences several threats that can trigger rage: a threat to life or limb, environment (her home is invaded by her husband), mate (Bill, her new lover, is attacked), and stopped (she is cornered and trapped, which will lead almost any creature to fight back). Her rage is justified, then, and felt by readers as well, who hope that Norman will receive his just deserts.

This leads to another human universal emotion, the desire for order, which, when violated, also may trigger a rage response. This sense of justice is strongly entrenched in society, which sanctions harsh penalties for violating human code of law. Thus, the idea of "an eye for an eye" and capital punishment have been a part of human culture since ancient times. For human societies to thrive and survive, outliers must be punished for misdeeds, which has resulted in a strong desire to see justice served. And when normal channels fail, vigilante justice is not only accepted but celebrated.

Readers receive an enormous sense of satisfaction when villains are punished, and the worse the crime, the harsher the punishment. In the case of Norman Daniels, being slowly devoured alive brings the ultimate sense of justice, although being beaten by Gert and urinated on is a rather satisfying first step in his collapse. In the end, justice is once again served in a Stephen King novel as the "bad guy" is humiliated, broken, tortured, and destroyed.

Evaluation

Rose Madder falls short, in my opinion, on several levels. Norman Daniels lacks the verisimilitude of a real person and quickly becomes a stereotyped villain. Rose herself is a much more believable and well-drawn character, but her strength is diminished in that she is saved through a magical device, which seems like an artificial element in the story. It's as if King felt the need to include a fantastic element in a story that would have, I think, been stronger without it. Rose could have defeated her husband in the real world rather than in a magical one. Furthermore, the magical elements in this story seemed to be disjointed and didn't really make narrative sense. King is correct in saying this isn't one of his best efforts, and I concur with his evaluation.

Interesting Fact

The madder plant, a member of the coffee family from which the red dye rose madder is made, was historically used to induce abortions.

Notable Quote

"It ain't the blows we're dealt that matter, but the ones we survive."

26

Insomnia
Miles to Go Before I Sleep

Background

Insomnia was published by Viking in 1994, and although not technically a "Dark Tower" novel, it incorporates many elements from King's "gunslinger" multiverse into its pages. Critics have pointed to it as an explanation of how the Dark Tower universe operates and can be thought of as one of the spokes of the Dark Tower wheel. Yet the book is a stand-alone novel for those unfamiliar with the Dark Tower series.

Summary and Narrative Devices

Insomnia is set in Derry, Maine, home to several other King novels (most notably, *It*). The story is rather complicated, particularly for readers unfamiliar with the Dark Tower series, yet can be understood as a stand-alone work. The premise of the plot concerns Ralph Roberts, who suffers from sleep maintenance insomnia, a condition where he wakes up earlier each morning until he is barely getting one hour's worth of sleep each night. As his condition worsens, he begins to see auras around people and little creatures in white coats whom he calls "little bald doctors." He then learns that his friend Lois Chasse is also seeing these creatures.

Once they confront these beings, Ralph and Lois learn that they are agents of death who free people from life when their time has come. Clotho and Lachesis, as they call themselves, represent "the purpose" and bring about death with dignity for those who are destined to die. A third agent of death, Atropos, personifies the random and brings about chaotic death and misery. Atropos is a servant of the Crimson King (a major force in the Dark Tower books), an immortal part of the multiverse who is dedicated to chaos and the destruction of the Dark Tower in that fictional series.

Atropos, under the Crimson King's direction, is sent to disrupt the order of the multiverse by manipulating Ed Deepneau, a rare character who is neither part of the Purpose nor the Random. Clotho and Lachesis have countered this action by inflicting Ralph and Lois with insomnia, which enables them to experience other planes of reality in the multiverse so that they might stop Deepneau and Atropos and thwart the plans of the Crimson King. The key to all of this is an artistic child named Patrick Danville, who will ultimately be the savior of the Dark Tower in that epic series. The forces of chaos have gathered in the *Insomnia* universe to bring about his death, and Ralph and Lois are the mechanism that the agents of the Purpose have selected to save him.

Insomnia is based on a what-if premise that inspires so many stories in the speculative fiction genre—in this case, what if someone were to sleep less and less each night? And what if this person found that someone else was in the same predicament and that the two issues were connected? The explanation for Ralph's insomnia opens the doors to the fantastic elements of the novel. As an interesting sidenote, King employs this technique again in *Elevation* when the protagonist gradually defies the laws of gravity. Since all living creatures sleep, the mystery of Ralph's insomnia becomes a puzzle to be solved. The appearance of the "little bald doctors" presents another enigma to be solved, as does Deepneau's erratic behavior. King tells the reader just what needs to be told and withholds information until the key moments when it is needed. The first third of the novel consists of solving the mystery of what is going on in Derry, the middle third provides solutions and plans for the future, and the last part of the novel puts the plans into action with direct conflict between the Purpose and the Random, where Ralph faces off against the Crimson King directly.

The characters in *Insomnia* are set up as chess pieces, with Ralph and Lois the mere pawns in the cosmic game. While all the other players wield much more power, the real battle is between the opposing pawns—the protagonists and Ed Deepneau. Once the terrorist threat is eliminated, then the protagonists take on Atropos, who, with his unpredictable movements, may be considered a knight (as is Roland, the gunslinger). Ralph and Lois are able to outmaneuver Atropos and threaten the king, but at the end of the novel, Ralph plays the pawn sacrifice that the game has demanded.

The novel is organized as an epic story with consequences far beyond the mere life of the protagonists. It is another hero's quest story with a reluctant hero who is chosen as an agent to save the universe from chaos and destruction. Ralph follows the hero's quest formula, leaving his comfortable world to become involved in a larger quest, meeting up with magical helpers on the way, traveling into the "belly of the whale" as he experiences higher dimensions, and ultimately defeating evil and restoring the universe to its normal state (at least temporarily).

Archetypes

Insomnia is steeped in the Greek mythology of the Fates, three sister goddesses who control human destiny. These three immortals, Clotho, Lachesis, and Atropos, controlled a person's lifespan, their unavoidable fate, so to speak, by spinning threads that dominate their life from birth to death. They knew one's destiny and controlled it, working together as a single force.

In *Insomnia*, the Fates are transformed into the personas of old men who oversee the forces of life, death, the Purpose, and the Random. Clotho and Lachesis are agents of death and work to facilitate the planned or purposeful death of human beings. Atropos, the embodiment of chaos, represents the Random, and brings about random, unplanned death by accident, catastrophe, and mayhem. He is the wildcard, the joker in the deck, who shows up when least expected and brings about death simply by misfortune and without purpose.

Stephen King's magnum opus, the massive eight-volume Dark Tower series, is also an archetype for *Insomnia*. Even though the Dark Tower books were nowhere near completion when *Insomnia* was published, this stand-alone novel is so intricately wound into King's epic that many critics and readers alike have considered it not only part of the series but an explanation for the mechanics of how King's multiverse is constructed. This novel, then, can be considered one of the spokes of the Dark Tower wheel.

Themes and Subtexts

Domestic violence is an important theme in King's novels, and *Insomnia* examines this issue by confronting it directly and indirectly through the lens of women's rights in general. Ed Deepneau is taken over by the forces of chaos and made to turn violent and fanatical in his beliefs on abortion and women. Since Deepneau is a man in a male-dominated culture, the Crimson King doesn't have to work too hard to turn him into a wife beater. His wife Helen leaves him and escapes to what appears to be the safety of a women's shelter. The shelter comes under attack by the forces of Atropos and is burned to the ground, demonstrating that battered women are not safe anywhere. The law is unable to protect women despite restraining orders, safe places, and good intentions. Deepneau's behavior is not part of the Purpose but serves the Crimson King and the forces of the Random.

Insomnia plunges directly into the abortion debate by featuring a character, Susan Day, who is an abortion rights activist. Deepneau is manipulated into becoming a fanatical pro-lifer who tries to carry out a terrorist attack against Susan Day's pro-choice women's rights rally. Although the object of this attack is really to accomplish the Crimson King's goal of killing Patrick Danville, who is destined to thwart attacks on the Dark Tower, the malevolent forces of chaos are just fine with the death of hundreds of pro-choice advocates as collateral damage. While Stephen King's views on the abortion issue are evident here, his theme about extremists resorting to violence is clear. The scenario of a terrorist crashing a plane into a crowded building is unintentionally prophetic in light of the 9-11 attacks that occurred seven years after *Insomnia*'s publication. The narrative depicts the polarization of America that would only get worse in the decades to follow and shows how disagreements over politics have turned violent.

Another major theme in King's fiction, free will—or the lack of it—forms the backbone of this novel and is presented in mythological terms. King presents the four constants: life, death, the Purpose, and the Random. According to this concept, there really is no such thing as free will. The Fates, the Purpose and the Random, dictate our lives. Our fates are decided at birth by the Purpose, and only random intervention can change this fate. Since we have absolutely no control over either force, free will does not exist in this universe.

Yet this narrative deconstructs itself in *Insomnia* since Ralph and Lois are able to intervene and defeat Atropos. Yes, it takes the divine intervention of Clotho and Lachesis to give them the power to understand what is happening, but the protagonists do freely choose to become involved once the Purpose is revealed to them. Their direct action saves Patrick Danville, who ultimately defeats the Crimson King and saves the Dark Tower (and the multiverse) in the last novel in the Dark Tower series. So it seems that there is a place for free will after all, and invoking this free will has cosmic consequences. While King's fiction tells us that the past is very difficult to change, apparently changing the predetermined future is within the realm of possibility.

Human Universals

Although not considered a human universal per se, sleep seems to be a biological universal. The details vary greatly, but scientists believe that

26. Insomnia

all living things sleep (or enter a restive state). The exact functions of sleep are still being debated by neuroscientists, but one thing is clear: human beings cannot survive without it. Without sleep, humans suffer from hallucinations, pressure around the head (known as "the hat phenomenon"), and eventually a malfunction of the brain that could bring about organ failure and even death.

In America, 30 percent of the population have suffered from short-term insomnia, and approximately 10 percent of adults have chronic insomnia. Furthermore, up to 75 percent of elderly Americans report insomnia symptoms. Therefore, while insomnia is not a human universal, it is quite widespread in the population and most Constant Readers will be familiar with the experience (especially after being unable to sleep after reading a Stephen King novel!).

The novel, as its title suggests, asks the question of what would happen if someone were to suffer continued insomnia to the point of being unable to sleep at all.

Evaluation

King is most critical of this novel, claiming that it was too plot-driven instead of going where the book naturally wanted to go. The book isn't one of my favorites on its own, but taken in context with the Dark Tower series, it does help to clarify the overall picture of the multiverse.

Interesting Fact

King says that he barely slept during the four months he spent writing *Insomnia*.

Notable Quote

"Of all the things which make up our Short-Time lives, sleep is surely the best."

27

The Green Mile
Rebirth of the Serial Novel

Background

As an English professor, I've had on more than one occasion to deflect some scorn for being a "Constant Reader" of Stephen King's novels (though I will say that my close colleagues at my university have been very supportive of my scholarship, even going so far as to grant me two fellowships for two separate projects to pursue my research). Horror and speculative fiction have often suffered from the disdain of snobbish critics such as the late Harold Bloom of Yale who disparaged King's works, accusing him of the "dumbing down of American letters." Incidentally, Bloom had no problem with cashing in on King's works by editing two critical studies about his fiction, reaffirming that the stories weren't worthy of critical study even while including over a dozen critical essays from other scholars who obviously thought otherwise. When I'm questioned by academics about my interest in King, I've found that most haven't actually read his books, though they may be aware of his stories from films. Interestingly, they praise *Stand by Me* and *The Shawshank Redemption*, unaware that these are based on novellas from the *Four Past Midnight* collection. And then I pull out my ace in the hole: *The Green Mile*. Despite its fantastic content, the film is universally beloved, and even English professors besides me are fond of it, again usually without realizing that it is a Stephen King story.

Of all of King's works, *The Green Mile* is special to me for several reasons. First, the book was originally released in monthly installments as a Dickens-type serial novel, with each part ending in a cliffhanger. I recall waiting anxiously for each new section to be released and rushing to the local department store with my $2.99 (plus tax, of course) to retrieve my copy before it sold out. This was in 1996, long before Amazon was even dreamed of. I'd bring the book home and read it in one ravenous sitting, like a juicy porterhouse steak, until the end, which for all but the last installment was "*To Be Continued.*" Although I was already the holder of a PhD in English and was gainfully employed as an assistant dean and professor, these monthly installments made me feel like a kid again, waiting for the next Hardy Boys book.

The Green Mile is also special to me because I own an autographed copy of the original manuscript of book 1, *The Two Dead Girls*. Part of the book's marketing strategy included a 50-word "essay" contest at the end of each section, where six winners per month would be awarded this autographed copy (36 winners in all), and I was fortunate enough to be one of the winners by answering the question posed in book 2, *The Mouse on the Mile*. It was probably this contest that pushed me from the point of being a Stephen King fan to a Stephen King scholar, and I was soon writing longer essays on his work and presenting papers at academic conferences.

Finally, *The Green Mile* is, in my opinion, one of those books that you just can't *not* love. It has unforgettable characters, a page-turning story, and themes that resonate long after the book has been finished. I have taught this book in my classes, and not only is it a student favorite, but it contains enough depth to support two weeks' worth of class discussion and debate.

As mentioned, the book was originally published in monthly installments from March to August 1996 by Signet paperbacks and was compiled into a single paperback edition in 1997. It was adapted into a film in 1999 starring Tom Hanks and was nominated for four Academy Awards and won two People's Choice Awards.

Summary and Narrative Devices

The Green Mile is the first-person account of Paul Edgecombe, a prison guard in charge of the death row ward at Cold Mountain Penitentiary during the 1930s. The book is written in the form of a memoir as Edgecombe, now a very old but still healthy man living in a nursing home, recalls his time spent on "The Green Mile," the nickname given to the cellblock he supervised, and where he was charged (no pun intended) with overseeing the execution of prisoners in the electric chair known as "Old Sparky." The central event in the book is the execution of John Coffey, a Black man wrongfully accused of the rape and murder of two young girls. In the novel, Edgecombe learns that Coffey possesses a special healing power, and instead of killing the girls, he was trying to heal them when he was found by the authorities holding them in his arms. He is powerless to stop the execution from going forward, and after doing his job as humanely as possible, he resigns from his position.

In the tradition of the serial novel, *The Green Mile* opens with a "hook" as Paul Edgecombe describes the electric chair, an object of fear and fascination, and states that he presided over 78 executions during his time as death row warden. The book is a page turner; with a faster pace than some of King's earlier novels, it jumps right into the story, immediately setting up the character of Edgecombe and the death row setting of E Block in intricate detail, showing the reader something that is seldom seen. The next chapter introduces the enigmatic John Coffey as the rapist and murderer of the Detterick twins. Chapter 4 dives into the murder of the two young girls, a horror worse than any supernatural element that a writer could imagine.

Since the book was serialized in six volumes, each of the volumes ends on a cliffhanger, posing a mystery or puzzle that forces the reader to continue reading in order to solve it. In English professor language, this is what the critic Roland Barthes termed the "hermeneutic code," the series of puzzles or enigmas that compel a reader to keep turning the pages. Only in the case of *The Green Mile*, the reader *couldn't* turn the page and read on—not until the next month when the new volume was released, bought, and paid for. Book 1, for example, concludes with Edgecombe and his friend Brutal taking an oath never to take part in another execution. The book ends with the line, "John Coffey was the last." To really understand the significance of this sentence, King's audience must read all six books, and only then are they rewarded with all the answers. This technique of planting seeds for future events (what we call foreshadowing or, in more technical terms, prolepsis) is a powerful tool for best-selling authors.

Point of view is an important element of this novel. The story is told in the first person by Paul Edgecombe, a very reliable narrator whom the reader comes to respect and trust. This point of view brings us deep into the story and allows us to experience Edgecombe's ethical dilemma firsthand. The manuscript, written in the form of a memoir recounting his time at Cold Mountain, is both a confessional and a revelation. Although Edgecombe is the protagonist, the central character is John Coffey, whom we see through the eyes of the warden, who can place Coffey's story into a larger framework.

Although the book has been described as magical realism, it doesn't really conform to that definition since in magical realism the fantastic element is presumed to be ordinary and part of the realistic world (as in the writing of Gabriel García Márquez). From an English professor's point of view, the book is fantasy, pure and simple, since Edgecombe sees Coffey's magic as being extraordinary and beyond the realm of the normal. The fantastic element does shed understanding on real issues, such as the death penalty and racism. Although Stephen King has been dubbed "the

King of horror," this novel, like so many of his books, is not horror, though it does contain some horrible moments, and the most horrible moments are not based on fantasy at all.

Archetypes

All great pieces of literature are based on works, ideas, or images that came before them, and one of the tasks of an English professor is to identify these elements, which T.S. Eliot called "objective correlatives." These universal stories may be what Jung terms archetypes, stories or images that have become part of the collective unconscious. Two objective correlatives in *The Green Mile* are the story of Jesus, as has already been mentioned, and John Steinbeck's masterful novel *Of Mice and Men*.

The plot of the novel correlates with the biblical story of Christ. Coffey has the ability to heal, is childlike in his innocence, and wants to help others with his magical powers. Unfortunately for Coffey, he is unable to raise the dead, but when taken before a court that has the power to sentence him to death, he, like Christ, does not defend himself. He allows himself to be captured, convicted, and put to death in a very public and gruesome way. The initials J.C. make this connection obvious.

King also connects the novel to *Of Mice and Men*, which, in turn, is based on the objective correlative of the Robert Burns poem "To a Mouse," best known for the line "the best laid schemes o' Mice and Men / Gang aft agley," or as it is better known in the modern translation, "the best laid plans of mice and men often go astray." *The Green Mile* mirrors Steinbeck's book by comparing John Coffey to Lenny, the powerful but mentally challenged protagonist who inadvertently kills with his strength. Lenny, like Coffey, dies at the end of the book.

To make the comparison plainer, King introduces the character of Mr. Jingles, the talented "mouse on the mile" who plays tricks with a wooden spool. The mouse is nearly killed by Percy and brought back to life by Coffey, who, in so doing, grants the mouse an unusually long life, a side effect of his powers. Paul Edgecombe, the protagonist of the novel, also receives this gift when Coffey heals his bladder infection.

Themes and Subtexts

In terms of theme and subtext (always a favorite among English professors), *The Green Mile* is multilayered and rich. I admire King's work and can teach it at the university level because his fiction contains so much to discuss (and so much opportunity to design essay questions!). *The Green Mile* is always a student favorite and leads to lots of class involvement.

One obvious subtext of the book concerns racism and the inequity of justice. Yes, the book is set in the South in the 1930s when racism was a cultural norm, but as we've seen in today's world, racial injustice hasn't gone away. King has been criticized for his stereotyping of African American characters as "magical" (Mother Abigail in *The Stand*, Dick Halloran in *The Shining*, and John Coffey in this novel). Yet, in *The Green Mile*, it is important that the magical character be African American as a vehicle to show the racial disparity of the time. Then, like now, a disproportionate number of death row inmates are males of color. Coffey, then, must be both innocent and Black for this theme to be expressed.

Coffey serves as a Christlike figure (the initials "J.C.") to illustrate that even *the* most innocent Black man is not safe from the law. Like Christ, Coffey has the power to heal, and he keeps his power hidden, though demonstrating it could have acquitted him of the murder charges. The stark contrast between his huge, powerful body and his submissive behavior drives home the biblical point that "the meek shall inherit the earth." Like Christ, he accepts and welcomes his execution without protest.

The Green Mile fictionally explores the themes of death and capital punishment in particular. The inhumane execution of Delacroix takes the definition of cruel and unusual punishment to new levels. And then there is the execution of Coffey, an innocent man who was convicted merely on circumstantial evidence, the need for swift justice for the two little girls, and blatant racism. Even Edgecombe, who supervised 78 executions, can no longer continue in his position and resigns despite the fact that work is hard to find and that it will put him at great hardship.

Aging is also under consideration in this novel. Edgecombe is granted the gift of an unnaturally long life, but it is a gift with a dark side as he must watch everyone he knows die before him. Reflecting the theme of Mary Shelley's "The Mortal Immortal," living past one's allotted time is more of a curse than a gift. And if that isn't horrible enough, he is condemned to spend his last years in a nursing home, a parallel to death row since both are places where people go to die. Instead of the sadistic guard, he suffers the abuse of a sadistic orderly. Indeed, in the Stephen King multiverse, people in power are inclined to abuse it.

Human Universals

One of the reasons that Stephen King has been so wildly successful is his ability to tap into human universal emotions, or human nature, if you will. One of the newest theories in the critical study of literature applies the sciences of evolutionary biology and evolutionary psychology to literature by examining how fiction captures universal human characteristics that all people possess and can relate to. In all his novels, King has mastered this technique, and *The Green Mile* is no exception.

One trait shared by nearly all members of the human species is the desire for justice. This trait is based on an evolutionary need to be able to trust all members of the group or tribe and has been demonstrated in the lab by those who study game theory. To put it simply, no one likes to be cheated, and if we feel cheated, we will retaliate. We have an instinctual desire to see that crime is punished and that people (particularly members of our social group) are treated fairly. We also have an instinctual desire to protect those who cannot protect themselves, a trait that is necessary in a species whose young are not self-sufficient for many years. Applying this approach (for which I've coined the term Darwinist hermeneutics—the close study of a text using both science and more traditional critical theory) shows that King engages the "Constant Reader" at a visceral, instinctual level.

The book highlights the murder of two innocent young girls, a crime that demands justice and retribution. Unfortunately, an innocent man is convicted, a Black man who is not a member of the "in-group" but an outsider. Readers see this miscarriage of justice and are drawn into the story by their desire to see the guilty punished and the innocent spared. King, of course, punishes the guilty. And the innocent Coffey proves his innocence to those that matter, Paul Edgecombe and the other guards. He then brings about retribution by destroying the girls' killer and giving the sadistic Percy exactly what he deserves—life in an insane asylum. This ending satisfies the reader's desire for both justice and revenge, traits that are part of human nature. And we feel that Coffey is no longer suffering from the harshness of the world.

Evaluation

From both a reader's and an English professor's point of view, *The Green Mile* is a tremendous success. All six of the installments placed on the *New York Times* bestseller list and most of the critics gave it high marks. From an English professor's point of view, the book is multilayered and meaningful, one of King's best works and one of my personal favorites.

Interesting Fact

In September 1996, all six installments of *The Green Mile* were listed on the *New York Times* bestseller list, which set a record and changed the way serial novels are classified on the list.

Iconic Moment

John Coffey transfers his sickness to Percy, then uses the guard to shoot Wild Bill—the revenge story at its best.

Notable Quote

John Coffey's last words: "I'm sorry for what I am."

28

Desperation
Even God Has a Price

Background

Desperation was published in 1996 and adapted into a film in 2006. *Desperation* and *The Regulators* are "mirror" novels. Both were released on the same day and represent parallel universes with the same characters. *The Regulators* represents the alternate universe where Richard Bachman exists, while *Desperation* occurs in the universe of Stephen King.

Summary and Narrative Devices

Desperation is set in a small desert mining town in New Mexico, appropriately named Desperation, that has been taken over by an evil force called Tak that kills everyone it encounters. The novel begins with a family being arrested by a cop who has been possessed by the entity, which, after parasitically killing him, jumps to another host to continue its work. The main characters all wind up prisoners of Tak in the town's jail where they will face certain death if they don't escape. Under the direction of David, a teenaged boy who has a calling from God, the survivors destroy the mine harboring Tak in a typical Stephen King purging by fire.

The novel is structured as a typical three-part horror novel. The story opens with the characters in a normal, mundane world. The Carver family is on a trip, Johnny Marinville is on a cross-country trek on his motorcycle, followed by his assistant Steve Ames. When the Carvers are pulled over by Entragian, it only slowly becomes apparent that the cop has something exquisitely wrong with him. The mundane event turns violent rather quickly as the conflict escalates. The brutal death of seven-year-old "Pie" alerts the reader that no one is exempt from the horror, not even an innocent little girl.

David's bargain with God is told in a very detailed and realistic flashback that makes the "miracle" very believable. Since this bargain with God is a central theme of the novel, it must be accepted as true. This story within the novel creates suspense of its own as the fate of David's friend Brian is in question—and the question of whether God will answer David's prayer.

Archetypes

Western ghost towns have always held a fascination for Americans and have been a featured element in the western genre, such as the 1956 film *Ghost Town*, where the occupants of a stagecoach hide in a ghost town to escape an attack by the Cheyenne. Perhaps a more specific archetype might be the story of Bannack, Montana, where a sheriff named Henry Plummer came to town during the gold rush and hired gang members to rob travelers. In 1863, the local miners took the law into their own hands and hanged Plummer and 24 gang members. Bannack then became a ghost town.

The novel also owes a debt to the 1956 film *Invasion of the Body Snatchers* and the Jack Finney novel from which it was adapted. This archetype will be discussed in more detail in chapter 29, which examines the companion novel *The Regulators*.

King's second published novel, *'Salem's Lot*, serves as an archetype of sorts for *Desperation*, being a small town that is taken over by evil and that destroys the residents. It, too, becomes a fictional ghost town.

Themes and Subtext

Various characters epitomize some of the themes of the novel. Marinville, the writer, represents the novel's theme of writing and creation. Twelve-year-old David Carver, who has made a deal with God to save his best friend's life, introduces the book's religious themes. And Tom Billingsley, the retired veterinarian, embodies alcoholism.

The theme of writing occurs in most of King's novels and is personified by the character of Johnny Marinville in *Desperation*. Marinville represents a highly successful writer who has allowed alcohol to destroy his career. Like Jack Torrance in *The Shining*, he allows substance abuse to distract him from his writing and leads to his becoming involved in scandals. He has had his moment of fame, and much of his fame comes from his image as a "bad boy," but as long as he is addicted to alcohol, he is unable

28. Desperation

to be productive. His cross-country motorcycle trip is a last-ditch attempt to reinvent himself as a writer.

The common stereotype says that the most talented writers rely on alcohol and drugs for their inspiration. King himself had a history of substance dependency and at that time feared he would be unable to write were he to become sober. After a family intervention where King did give up drugs and alcohol, he discovered that he was able to remain productive, and in fact, most critics believe that his post-drug writing is better. Marinville's tragedy is that he did overcome his addiction and would have had a fighting chance of reclaiming his career.

Tom Billingsley also portrays an alcoholic whose life has been ruined by drinking. He draws fish on the walls in magic marker when he's drunk. But his drunken lifestyle has prevented him from doing much more than drawing the equivalent of beautiful graffiti.

Religion is a double-edged sword in King's fiction and usually comes with dire consequences. Much of Carrie White's misery stems from her mother's fanatical religious beliefs, Father Callahan from *'Salem's Lot* is shown to be wanting (though he is redeemed much later in the Dark Tower series), and the preacher in *Revival* proves to be a fraud. In *Desperation*, having a prayer answered turns out to be a deal with the devil of sorts—yes, David's request is answered, but there will be a heavy price to pay in return. Indeed, Satan also comes to David and asks him to worship him instead of God, making the case that a God that kills babysitters is no better than the devil himself. Even David's preacher admits that "God is cruel," a prediction that turns out to be true. As God grants a life, so he later demands one in return. Perhaps worst of all, the price that God exacts remains a mystery until it is required.

Human Universals

The most basic human universal trait is survival (life and limb), which, of course, occurs in all of King's fiction. Couple this with concern for one's family, and it forms a plot for a story. Fear is part of this universal, and a fear of being trapped or confined is a common and natural phobia. *Desperation* leads the protagonists from one confinement to another. First, they are confined by the sheriff in the patrol car, then in the jail, then in the town itself, which seems to hold no hope of escape. The attraction of the novel is when they turn from being victims and survivors and go on the offensive against Tak. Since being "trapped" is one of the triggers that turn on the rage impulse (when flight or freeze doesn't work, even the meekest creature is liable to fight back), the reader is pulled into the story as an active participant and achieves the satisfaction of overcoming the odds.

Altruism is a particularly human trait that, according to evolutionary psychologists, has enabled *Homo sapiens* to survive as a social species. Rather than evolution being the "survival of the fittest," it is really survival of the fittest genes. Kin selection theory postulates that humans show more altruism and are more likely to sacrifice themselves or take risks for their kin (who share genes) than for outsiders. This is quantified in Hamilton's rule, which calculates the closeness of kin through genetics to predict the likelihood of sacrificing oneself for another. Thus, a parent is more likely to take risks for their child than for their cousin or a stranger. Although this might seem self-evident, the theory fairly accurately predicts the likelihood of persons engaging in altruistic behavior.

Several of Stephen King's novels illustrate this idea of altruism, especially the willingness of parents to risk their lives for their children. This occurs in *Firestarter, Cujo, Dolores Claiborne,* and others, where parents put themselves at great peril for their children. In *Desperation*, Ralph Carver gives his life to save his son, an act that resonates with readers who are parents.

General altruism has also been a survival mechanism for the human species and may be considered a distinctly human characteristic. True heroes are people (firefighters, for example) who put themselves at risk for others, usually strangers, and they are revered by society. Indeed, heroic epics wouldn't exist without them. *Desperation* features an unlikely hero, Marinville, who also sacrifices himself for David and for the rest of the group by entering the mine and destroying Tak. Marinville demonstrates that even flawed characters can change and become heroic.

Evaluation

Desperation is a fun book to read, and I prefer it over its companion *The Regulators*. From an English professor's point of view, I think it handles some very interesting and important themes, most notably addiction and religion. The book's showing the similarities of God and Satan may upset some conservative readers, but it does make an interesting premise and looks at religion in a different way. The book is more complex than it seems at first and does benefit from a second reading and more detailed analysis. I'd place it among the top one-third of King's novels.

28. *Desperation*

Interesting Fact

Stephen King says he was inspired to write *Desperation* as a result of a cross-country drive in 1991, where he stopped in the small desert town of Ruth, Nevada. Thinking that all the townsfolk were dead, he imagined that their sheriff had killed them, and thus the story was born.

Notable Quote

"When a person stops changing, stops feeling, they die."

29

The Regulators

Horror in the Burbs

Background

The Regulators, the "mirror" novel to *Desperation*, was published in 1996 under the Richard Bachman pen name, even though by this time it was common knowledge that Bachman was, in fact, King. In an unusual publishing move, the two books were released at the same time and had dust jacket covers that, when placed side by side, formed a complete picture. Each book also featured a small view of the other's cover on the back of the book. The novel features the same characters as its mirror volume, though in a different multiverse and under different circumstances. The novel originally began as a screenplay called *Shotgunners* but was never finalized or produced.

Summary and Narrative Devices

The Regulators is set in the suburb of Wentworth, Ohio, where a neighborhood is taken over and terrorized by Tak, the evil entity from *Desperation*. In Bachman's alternate world, a family with an autistic child, Seth, travels through the mining town of Desperation and visits the mine where Tak has been trapped, giving the entity the opportunity to invade the autistic boy's mind and ultimately take control of him. The family is later killed, and Seth is moved to the Poplar Street neighborhood, where Tak grows stronger and turns the neighborhood into a war zone by creating characters from western television shows and a children's superhero cartoon and having these characters attack the neighborhood. Many of the residents die horrible deaths, but the survivors of Tak's rage learn that the monster lives inside Seth and are eventually able to destroy it.

Some critics have suggested that the "Bachman" books are grittier than those published under the Stephen King name, and this novel lends some evidence to that claim. The work is particularly graphic, with a heavy reliance on what King terms "the gross-out." The book opens with the murder of a child and a dog, immediately setting the tone that no one is safe, not even the "nice" characters. The omniscient narrator shows the murder and initial violence through the rapidly shifting points of view of each of the neighbors, making the carnage a reality and the danger imminent. This device engages readers and puts them into the action of the story. The novel contains harrowing descriptions of violence throughout its pages. The description of Marielle's wound and subsequent suffering is particularly graphic and disturbing.

The Regulators effectively uses foreshadowing devices early in the novel when it previews the fact that Cary Ripton is "unaware that he will die both a virgin and a backup shortstop." Although this device may be a bit heavy-handed (in true Bachman style), it does give a taste to the bad things that are about to occur in this novel. The newspaper carrier is set up as a likable, innocent kid, and now we're about to see the doom of King's multiverse descend on him.

King effectively withholds information later in the novel when Seth shares his plan with Audrey Wyler, but King allows the details of that to occur offstage. All we know is that it is "such a simple thing ... but it might solve a lot." This use of hermeneutic code not only builds suspense but, by introducing a mystery, invites readers to figure it out for themselves. We are given just enough of a clue to know that there is a plan and that it might work. We must continue reading to find out exactly what this strategy entails.

Another interesting technique is King's inclusion of ancillary material: letters, memos, newspaper accounts, even a postcard. This approach, which he used to great advantage in *Carrie*, allows King to examine other points of view that would not be available even to the omniscient narrator. Audrey's journal gives us the backstory of Seth's possession by Tak, and the long letter by Allen Symes of the Deep Earth Mining Corporation serves as a short story within the novel, with a definite short story structure. Even within this story, we experience the hermeneutic code when the "little scare" is introduced. Readers can only wonder, what is the "big scare"? This short story creatively reveals the backstory of Tak and the mine in Desperation. Readers who have also read *Desperation* receive an extra bonus.

Archetypes

One of the archetypes for both *Desperation* and *The Regulators* is the Jack Finney novel *The Body Snatchers*, which was adapted into the iconic

1956 film *Invasion of the Body Snatchers*. In this story, alien invaders take over the bodies of everyday human beings and slowly assimilate their victims until they become "pod people." Although it is not clear if Tak is an alien, a demon, or something else, the entity does enter the bodies of its victims and takes over their minds and their will. In *Desperation*, Tak is able to assimilate anyone it likes; however, it uses up the bodies and must move on to new hosts. In *The Regulators*, most human minds and wills are too strong for Tak to take over, hence his victimization of Seth, the autistic child. Tak feeds on death and misery to stay strong and doesn't need to move on to a new host.

A more recent archetype is the Dan Simmons novel *Carrion Comfort*, published as a novella in 1983 and published as a full-length novel in 1989. In this work, psychically gifted villains are able to take over people's minds, incite them to violence, and vampire-like, feed off the resulting energy. Tak, like Simmons's villains, controls its victims, creates violence, and feeds off the results.

The Regulators also calls to mind the popular children's television cartoon *Mighty Morphin Power Rangers*, which debuted in August 1993. In this series, teenagers were able to morph into powerful superheroes who drove vehicles similar to those in *The Regulators*. The series was criticized for its violence, yet was spun off into films, action figures, and toys.

Finally, as in *Desperation*, Westerns are a prominent part of the novel. King goes so far as to create a mythical western movie, titled "The Regulators," and includes a sample script from the film as an ancillary piece in his novel. The irony of both the superhero and western motif is how easily the heroes can be transformed into villains.

Themes and Subtexts

The familiar theme of writing and creativity is present in *The Regulators*, once again in the persona of John Marinville, who is a professional writer in this novel as well. In this case, there are two Marinvilles: the literary novelist who is a critical success and the children's book writer who has made a small fortune with his books for kids. The literary writer was plagued by self-doubt and substance abuse issues, which caused him to do a complete career pivot. He stopped worrying about the critics, cleaned up his personal life and went sober, and wrote children's books for enjoyment. The kids' books made much more money than the literary novels, which were praised by the critics. This once again illustrates King's idea of the different types of writers and shows how critical success is not the key to a successful career. This mirrors King's own writing. He writes horror and fantasy because that is the type of writing that brings him the most joy. Early in his career, King freely admitted that he hoped his writing would be financially successful. After the publication of *Carrie*, he was warned that he would be typecast as a horror writer. After thinking over the consequences, he decided that authoring horror fiction was fine with him, and he never looked back, jokingly admitting that he was "the literary equivalent of a Big Mac and french fries." Even now that he is beginning to be accepted in critical circles and even publishes short stories in literary journals, he still considers himself a genre writer and his work is marketed that way by his publishers.

Autism is an interesting subtext in this novel, as King explores it through the character of Seth, who seems to be nonfunctional in the traditional sense. Unable to communicate, he is stereotyped as being an outsider, less than human, in society. Yet King makes it very clear that Seth is quite human, with all the thoughts and emotions that define us. He experiences love, excitement, pleasure, and pain, even if he is unable to communicate using language. His takeover by Tak is even more tragic because he comes to understand what is happening to him. He demonstrates uniquely human moral values in his efforts to fight against the intruder in his mind and clearly shows love and empathy toward his family and especially toward his aunt. He also exhibits altruism as he sacrifices himself in his effort to save his aunt and the others, clearly putting himself in tremendous danger. This theme of looking deeper into the characters of others, whom we might otherwise dismiss, also appears in *The Stand* where the mentally challenged Tom Cullen and the deaf-mute Nick Andros play very powerful roles in bringing about the destruction of Randall Flagg's empire.

Human Universals

Like virtually all horror novels, *The Regulators* evokes the twin human universal emotions of survival and fear. As H.P. Lovecraft has stated, fear is the "oldest and strongest emotion." And survival is the most basic instinct of all living things.

Traditionally, horror novels are set in "creepy" places—haunted houses, ancient tombs, graveyards—and the story usually occurs in the dark. In *The Regulators*, King turns tradition on its side by placing the horror in what we would assume to be one of the safest places on the planet, a small, American suburban neighborhood. Poplar Street isn't your isolated hotel with a checkered past (*The Shining*), a sequestered tiny Maine town with a history of weirdness (Derry, Castle Rock, or Jerusalem's Lot), or the death row unit of a maximum-security prison (*The Green Mile*), all of which have become tropes of horror fiction largely due to King's influence. On the contrary, this Ohio suburb is classic Americana, a setting more suitable for a Hallmark feel-good film than to a gory tale of terror. The opening pages of *The Regulators*, in fact, are reminiscent of Ray Bradbury's *Dandelion Wine*, as they describe an idyllic summer day in the Midwest experienced by young people enjoying their summer vacation. In fact, a Constant Reader might wonder if King has changed literary genres until the scene explodes with sudden, savage violence beginning immediately in the next chapter.

Cary, the 14-year-old boy who delivers the newspaper, resembles Douglas Spaulding, Bradbury's hero of his "feel-good" novel. In the world of Stephen King, however, the likable young protagonist is mercilessly slaughtered in the first two-dozen pages, and the sweet, peaceful neighborhood turns into a battlefield for the rest of the novel. Just when readers are being lulled into a pleasant and comfortable setting, King twists Poplar Street into a nightmare. This begs the question, if we are not safe in this perfect Norman Rockwell world, can we be safe anywhere? The answer, in King's world, is a resounding no. Horror can appear unannounced at any time and in any place to anyone.

Another human universal emotion concerns our sense of SELF, according to Jaak Panksepp and Lucy Biven, in their theory of neuroevolutionary origins of emotions. Even though we can't know what occurs inside the brains (minds?) of animals, humans have what appears to be a capacity for self-awareness that is unique in biology. We can know ourselves, so to speak, and are aware of what may happen to us in the future, even to the point of understanding our own mortality. In the case of Seth, his "self" has been invaded by Tak, and he will do anything to regain control of his "self," even if it results in his death. An invasion like this is one of the most horrifying things we can imagine. Indeed, the loss of "self" is one of the most disturbing aspects of dementia and Alzheimer's disease, where patients no longer recall who they are. This human universal emotion triggers strong feelings in us and, in the case of Seth, makes him a sympathetic character rather than the monster he is seen as by some of the other survivors.

Evaluation

The Regulators is a gritty novel in the pulp fiction tradition that is typical of the Bachman books. It is easy to read, fast paced, and enjoyable. From a critical standpoint, it's not a novel that I'd choose as required reading for a Stephen King seminar, and I'd consider it in the lower middle third of King's books in general.

Interesting Fact

King says that *Desperation* is about God and *The Regulators* is about television, making them "both about higher powers."

Notable Quote

"Sometimes all you can do is get moving, keep moving, and hope that God will hold up the roof."

30

Bag of Bones

Digging Up the Past

Background

Unhappy with his royalty deals with Viking, Stephen King signed a three-book contract with Scribner in 1997, who published *Bag of Bones* in 1998. The novel won the Bram Stoker Award, the British Fantasy Award, and the Locus Award for best novel. Billed as "a haunted love story," *Bag of Bones* shows a much more literary style of writing than in King's previous books, a style that he successfully developed under his new publisher. The book was adapted into a television miniseries in 2011 starring Pierce Brosnan as Mike Noonan.

Summary and Narrative Devices

Mike Noonan, a best-selling author, suffers from writer's block after his wife's death. Although he has several completed manuscripts that he has held back from his publisher and can now use to fulfill his writing obligations, he is plagued by the writer's block, nonetheless, and decides to move to his rural summerhouse, which the locals refer to as "Sara Laughs," hoping to recover his creativity. Once there, he encounters a child, Kyra Devore, and her mother Mattie, who are involved in a custody battle with the child's 80-some-year-old wealthy and powerful grandfather, Max. Noonan helps Mattie with her legal troubles despite interference from Max, who nearly kills him.

Once at Sara Laughs, Noonan begins to write again and falls under the influence of the ghost of the blues singer Sara Tidwell, which is haunting the house and has, in fact, put a curse on the township. With the help of his dead wife's spirit, Noonan is able to find the ghost's bones and destroy them, ridding the township of the curse. Unfortunately, the living evil of

30. Bag of Bones

Max and his henchmen return and kill Mattie. At the end of the novel, Noonan is adopting the little girl.

King uses a number of techniques to create suspense in *Bag of Bones*, which uses the parallel plots of Noonan's writer's block, the custody battle over the child and the danger that entails, and the mystery of the curse of Sara Tidwell. Coupled with this is the issue of Noonan's wife Jo, who was involved in some mysterious doings before she died.

The novel opens with Noonan recounting his wife's death in a prolonged narrative that reveals that she died from a brain aneurysm while running to the scene of a car accident to try to help out. Her unexpected death is compounded by the fact that she has purchased a home pregnancy kit, which Noonan knew nothing about, leading him to wonder if she had some sort of secret life. This puzzle is later shown to be connected to the curse of Sara Tidwell, and Jo's "secret life" has been to try to unravel the mystery of the jazz singer's history.

King also builds suspense around the problem of Noonan's writer's block. Although nonwriters might not consider this such a severe problem—after all, Noonan does have spare novels to sell and certainly has enough money to support himself—King links this problem to the protagonist's mental health. Writing is more than just a job to Noonan—it is life itself, and without his creative outlet, he is just a shell of a person. As time goes on, the reader can see just how vital writing is to the protagonist. This becomes even more apparent as Noonan publishes the books in his "backup file" and needs new work to sustain both his image and his sense of being.

Mattie's custody battle introduces another plot element into the story. Noonan's involvement puts him in physical danger, forcing him to literally fight for his life. The dread that comes with infuriating a powerful man hangs over the entire novel like a dark cloud.

Finally, and most integral to the horror aspect of the story, is the curse of Sara Tidwell. King presents the enigma of there being something terribly wrong at Sara Laughs and challenges Noonan to solve the puzzle. When he stumbles upon his wife's research into the mystery, the ante is raised. As in a good mystery story, the clues are released slowly until the dark history of Sara Laughs is revealed.

Archetypes

Daphne du Maurier's *Rebecca* is referred to several times in *Bag of Bones* and does serve as an archetype of a house that is "haunted" by the presence of a dead wife. Although *Rebecca* differs markedly in its plot from

King's novel, the two books share several elements. Both are set in named estates (Sara Laughs and Manderley) that have a Gothic flavor. Both places feature the overhanging presence of a dead wife (a supportive one in the King novel and a destructive one in *Rebecca*). Both wives have secrets, which are slowly revealed to the reader. Both estates employ staff members that turn out to be sleeping with the enemy, at least in a figurative sense. Both husbands enter into relationships with younger women after their wives' deaths. Finally, both novels feature the presence of wicked females (Sara and Rebecca) who flavor the atmosphere.

Bag of Bones also references Melville's *Bartleby, the Scrivener*, a novel about a writer (more like a copier) who chooses to put down his pen. Noonan doesn't initially choose to stop writing but is forced to by his debilitating writer's block. At the end of the story, though, he does make this conscious decision to stop writing.

Finally, there is the reference to Thomas Hardy, who supposedly said the quote about fictional characters being nothing more than a "bag of bones" when compared to real people. It is interesting that King chose Hardy to attribute this quote to since Hardy is generally recognized by critics as being a master of character, having created some of the most memorable protagonists in literature: Tess Durbeyfield, Diggory Venn, Jude Fawley, and others. If these characters are just shadows of real life, we must ask, what are characters created by less-skilled novelists? This is the challenge that every storyteller faces, according to King—the herculean task of creating realistic characters using only words on the page.

Themes and Subtexts

Perhaps the most important theme of *Bag of Bones* concerns the issues of racism and misogyny. Racism underlies the history of both Sara Laughs and the entire unincorporated township, staining it with a past that all the old-time locals know but that is buried (literally and figuratively) and can't be acknowledged or discussed. The gang rape of Sara Tidwell and the murder of her and her child are motivated by both racism and male dominance (though the perpetrators would never commit such violence against a white woman), and with Sara's death, the curse of racism is leveled against the men and their ancestors, claiming the lives of their sons as part of Sara's legacy. Symbolically, then, this curse of racism is passed down through the generations and like the institution of racism in society, it cannot easily be purged or terminated. Like racism in American society, this blight remains despite all efforts to move on and end this inheritance. Whereas Noonan may extinguish the curse that Sara Tidwell has placed on the community, the overall institution of racism cannot be so easily expunged.

Misogyny forms another part of the curse of Sara Tidwell, which is why she targets the male heirs of those who raped her, plaguing them with the same horror that they inflicted on her as she was forced to watch them drown her son. As a result, these men and their ancestors will drown their own sons until the curse can be lifted. The rapists look at Sara Tidwell as nothing more than a sex object, someone who can be taken and used however they desire. They justify their violence with an excuse common to rapists—that she "teased" them with her singing and sexy movements, and therefore she must have wanted it. Needless to say, this "justification" is wrong and will not shield them from Sara's curse.

Misogyny appears again in the character of Max Devore, who has no respect for Mattie, the mother of his granddaughter. He will stop at nothing to gain custody of the child, presumably so he can kill her and stop the curse from spreading to another generation. He is symbolic of the "old boy" network of powerful men who use their money and influence for their own ends with little thought to the well-being of others. His actions result in Mattie's death; Noonan and the child are nearly murdered as well.

Gloria Naylor, a prominent African American novelist, observed that *Bag of Bones* is "a love story about the dark places within us all," which reveals another interesting subtext—that of secret or forbidden knowledge (a theme that is also prevalent in *Rebecca*). The uncovering of a terrible secret is a common feature of the horror story. In some tales, like those of Lovecraft, for example, the discovery of forbidden knowledge destroys the protagonists. In *Bag of Bones*, however, the forbidden secret must be brought to light for the protagonist to be saved. Noonan's wife Jo had been in the process of uncovering the secret when she died, and with the help of her ghost, Noonan can bring the sordid history of the township to light, discover the source of the curse and end it. Acknowledging racism and calling it out is the first step in ending it. Noonan is able to do his part in the small community of rural Maine; however, this is but a microcosm of the world at large. Racism remains buried deep in society and rooting it out and eliminating it is no easy task.

Writing makes its appearance once again in this story in the character of Noonan, a best-selling author. As the novel opens, writing is such an important part of Noonan's life that he has difficulty functioning when he finds he is unable to write. King has claimed that he is "addicted to writing"; for King, and for Noonan, storytelling defines who they are. Although the end of the novel finds Noonan putting down his pen, his magic wand, like the sorcerer in Shakespeare's *The Tempest*, he must first experience a death of sorts and then a rebirth to accept a life without writing in it. In King's world, writing is not a profession but a way of life, something that one cannot easily retire from.

Noonan finds that he can no longer write after his wife's death and is only able to resume writing once her spirit begins guiding him. Even then, Jo's "inspiration" is her method to help her husband discover the secret behind the curse.

In his novels, Stephen King always credits his wife Tabitha as being his support person, either in the dedication or in the acknowledgments. No doubt the reference to Noonan's being unable to write is a shout-out to Tabitha as well, who he says in this novel's acknowledgment page "was there for me again when things got hard."

Human Universals

Grief is a human universal emotion that every person on the planet has suffered from, from the loss of a beloved pet to the loss of a parent, spouse, or perhaps worst of all, a child. *Bag of Bones* opens with Mike Noonan chronicling the death of his wife and then detailing the crippling grief that he suffered thereafter. King describes the period of numb grief that Noonan suffers after his wife's unexpected death and his shock at the fact that she was pregnant, and thus, two lives were lost. He seems to exist on autopilot with the support of family and friends and finishes the book. After that, he is unable to write.

Neuroscience acknowledges grief as a result of the panic instinct that young mammals have hardwired into their brains when they are separated from their caregivers. This is observed directly as a crying response in animals and, of course, human babies and can be directly observed in mammalian brains through fMRI scans. Since humans are also hardwired to form social relationships and pair bonds—a favorable condition for raising children from birth until they become self-sufficient—this same caring/loving response is transferred to a partner, and the loss of the partner triggers the grief response. It has been well documented that when a long-term partner dies, the remaining partner often dies of a "broken heart" soon thereafter. Although Noonan doesn't suffer this condition, his grief manifests itself in depression, a common response, and his inability to write. His refusal to seek help or counseling, or to even talk about his grief with anyone, only compounds the issue. And although the average nonwriter probably can't relate to writer's block, depression, grief, and the inability to work connect with any audience.

CARE is another universal emotion that everyone understands. This emotion presents itself in several ways in *Bag of Bones*. First, there is the care that Noonan has for his wife, which is shown in the flashbacks of their time together. In neurological terms, romantic love is a combination of two human universals: care and lust. It is obvious the Noonans share both emotions, the loss of which triggers the grief response previously mentioned. In addition, since Jo is pregnant, her husband also experiences the loss of a child; the care response for one's offspring is instinctual in all mammals and is especially strong in humans since child-rearing is a long and complicated process that requires a strong bond between parents and children.

The care response also appears in the character of Mattie, who is in danger of losing custody of her child. Noonan, who is grieving for his wife and, to a lesser extent, the unborn child, identifies with Mattie so much so that at the novel's conclusion, he seeks custody of the girl. This subplot adds suspense to the novel and raises the stakes for Noonan; the life of both Mattie and her daughter are in jeopardy, not to mention his own, once he becomes involved. The mystery of Sara Laughs, then, becomes not just a puzzle to solve but a matter of survival for the major characters.

Finally, lust, another universal emotion, plays a role in the novel. Evolutionary psychology predicts that men value sex without commitment much more than women. The biology behind this is simple: during the course of his lifetime, a man may theoretically produce thousands of offspring, while women are limited to approximately one child per year and for only 30-some years. Women, then, have a lot more invested in a child and are therefore choosy about whom they partner with. Men, on the other hand, can (again, theoretically) partner with any fertile woman without commitment. Civilization and society have, of course, tempered this lustful behavior in the acceptable institution of marriage. Yet statistics show that men are more likely to cheat on their partners than women, and virtually all rapes are committed by males.

The rape of Sara Tidwell by several men set off the events behind the history of the story. Whereas they justify their actions by the belief that Sara "wants it," this conclusion is inconsistent with both the theory of evolutionary psychology and common sense. By following their baser instincts to rape and murder, the men set off the curse. Noonan, who is in control of his lust instinct, is able to end the curse. Yet even he needs the assistance of a woman, the spirit of his wife, to do so.

Evaluation

Bag of Bones marks a transition in the King canon as he signed on with Scribner, a new publisher. Beginning with this novel, King began enjoying more critical acceptance of his work, and rightly so. Although technically a horror story, the horror element was downplayed in its marketing in an attempt to attract a wider audience. In my opinion, *Bag of Bones* is one of King's better books because of its multiple layers of meaning, psychological insights, and effective treatment of social issues.

Interesting Fact

A character in the film tells Noonan that he is his "number one fan," a reference to *Misery*.

Notable Quote

"Compared to the dullest human being actually walking about on the face of the earth ... the most brilliantly drawn character in a novel is but a bag of bones."

31

The Girl Who Loved Tom Gordon
Gretel Goes It Alone

Background

The Girl Who Loved Tom Gordon was published in 1999 by Scribner and in 2004 was adapted into a pop-up book. A film adaptation has been planned but as of the time of this writing, has not moved into the production stage. The book was inspired by Stephen King's love of baseball and particularly the Boston Red Sox. Tom Gordon, referenced in the title and throughout the novel, was a relief pitcher for the Red Sox from 1996 to 1999. After pitching for several other teams, he retired from baseball in 2010 as the only pitcher to accumulate 100 wins, 100 saves, and 100 holds. Gordon was beloved by Red Sox fans during his tenure with the team.

Summary and Narrative Devices

The Girl Who Loved Tom Gordon is about a nine-year-old girl named Tricia McFarland who gets lost in the vast Maine woods after wandering off the path of the Appalachian Trail. Tricia's parents have split up, and she and her brother are caught in the middle of parents who live in separate states and can't get along. Baseball is the one stabilizing influence in her life, epitomized by her infatuation with Tom Gordon, the star relief pitcher for the Boston Red Sox. Once Tricia is lost, she moves deeper and deeper into the wilderness, far from where rescue parties are looking. Her only comfort is her radio, where she can listen to the broadcast of the Red Sox games on the local channel. Using her own resourcefulness, courage, and strength of will, she is able to survive, channeling the energy from her baseball hero to overcome almost impossible odds.

Rather than typical chapter headings, the novel is organized by innings, beginning with pregame, each of the nine innings of a baseball game, and the postgame. This device gives the reader a sort of countdown, marking Tricia's progress in the game. Unlike other sports, baseball isn't governed by time but by at-bats; theoretically, a game can last forever, as long as a team doesn't make a third out (a device that Kinsella used very successfully in his novel *The Iowa Baseball Confederacy*). Since Tricia doesn't have a watch or a calendar, this organizational structure is an effective way to keep track of the narrative and its timeline.

As in several of King's stories, the author is faced with the problem of following a single viewpoint character who is alone and can't have interactions with others. Any dialogue she has is with herself, and she can't count on anyone else to help her survive in the woods. King's third-person point of view does occasionally allow him to shift focus and observe Tricia's parents. And the radio announcers' play-by-play of the Red Sox games brings another interesting perspective. Much of the narrative, however, is composed of Tricia's internal thoughts, some of which she vocalizes, and her remembrance of the past, which serves the role of flashbacks.

The book is highly suspenseful, of course, because the woods are a dangerous place: "these weren't toy woods," Tricia says. She must face the elements—heat, cold, and rain—as well as wildlife that calls the woods home. The terrain is unforgiving, with its steep hills, sharp rocks, and swampland and the black bear that stalks her for the entire journey. Finally, there is the internal conflict of being alone and overcoming the very real fear that she might die without ever being found.

Although King is best known for his horror stories, *The Girl Who Loved Tom Gordon* is a realistic novel without the usual horror trappings. It is a book about fear, of course, fear of being lost in the woods and stalked by a bear. But this is a fear that anyone can relate to without really having to suspend their disbelief. Although Trisha believes that a monster is stalking her, the monster, far from being supernatural, is shown to be a black bear, an animal that can easily kill and eat a human in the wild.

The details of the woods are specific, concrete, and very accurate. King captures the fear of the vastness of the woods very effectively and populates it with dangers that would be considered slight in someone's backyard but are momentous when placed in a huge, isolated forest. Wasps, snakes, insects, and even fallen trees and logs become terrifying. A small injury, easily treated in the emergency room, becomes deadly in the deep woods.

King has acknowledged that in his fiction, "story is boss," and in typical storyteller fashion he makes use of narrative techniques designed to heighten suspense. The opening lines of the novel immediately introduce the issue of a nine-year-old girl learning that "the world had teeth and it could bite you with them any time it wanted." In a King novel, we know that this lesson will be a difficult one that a child should not have to learn at such a young age. King's Constant Readers also know that the author has no qualms about killing children in his books and making them suffer. Before we know anything about the protagonist, our sympathies are already with her. She is in for a rough time, and we are destined to take the journey with her.

King heightens suspense with foreshadowing, letting readers know that things will get even worse as, for example, when the third-person narrator interrupts the story and notes, "this was the worst mistake," and to observe that something was watching her (presumably the bear that appears in the last chapter) and that it stayed close to her. The third-person narrator also provides brief glimpses about what was happening behind the scenes: that search parties were looking in the wrong place and, later, that they thought she had been kidnapped and that her family had accepted her death and was making plans for her funeral. While readers may root for her, much as they root for their favorite baseball team, the outcome is never certain.

Archetypes

This novel is another variation of Joseph Campbell's "hero's journey" with the hero, in this case, being a heroine. She does not go out seeking adventure, of course, but like many heroic figures, she finds herself trapped in an unplanned quest. The departure occurs when she leaves the marked trail and is separated from her mother and brother. She tries to refuse the call to adventure by taking a path that will lead her to safety quickly, but her wrong decision leads her to cross the threshold and embark on a series of trials—the battle with insects, falling down a ravine, and eventually facing down a bear. She symbolically receives supernatural help from Tom Gordon, both by listening to baseball games on her Walkman (which miraculously still works) and by "seeing" him in her visions. She survives the "belly of the whale" when she passes through the almost unpassable swamp, which brings her out of the zone where rescuers would believe her to be. She is "reborn" from the experience and is tempted to give up after seeing three figures (Tom Gordon, who says he can't help her; her father as a representation of the inaudible, which also can't help her; and the monster, which has claimed her). Yet she carries on, achieves apotheosis when she stands down the attacking bear, receives the ultimate boon of being rescued, and returns to the civilized world, much more mature than her 14-year-old brother.

As with many hero's quest stories, *The Girl Who Loved Tom Gordon* is a bildungsroman where the protagonist undergoes a rite of passage and emerges from the experience as an adult. Although Tricia may still be nine years old after her ordeal in the woods, the novel ends with her symbolically saving the game in the bottom of the ninth and realizing that she is well on her way to becoming a strong, successful woman. Her final gesture, holding her cap and pointing to the sky, mirrors the action of Tom Gordon and articulates her newfound confidence and maturity in a way that words cannot express.

Finally, the book is a fairy tale of sorts, a Hansel and Gretel story, without Hansel, according to King.

Themes and Subtexts

King uses the game of baseball as an important symbol in *The Girl Who Loved Tom Gordon*. Baseball is structured on the concept of getting home safe, but King takes this symbol to the next step with the idea of a relief pitcher saving a game. A save is recorded if the relief pitcher enters the game with a lead of no more than three runs and keeps the opposing team from winning. It is a high-stress position with little room for error.

By channeling Tom Gordon, one of the game's best relief pitchers, Tricia symbolically "saves" her game, which is her life, and is able to reach home. Her successful management of her own emotions and her ability to remain focused and, for the most part, calm under pressure mirrors the traits of a successful reliever. These are exactly the traits that she needs to survive. Although she is tested often and sometime succumbs to emotion, she always pulls herself together and never gives up. Because of this, she overcomes overwhelming odds and survives, even when the authorities, and her parents presume she is dead.

King has been accused of being unable to create strong adult female characters (a criticism that, I believe, he overcame in his later novels). Although Tricia McFarland is not an adult physically, her adventure in this book does transform her from a girl into a woman emotionally and mentally. Physically, she beats the odds and survives in a most inhospitable environment, one where it is presumed that a "girl" could not overcome. She accomplishes this through her strength of will, her determination, and by ultimately learning to believe in herself. She begins the novel as a helpless little girl who plays with dolls but ends the book as a force to be reckoned with, even standing up to a charging bear which, I believe, she would have defeated even without the help of the hunter who arrived on the scene.

Interestingly, Tricia has learned survival skills from her mother, not her father, in a reversal of the traditional role models of American society. Her mother has provided lessons on which foods to eat in the wilderness and how to think like an adult when in a dangerous situation. Her mother Quilla is undoubtedly the stronger parent in the family. Her father, although he may be loving and supportive, allowed himself to use alcohol as a crutch, at great cost to his family.

Divorce and the breakup of the family is another important theme that runs through the novel. The problem of adults not being able to get along is transferred to the children. Tricia's brother is especially affected by this situation, which results in the conflict with his mother that leads to Tricia's becoming lost. The two are so consumed with their bickering that they don't realize that Tricia is no longer with them. She is hopelessly lost and off the path before they realize that she is gone.

Human Universals

Survival is the most basic instinct shared by all living things (although Richard Dawkins would claim that survival of one's genes is even more universal), and this novel is a book about survival. The main plot element pits the protagonist against nature and all its most elemental forces: rain, harsh terrain, insects and dangerous wildlife, sickness and disease, darkness, and lack of food. Tricia is an unlikely candidate to overcome the harsh environment she finds herself in, and her struggle to survive is a compelling read. King's detailed account of her ordeal is enough to carry the story on its own. Couple this with the human aversion to the suffering of children, and the conflict rises to a new level.

But Tricia's conflict with nature is only part of the story. Her harrowing experience forces her to dig deep within herself and to understand her core SELF, another human universal that neurologists have identified as being central to the human species. The question remains as to whether animals experience a sense of self (I, for one, believe they do), but humans undeniably comprehend their own sense of being. Tricia's journey from childhood to adulthood involves getting to know and understand who she is as a person. She realizes that she can no longer think like a child but must instantly become an adult if she is to survive. To accomplish this, she must gain an understanding of who she really is. She must grow up, literally overnight, and vanquish her childish fears, perceived inadequacies, and doubts. This basic human instinct, for each of us to "find ourselves," so to speak, is a universal element in narrative.

Interesting Fact

Stephen King has written several books about baseball, including *Blockade Billy*; *A Face in the Crowd* (with Stewart O'Nan); and *Faithful* (also with Stewart O'Nan), a nonfiction personal account of the 2004 Red Sox baseball season.

Notable Quote

"The world has teeth and it can bite you with them any time it wants."

32

Dreamcatcher
A Winter's Tale

Background

Originally titled *Cancer* until King's wife convinced him to change the title, *Dreamcatcher* was published in 2001 by Scribner. The novel is one of King's least favorite books and was written while he was taking prescription pain medicine for his injuries after being hit by a van. A film version appeared in 1993. The book is set near King's fictional town of Derry, Maine.

Summary and Narrative Devices

Dreamcatcher is a science fiction alien invasion story reminiscent of *The Tommyknockers*. The novel features four friends from junior high school (Beaver, Pete, Henry, and Jonesy) who befriended a child with Down syndrome, Douglas Cavell (Duddits). They are now grown up and taking part in their annual hunting trip to The Hole in the Wall, Beaver's cabin deep in the Maine woods, and they find themselves directly in the middle of an alien invasion.

Although Duddits has the mind of a child and has trouble communicating, he does have psychic powers, which he shares with his new friends, enabling them to also have some extrasensory abilities, such as being able to communicate thoughts and find lost things. These powers also make Jonesy immune to being taken over by an alien entity (Mr. Gray), though Jonesy doesn't realize it at the time. Along with Duddits, who at the end of the novel is dying from leukemia, and a soldier named Owen, Jonesy and Henry are able to stop the alien invasion despite interference from an insane military officer, Colonel Kurtz, whose mission is to exterminate everyone in the area, alien and human alike.

Dreamcatcher is an interesting twist on the typical alien invasion story. The aliens come in different forms: as a red fungus, reminiscent of a "red tide" that would be found in the ocean; as a vicious eel with razor-sharp teeth that incubates in the human digestive system; and as the more typical "grays" that are the subject of extraterrestrial encounter stories. King does use the typical crazed military figure that has become a trope in such stories, but he links him to the literary tradition of Joseph Conrad's *Heart of Darkness*. The extraterrestrial invasion is hampered by the harsh Maine weather, which acts like the earth microbes in H.G. Wells's *War of the Worlds*, but it ultimately takes a dying character with Down syndrome to bring about the aliens' destruction.

Structurally, the novel begins by introducing four characters as protagonists, but King kills two of them early in the novel and the third, Jonesy, appears to have been completely assimilated by the alien known as Mr. Gray. Duddits, the "dreamcatcher" that links the four protagonists, appears only in flashbacks for most of the novel and only makes a real-time appearance in the endgame. This narrative technique helps to keep Duddits's powers mysterious for most of the book.

King also poses the question of why Duddits has the powers he does and why he is able to transfer some of this power to his friends. The film version of *Dreamcatcher* speculates that Duddits is really an alien himself, a beneficent being sent to earth to stop the invasion, which he has foreseen. The novel, however, never answers this question completely, leaving us to wonder if there is a more far-reaching purpose to the friendship between the five characters. The answer seems to be that there is more to the story than just coincidence, but the enigma is never definitively solved.

King's use of the omniscient point of view allows him to easily jump from one character to another across both time and space. This enables him to selectively withhold information to build suspense and then supply it when needed. As the novel progresses and the characters become telepathic, the reader is allowed to live simultaneously in more than one character's head, presenting a more global picture of the events as they unfold.

Archetypes

King alludes to plenty of literary references in *Dreamcatcher*, including his own previous novel *The Tommyknockers*, which is also about an attempted alien invasion in the Maine woods. The plot of the story does follow the idea of *War of the Worlds*, where aliens are thwarted by an inhospitable earth environment, in this case the bitter New England weather rather than deadly earth microbes. John Wyndham's 1951 novel

The Day of the Triffids uses an invasion by plantlike aliens similar to the red fungi in King's story. And, of course, Colonel Abraham Kurtz is emblematic of the Kurtz character from Conrad's *Heart of Darkness* and Colonel Kurtz in Francis Ford Coppola's *Apocalypse Now*.

Themes and Subtexts

The image of coldness dominates *Dreamcatcher*. A freak November nor'easter strikes northern New England just as the alien spacecraft crashes into an isolated part of the Maine woods, making the environment almost uninhabitable for the extraterrestrials. The blizzard, though not common, is not abnormal either for New England. The weather plays a major role in the plot, however, by containing the aliens and keeping them from spreading too rapidly and by isolating the human population. The novel would have been much different if the ETs had crashed in Manhattan in July. The weather and the remoteness of the land allow the government to keep the disaster a secret and to manage their clandestine mission without troublesome coverage from the press. The area is easily quarantined, and the aliens could be easily contained were it not for Mr. Gray's takeover of Jonesy and his mission to infect the drinking supply of Boston with alien spores and contaminants. This setting keeps the battle limited and allows the novel's main characters, Jonesy, Henry, Duddits, and Owen, to play their heroic roles.

The images of cold, snow, and ice also project a mood of freezing bitterness into the novel. These images make the reader uncomfortable throughout the entire book and wishing for a warm blanket and a hot beverage. This visceral reaction enhances both the horror of the book and the unnatural situation. Much like the setting of *The Shining*, the harsh weather couples with the isolated setting to bring further discomfort.

The coldness of the climate is reflected in the coldness of the alien invader, which has absolutely no human emotions. The creatures are basic biology and demonstrate only the need to reproduce, to replicate their kind and take over the ecosystem. Mr. Gray epitomizes what it is to be inhuman when he begins to enjoy human emotions. He cannot understand love, creativity, or caring but embraces gluttony and murder instead. His coexisting with Jonesy would be impossible because Jonesy, for all his human faults and frailties (petty sins, really), is a caring, empathetic individual who cares about his friends—and even about the student who plagiarizes an exam. Mr. Gray and the alien entities would not be able to accept or even understand these emotions. Instead, they succumb to both the freezing environment and to the positive human emotions that are such an important part of Jonesy, Henry, Duddits, and even Owen.

Addiction plays a small but important role in *Dreamcatcher*. The two characters who have addiction problems (Pete, an alcoholic, and Beaver, who hangs out in dive bars and has an unhealthy obsession with chewing toothpicks) are both killed early in the novel. Pete's returning to the accident scene to retrieve beer (and not food or a rifle) plays a role in his death, as does Beaver's allowing the alien to escape from the toilet when he leans over to retrieve his dropped toothpicks. In both cases, their weakness winds up costing them their lives.

Henry, on the other hand, contemplates suicide from early in the novel, yet he never crosses the line and doesn't act on his impulses. He manages to keep his depression and his self-destructive thoughts at bay. Although he is aware of them, he doesn't allow them to control his actions. Instead, his strength of character keeps him going, especially when he realizes that there is something greater than himself that is happening in the world and that he must become one of the "heroes."

Jonesy also harnesses an inner strength he doesn't realize he has, first to overcome the near-fatal injuries he has suffered and then to win the fight against Mr. Gray and the alien influences conspiring to take over his brain and the world as he knows it. Once he is taken over by the alien, it seems likely that he will suffer the same fate as Paul and Beaver. But he fights on, perseveres, and with the help of Duddits and his friends, he surmounts what seems like an impossible situation. It is no coincidence that the two characters with the strongest wills survive and ultimately thrive.

Creativity forms a strong subtext in this novel, and in King's world, creativity comes from dreams—both the literal dreams that we have in our sleep and the dreams that we dare to dream and strive for. Humanity defeats the alien invader because the major characters are able to think creatively, to dream, and connect the dots of things that seem unconnected.

To begin with, the four boys at the beginning of the novel are able to enjoy Duddits's psychic gift because they are children and their minds were still impressionable enough and open enough to accept what seemed impossible. Had they been older when they met Duddits, they would not have been open to receiving his psychic powers. And Duddits, with the innocent mind of a child, is the perfect conduit for such powers. In the Stephen King multiverse, psychic ability seems to reside in the young— Carrie, Charlie McGee, and the children in *The Institute*—and in those like John Smith, who is reborn in *The Dead Zone*. Adults have become too hardened to believe in such things, and so they are less likely to be receptive.

Physical dreams are also a theme of this novel. The four boys and

Duddits dream Richie's death, and it occurs in the real world. Their minds have become a powerful force. Jonesy uses this knowledge to his advantage to defeat Mr. Gray. The dreamcatcher, a symbol of the mind's power to create, becomes an actual weapon to use against the alien.

It is worthwhile to note that Kurtz is unable to dream, either physically or metaphorically. And the alien invaders can't think creatively; they can't connect the dots and so are doomed to destruction by those who can.

Finally, like many of King's novels, *Dreamcatcher* explores the problem of government overreach and the possibility of powerful government officials going rogue. This theme is most apparent in novels like *Firestarter* that speculate that "The Shop" is more than willing to destroy civil liberties for its own benefit. In *Dreamcatcher*, Colonel Kurtz suspends all freedoms to contain the invasion and keep it a secret. Although the quarantine of the inhabitants of this section of rural Maine might be a case of utilitarianism—the safety of the many outweighing the rights of the few—Kurtz goes from quarantine to extermination and murder. Even when he learns that the infected develop an immunity and fight the disease off, he still insists on killing everyone, though he no longer has a logical reason. This fear of government power and insensitivity is a common element in so many of King's works.

Human Universals

FEAR is the human universal that is common in King's novels, whether it be fear of the supernatural, fear of the government, fear of "bad people," or fear of the natural world. *Dreamcatcher* does rely on fear to propel the narrative. But in addition to fear of the alien invasion and a messy death, this book capitalizes on another human universal, SELF, and the fear of losing it.

Regardless of what people may think of themselves, they do, for the most part, recognize themselves as individuals with hopes, dreams, desires, strengths, weaknesses, insecurities, and a unique way of looking at the world. This core being, if you will, is what drives human beings to do everything they do, good, bad, and neutral. The thought of losing control of this "self" to an invader is terrifying on many different levels. Our core beliefs involve knowing and recognizing the self; the horror of the self being highjacked by an intruder in the brain is almost incomprehensible. This is the horror of dementia and Alzheimer's, the losing the sense of self, and is why this disease is dreaded perhaps above all others.

Dreamcatcher does present conflict over possession of the self as Mr. Gray takes over Jonesy's mind, controlling his body and his actions. Jonesy carries on a mental battle with the alien (a battle that turns out to be a battle against himself). This proves to be the most important struggle in the novel, not only for Jonesy but for the survival of the human species as well. Once our humanity is taken, nothing worthwhile is left. Metaphorically speaking, human emotions, the human "self," is the most important part of life. Without it, we are little more than the red fungus that threatens to take over the earth. When Jonesy reclaims his own self, he reasserts the qualities that make humans human, and despite the bad things that go along with the species, most of the self turns out to be a good thing after all. *Homo sapiens* enjoys the full range of emotions, including love, altruism, caring, and self-preservation, not to mention perks such as creativity and the ability to think out of the box to solve problems. Compared to the mindless replicating fungi of the alien world that King presents, human beings aren't so bad after all, even if there are bad apples like Kurtz.

Evaluation

I don't know if it's because I really don't like the cold (and, hence, left New England for warmer climes), but *Dreamcatcher* is a difficult read for me, and I'd rank it in the lower third of his novels. It's one of those books that's just tough to get through and could probably benefit from some cutting. It might also have something to do with the fact that King was taking painkillers at the time and recovering from injuries he suffered after being hit by a car. At any rate, the book, for me, becomes tedious in places (as does the film adaptation, for that matter).

Interesting Fact

Stephen King wrote the entire first draft of *Dreamcatcher* in cursive while recovering from an accident where he was run down while walking and nearly killed.

Notable Quote

"Hearts were made to be broken and minds were made to be changed."

33

From a Buick 8
The One-Way Portal

Background

From a Buick 8 was published in September 2002 by Scribner. The idea came to King when he was driving across western Pennsylvania, and during at a restroom stop, he slid down a slope and almost fell into a river while exploring the area behind a Conoco station. Rather than transfer the story to a more familiar Maine setting, King returned to Pennsylvania later and spent some time with the state troopers there to gain authenticity for the book.

A film version of the story has been optioned and, as of the time of this writing, is in preproduction.

Summary and Narrative Devices

From a Buick 8 begins with the abandonment of an old Buick Roadmaster in a gas station in rural western Pennsylvania. The driver mysteriously disappears, and the vehicle is towed back to the state police barracks of Troop D. The car, however, proves to be strange in many ways, and when one of their own troopers disappears inside the car, the police know they have an inexplicable phenomenon on their hands. They speculate the Buick is really a portal to another world or universe, as it will erupt in weird light shows and sounds and will transport things away or deposit otherworldly things in the garage where the troopers have hidden it. True to the line from the gunslinger books, "there are other worlds than these." The car is kept a secret until Sandy Dearborn tells its story to Ned Wilcox, the 18-year-old son of an officer who was killed in an accident and who was investigating the Buick 8. Once he learns the story, Ned attempts to destroy the vehicle and is nearly consumed by it himself in the attempt.

In *From a Buick 8*, King uses the narrative device of storytelling to explain the history of the strange vehicle to Ned and, of course, to the novel's readers. The tale begins with Sandy's telling of it, but as the narrative grows, other members of Troop D add to the story, giving their own accounts of things that happened and their perspective on them. Each of the characters tells the story to Ned. The narrative moves back and forth from present to past tense this way, with breaks in the present between each account. Most of the novel, then, is set in the past and recounts the mystery and the horrors of the Buick 8 over a 20-year past. The real story of Ned trying to destroy the car comes at the very end of the book. Everything else leads to this.

The long history of the car is a slow building of suspense from 1979 to 2001, the story's "present," where Ned is listening to the bizarre tale of the Buick. Ned grows increasingly anxious about the car as the story progresses, and it becomes apparent toward the end that he somehow blames the vehicle for his father's death. It isn't much of a leap, then, for him to try to exact revenge by destroying the thing, though it soon becomes clear that the Buick's strategy is to lure him into its clutches so that it can destroy him first.

The use of the storytelling flashbacks is a very effective device because it not only fills in the backstory in a particularly vivid way and through multiple points of view, but it also involves Ned in the narrative and allows readers to observe his fascination with the tale firsthand. Although a good part of the story concerns the Buick, a major part, which is more subtle, concerns Ned and his reactions to the narratives. In the end, of course, this proves to be the real story all along, as the Buick's history becomes the narrative present and plays out with Ned's attempt to destroy it.

The multiple points of view also give authenticity to the story since each narrative supports the one before it and leads to the one following it. The storytellers are all seasoned police officers who are both trustworthy and accurate and who have the ability to write truthful police reports that will hold up in a court of law. The narratives are accurate, journalistic accounts of the Buick's history without exaggeration and told by very reliable narrators. There is no reason for either Ned or the reader to doubt the veracity of the account despite its strangeness.

Archetypes

The cosmic horror genre that was invented by H.P. Lovecraft serves as the archetype for *From a Buick 8*. One story in particular, "The Colour out of Space," seems to be a good model for King's novel. In the Lovecraft short story, a weird meteorite falls in a field and spawns a host of strange happenings. The meteorite emits a color unlike anything known to man and, thus, not on the known spectrum of elements in the periodic table. King's Buick also emits strange colors and sounds and seems to have geometric shapes that defy the conventional three-dimensional world. This all contributes to the idea that earth and its people are just one tiny and insignificant part of the universe, an idea that Lovecraft championed. King's concept of the multiverse takes this frightening thought to even deeper levels and forces us to contemplate our own insignificance.

Themes and Subtexts

King's fascination with old cars is evident in this novel and in *Christine*. Old cars have become an iconic part of American culture, and as newer automobiles become more and more standard-looking, there is definitely nostalgia for classic cars from the past. This nostalgia is particularly evident in *Christine* but reappears in this novel as well.

It is notable that this portal to other worlds takes the shape of a classic car. If the Buick 8 is a trap of some sort to lure in victims, like a Venus flytrap, a classic car shape would be a perfect vehicle (pardon the pun) for attracting young men. Whatever force created the Buick is unable to duplicate the car exactly, but the nonworking reasonable facsimile functions quite nicely. It is an object of fascination from the get-go and must, in fact, be hidden away to keep from drawing attention to itself.

Since the Buick seems to draw victims from other worlds into its clutches, another unanswered question arises: What does the thing look like in these other worlds? Probably not a classic automobile. Does it morph its shape into something attractive in the other places it inhabits? If it sucks alien creatures into its clutches, we must presume that it is fascinating to them in some way that draws them in. This concept only adds to the cosmic horror theme that King presents.

One of the main points of King's epic Dark Tower series of books is the idea that "there are other worlds than these." The Dark Tower books feature portals that allow characters to travel between worlds. Some of these are one-way doors, and some allow travel in both directions. Some only open to a specific place and time. The Buick in this novel fits nicely into the portal concept in King's other multiverse novels as well (*Revival*, *11/22/63*, and *Insomnia* are some examples). The Buick 8 is a portal that leads to and from *somewhere* (or somewhen), like Alice's rabbit hole, and this mysterious place is nothing like 20th-century planet Earth. It might represent a different planet, a different time on Earth, a different world, or even a different universe. The cosmic horror is in not knowing the answer. The human race is not intelligent enough or important enough to understand.

This leads to the theme of curiosity, the need to know. Much of Lovecraft's fiction concerns the pursuit of forbidden knowledge, how humans will pursue answers even when finding answers causes anguish and even harm. And once knowledge is learned (the atomic bomb, for example), it can't be unlearned, no matter the dire consequences.

King runs with this idea in *From a Buick 8*, only with one difference—the knowledge is never discovered. Only the mystery remains. Whether real scientists would have been able to solve the enigma of the Buick is debatable, but it seems unlikely. Rather than risk the harm that even the knowledge that the Buick exists might cause, the troopers decide to keep it a secret. The true miracle of the novel is that they are able to. In Lovecraft's stories, the secrets are always uncovered, no matter how hard their keepers try to bury them. In King's novel, though, the secret is only known to a select few who manage to keep it under wraps. As the novel ends, with a crack in the Buick's windshield, it seems likely that the secret will die of old age.

The point of the book is that some things will never be known or understood. We like the world to be a story, with a beginning, a middle, and an end. But real life has loose endings, some, like the Buick 8, that are simply unknowable—they are beyond the comprehension of mere mortals.

Human Universals

The refrain of "curiosity killed the cat, but satisfaction brought it back" is the essence of the human universal emotion of SEEKING. Humans are hardwired to seek out answers, to pursue truth, and to explore the unknown, no matter where the journey takes them. This human universal is one of the factors that has propelled *Homo sapiens* to the top of the food chain. It is also the emotion that fascinates readers of both fiction and nonfiction—we want answers. King exploits this seeking response in *From a Buick 8* by presenting a totally alien and mysterious object that gets weirder as the narrative progresses. Any normal reader cannot help but want to know what this thing is all about. More and more details and weird events are presented, making the mystery both clearer and more enigmatic at the same time. King is able to present this puzzle in a fascinating way that does defy the usual stereotype. Furthermore, it doesn't present any easy solutions. Instead, the reader continues to seek answers even after the novel has ended.

Not knowing the answer triggers the human universal emotion of FEAR. The human species has an instinctive fear of the unknown because in prehistoric times the unknown could lead to death. Hence, we fear the dark (an unseen predator might lurk nearby), we fear sticking our hand into an unknown hole or crack in the rocks (we might be bitten by something nasty), and we fear creatures or things that we can't easily identify (they might be dangerous). The Buick 8 qualifies as an object of fear on many levels. We also fear having our bodies or minds being taken over by something else or being unable to control our actions—the Buick 8 has the power to lure people into danger.

Finally, we fear our own insignificance in the cosmic scheme of things. All religions and mythologies attempt to explain the unknown in ways that we can understand. The Buick 8 doesn't fit into any mythology or religion. Indeed, science and religion often clash because science admits that there are things that are unknown, questions that can't be answered. Religion offers a safe way of looking at the world. Science, on the other hand, can be quite unsettling, especially when studied at the cosmic level. *From a Buick 8* effectively captures that uncanny, disquieting fear of the unknown in a way that is both concrete and quite mysterious at the same time.

Evaluation

I'd place *From a Buick 8* in the middle third of King's novels. It's fast pace and interesting use of point of view make it an enjoyable read, and quite frankly, this English professor is a sucker for cosmic horror.

Interesting Fact

The title of the novel is derived a Bob Dylan song, "From a Buick 6."

Notable Quote

"People can get used to just about anything. That's the best of our lives, I guess. Of course, it's the horror of them, too."

34

The Colorado Kid
The Unsolved Mystery

Background

The Colorado Kid was published in 2005 as a paperback original by the Hard Case Crime imprint of Titan Books. Charles Ardai, founder of the imprint, asked King's agent for a blurb introducing the new imprint. King responded with a novel of his own and has since published *Joyland* and *Later* with this publisher as well. The book was the inspiration for the television series *Haven*, which ran from 2010 to 2015.

Summary and Narrative Devices

One of King's shorter books, *The Colorado Kid* is closer to a novella than a novel and, like *From a Buick 8*, is told in the form of a story within a story. Two elderly seasoned newspaper reporters who publish the local newspaper, *The Weekly Islander*, tell the story of an unexplained mystery to Stephanie McCann, a graduate student who is interning with the paper. Their narrative is really a job interview for Stephanie, who they hope will stay with the paper after she graduates. They use the mystery as both a teaching lesson and a final exam for her to assess her thinking skills, knowing full well that she will pass the test.

The story itself describes the case of an unidentified body of a man found on the beach some years previously and the puzzle of who he was, how he came to be there, and what caused his death. While the newspapermen walk Stephanie through how they solved parts of the mystery and ask her to solve it with them, the ultimate answer about his death is never answered. Those who want a clear-cut solution to typical "whodunit" will be frustrated because as Stephanie and the reader learn, the answers to most of the world's most difficult questions will remain unsolved. This novel, coming immediately after *From a Buick 8*, is the "mundane" world's take on this theme of the unknowable.

True to the crime novel format, the mystery is presented in steps and stages with clues dropped like breadcrumbs to be picked up and analyzed, both by Stephanie and by the Constant Reader. King dutifully provides an opportunity for readers to think about the clues as the storytellers take coffee breaks and engage in small talk while narrating the events of the mystery, and readers are thereby invited to come up with their own theories and ideas. Some of the puzzles have been solved by the reporters, such as the victim's name and background. But although we might speculate on what brought him halfway across the country to a tiny island in Maine, it is made clear at the end of the book that we will never know. Some answers are withheld until readers have had time to think about the puzzles, and other answers remain mysteries.

Archetypes

The Colorado Kid is a version of "The Lady or the Tiger," an 1882 story by Frank Stockton, where readers are given an enigma and then are left hanging. This story has become emblematic of the unsolvable problem. And although King's stories have no clear choice of a "Lady" or "Tiger" solution, the multiple levels of mystery make it even more perplexing.

The novel is also built on the model of the traditional detective story where a mystery is presented, clues are revealed, and the detectives, in this case the newspapermen, follow the leads to solve the crime. Some clues are presented immediately, while others take more time to be unearthed. Since a solution to the mystery is expected, the reader embarks on and continues the journey with the expectation that all will be revealed in the final chapter. King plays with this formula by not revealing an answer; it is doubtful that even the author of this tale has identified one. And so, we are back to the unsolvable mystery.

Themes and Subtexts

If *From a Buick 8* is the science fiction/horror example of some things being unknowable, then *The Colorado Kid* proposes the same theme in the form of a mystery novel. In this case, the mystery has no supernatural basis as far as we know at least (but in a King novel, anything is possible!). Just as the true nature of the Buick 8 will never be known, this novel reminds us that not all mysteries will be explained, and not all murders will be solved.

This knowledge of our lack of knowledge is uncomfortable but true. True-life mysteries surround us in the real world, cold cases that will remain cold, and missing persons who will never be found. Causes of death are not always certain. People behave in irrational ways that defy explanation. Sometimes the motive for a killing can only be guessed at and never known. King uses the vehicle of the murder mystery, which usually wraps up all the loose ends as the brilliant detective explains everything to the uninitiated, to explore this theme of the unknown to its fullest. What seems like a very ordinary event in a mystery novel—the body of a dead man found on the beach—proves to be everything but ordinary. Even the clues that are left behind are unremarkable. The entire thing seems to be quite average except for the fact that a man is dead and possibly murdered.

The education of Stephanie is another theme of this novel. And even though it might seem that the elderly reporters are patronizing their student (which causes this English professor more than a little discomfort), they may be forgiven because of their age and the fact that their intern is, at least technically, still a student. They serve as mentors to her, helping her understand the real world of journalism and how it differs from the textbook world. This lesson—that there isn't an answer to every question—is an important part of the curriculum. The fact that Stephanie is charmed rather than offended by their treatment of her does clarify their attitude as being harmless and grandfatherly. Still, in the #MeToo environment, it does seem somewhat outdated, even for men who are long past retirement age.

King is trying to show the passing on of not only knowledge but wisdom, especially since not everything can be known. Part of this wisdom is recognizing and accepting the unknowable. This lesson, the novel shows, can only be learned from experience and the help of sagacious mentors.

Human Universals

One of the most basic human universal emotions is what Jaak Panksepp terms SEEKING—the need for human beings to know everything about their world. This affective emotion is instinctual, according to evolutionary psychologists, because for prehistoric people, knowledge was power. Knowledge of the world allowed them to find food, invent tools, forecast the weather, understand the seasons, and through story, communicate the knowledge they found to their fellows. This seeking response is more than just play; it represents survival of the species. Our curiosity has led our species to the top of the food chain, where we have colonized every continent and even set foot on the moon.

This seeking response may sometimes lead to danger and death. But humans are a resourceful species and have learned through their own mistakes and the mistakes of others—again, often told in stories. This emotion of curiosity not only drives science and exploration but is ingrained within us as readers when we engage in storytelling. Stephen King calls this the "gotta know" response that keeps his audience turning the page, chapter after chapter and book after book. We have to finish the story to learn how things turn out. Or as is the refrain of both *From a Buick 8* and *The Colorado Kid*, "curiosity killed the cat, but satisfaction brought it back."

In *The Colorado Kid*, King effectively strings the reader along with the expectation that there will be a climax, an explanation, and the denouement where any loose ends are neatly tied up. In this novel, however, the answer is that there is no answer. King teases us by asking us to seek and then proving how strong the seeking instinct is by frustrating us. The loose ends and unanswered questions make the point much better than any answer possibly could. We experience the seeking emotion throughout the book, and then, when the novel ends, we experience the reality of life and are left still wondering. Although the book may be frustrating from a traditional point of view, its unorthodox ending does answer questions by reminding us that there are no answers.

Evaluation

The Colorado Kid is a frustrating book for those seeking a traditional story with a beginning, middle, and end, but the premise that not all mysteries can be solved is interesting. I'd rank this book somewhere in the lower end of King's novels. As a novella, it is tightly written, but the story isn't complicated enough thematically to warrant much more analysis.

Interesting Fact

The Colorado Kid helped to launch the Hard Case Crime imprint in 2005.

Notable Quote

"It was that kind of story. The kind that's like a sneeze which threatens but never quite arrives."

35

Cell

The Techno-Zombie Attack

Background

Cell was published in 2006 by Scribner, and it was adapted into a feature film in 2016. King wrote the novel between the first and revised drafts of *Lisey's Story*. King considers the story more of an "entertainment" than a novel, yet the story does have some interesting subtexts about the modern world in general and technology in particular.

Summary and Narrative Devices

Cell is a zombie apocalypse story with a twist: people are turned into walking dead when their cell phones emit a mysterious pulse. The protagonist, Clayton Riddell, is one of the few people who doesn't own a cell phone. The Pulse occurs when he is walking the streets of downtown Boston, and suddenly everyone with a cell phone turns violent. Clay and a few other survivors manage to escape the immediate mayhem. His immediate goal is to escape from the city and return home where he can reunite with his son and wife.

The novel is a survival story where those who have not been affected by the Pulse must find a way to avoid being killed by the "phone crazies" and, ultimately, destroy them. The zombies themselves undergo an evolution of sorts, turning from violent individual units into a hive mind. Through this evolution, they transform into a new species of humans in competition with the surviving *Homo sapiens*. The need to exterminate this new species becomes more than just an individual survival mission but a quest to save the human race from extinction.

Cell is packed with narrative devices that increase suspense and excitement. The novel opens in the middle of a disaster. The very first paragraph hints at the horrors that are to follow, and the book turns violent almost immediately. The beginning pages feature a man biting off a dog's ear, a girl biting into a woman's carotid artery, vehicles running down pedestrians, and a body flying out of the window of a tall building to splatter on the pavement. One of the characters questions if they are in the middle of a terrorist attack.

Another attention-getting device involves the very first line, which introduces the protagonist, Clayton Riddell, as a "young man of no particular importance" who, the narrative suggests, will change history. These first lines are written from a historical perspective, as if the narrator were writing from some time far in the future and recounting the epic events that occurred during the time of the Pulse. This point of view implies that not only was Clay a hero but that the outcome was positive and that the apocalypse was avoided and that civilization (and history) has survived and prospered. The story of how this average comic book illustrator brought this about immediately arouses interest.

While King uses all the traditional narrative devices to create suspense and move his story forward, he presents a very human problem—the safety of Clayton's son—and puts this issue before the reader early in the story. While the big picture involves the survival of the human species as we know it, King also poses a smaller but very emotional problem. Clay's son, who owns a cell phone, is immediately shown to be at risk of having suffered the effects of the Pulse. Clay can't contact him, of course, and has no way of knowing if the boy is alive or not or if he's been turned into a zombie. The issue is complicated by the fact that Clay and his wife are having marital problems, and he can't reach her either. His quest to reunite with his son is presented quickly and is not resolved until the very end. The questions of whether the boy has survived and if the family will be reunited help to drive the plot forward at a very emotional level.

Archetypes

Cell is dedicated to two masters of the zombie horror genre, Richard Matheson and George Romero, who created, respectively, the classic zombie stories *I Am Legend* and *The Night of the Living Dead*. *I Am Legend* began as a novel in 1954 and was adapted into a film in 2007. Romero's *Night of the Living Dead*, a low-budget 1968 horror film, is credited with inventing the zombie genre as we know it today. *Cell* owes much of its existence to these two works.

The zombie genre itself began with a book titled *The Magic Island*, a nonfiction travel book on Haitian voodoo written by William Seabrook and published in 1929. This book, and a 1932 film, *The White Zombie*, dealt with the idea that wealthy plantation owners would enslave workers and drug them until they became mindless, robotic zombies to harvest the sugar crops on the island. The horror in these stories was in being captured and turned into a zombie slave.

Romero turned the zombies from victims into undead predators in his film, and this model has become a trope in the horror field, yielding books, films, and television shows, most notably the wildly popular *Walking Dead* series based on the graphic novels of Robert Kirkman. In the spirit of these aggressive zombies, the "phone crazies" in *Cell* are predatory and capable of turning survivors into inhuman monsters as well.

The novel is also patterned on the hero's quest that is a blueprint for so many stories, both ancient and modern. This is truly the reluctant hero version of the quest; at the outset of the narrative, Clay has just landed his dream job and is only interested in returning home to celebrate his success and, hopefully, save his struggling marriage. The Pulse changes all of that, of course. He modifies his goals to just returning home to his family. But as the tale goes on, it becomes clear that this quest involves much more than just going home. To be successful, he will have to become a major player in the battle against the cell phone zombies that are taking over the planet. And as is suggested by the first few lines of the book, he goes on to become an epic hero worthy of remembrance in the historical record.

Themes and Subtexts

Although King doesn't seem to take *Cell* as seriously as some of his other novels, the book does pose some important questions about life and the human species. Most notably, the story asks the question, "What does it mean to be human?" and attempts to answer it by contrasting *Homo sapiens* with the new species of hominoids that are being spawned by the Pulse. The difference between humans and the phone crazies is the concept of speech and communication, which sets humans apart. Humans have been labeled "the storytelling animal" by Jonathan Gottschall, and this ability does seem to be one of the things that sets us apart from all other creatures on the planet. The ability to communicate through language is uniquely human, and in *Cell* it is the litmus test that proves that the zombies have lost their humanity.

Much of King's fiction criticizes technology and/or the government. *Cell* combines both themes in a single novel as it suggests that the government, or a government, might be responsible for the Pulse, either through negligence or a terrorist attack. It is no secret that governments engage in cyberwarfare, hacking computers, cell phones, and other sensitive devices that store information. Hackers have used ransomware to extort governments and private entities, and the threat of a hostile government shutting down the power grid or hacking into defense systems is all too real. Indeed, few of us have not been victims of some sort of scam or virus; as a result, cybersecurity has become big business.

Although the book never explains the answer in detail, it is probable that the Pulse is the result of a cyberattack, either accidental or hostile. In a Stephen King novel, technology in the hands of the government is always dangerous. A portal to another hostile world is opened in "The Mist," the harnessing of psychic powers destroys individual freedoms in *Firestarter* and *The Institute*, and tinkering with biological warfare leads to the apocalypse in *The Stand*. It is only natural that cell phones would be put to nefarious uses in a King novel.

King is also critical of cell phone technology itself, and this novel metaphorically shows how it is dehumanizing humanity, destroying social structures as people have become addicted to their phones. Rather than interact with one another, people communicate through text messages, e-mails, and chats, which leads to the lack of communication exhibited by the zombies. Eventually, they develop a hive mind, but this hive mind allows for no individual thought, no creativity, and no real understanding. The technology that was supposed to help us communicate more efficiently has turned us into zombies, according to King, who, at the time that he wrote *Cell*, did not own a mobile phone.

Finally, King also attacks our consumer society. The very opening of the novel is all about appearances, brand names, and status, as the pedestrians of Boston sport designer labels, credit cards, power suits, and expensive cell phones. When the Pulse hits, their technology turns against them as the phones transform them into zombies. Within minutes, all thoughts of possessions and status disappear into a fight for survival. Clay even discards his artwork, the precious items that landed him his dream job, as he flees for his life. This novel is a reminder of what is truly precious in life—the people we love and care about, not the things we own.

Human Universals

From a Darwinist point of view, several human universals are presented in this novel. The most obvious is the CARE response that humans have for their offspring. Once his immediate survival is secured, at least for the moment, Clay turns his thoughts to his son. From the point of view of evolutionary psychology, this "selfish gene" impulse to save our descendants trumps almost all other human emotions and instincts. Clay's major issue is worrying about his son and his desire to make sure that he is safe.

Taken one step further, there is the desire to save all human genes—in other words, to prevent the extinction of the human race. This idea is common in apocalyptic stories, whether it be destruction of the planet by a rogue comet, an alien invasion, or an extinction event brought about by zombies. No matter our views on almost anything, we always root for *Homo sapiens* in any battle with the "other."

Language and storytelling is another human universal that is addressed in this novel. According to evolutionary psychologists, much of our survival as a species can be linked to our ability to master language and communication. Although the debate is still open, many linguists believe that the ability to learn and use language is actually coded in human DNA, much like the specific song of a bird is instinctual to its species. This explains why children master language at an incredibly rapid pace very early in their development. This ability to tell stories, to pass on knowledge and life lessons, and to communicate our desires and intentions to one another served prehistoric peoples well. The phone crazies in *Cell* lack this skill. Even their psychic abilities are an ineffective means of communication since the hive mind is incapable of independent thought and is easily destroyed by the creative thinking of humans.

Evaluation

Cell is an interesting novel, and even though not King's best, I believe it is better than the critics claim. Its theme of communication is especially poignant, as is its social commentary on people and their technology.

Interesting Fact

The name and description of one character was sold in a charity auction on eBay. The winner of the auction, Pam Alexander, paid $25,100 and gave the honor as a gift to her brother Ray Huizenga, who was portrayed as a construction worker who specializes in explosives and proves to be a heroic zombie killer.

Notable Quote

"Who can resist a ringing phone?"

36

Lisey's Story

The Literary Best Seller

Background

Lisey's Story was published in October 2006 by Scribner. It won the Stoker Award for best novel in 2006 and was nominated for a World Fantasy Award. It was adapted into an eight-part miniseries that premiered on Apple TV+ on June 4, 2021, and that was scripted by King. King considers this one of his best novels.

Summary and Narrative Devices

The protagonist of this novel, Lisey Landon, is the widow of Scott Landon, a best-selling novelist who is also a critical success. In one plot thread, Lisey finds herself threatened by Zack McCool, a criminal who has been hired by a professor to secure Scott's documents and unfinished manuscripts for a university. In a parallel plot, her sister Amanda attempts suicide and lapses into a coma. As Lisey reminisces about her late husband, she begins to recall repressed memories and realizes that Scott had the power to enter an alternate world. She also learns that he has left her clues so that she might enter it as well. By solving the "bool" hunt (Scott's word for a scavenger hunt) that Scott has left her, she is able to enter this world and rescue her sister from her coma and destroy Zack.

Always the master of suspense, King sets up Scott Landon's death from the beginning of the novel, but instead of revealing how he died, King dives into a prolonged flashback about how Scott was almost killed by an insane stalker some years before. The cause of his death isn't revealed until page 368, well into the novel, and the cause appears to be natural: pneumonia. Yet this does come into question as it seems likely that Scott may have brought back an infection from Boo'ya Moon, an alternate universe, which would make his untimely death more unusual and would cause Lisey to worry that she might have become infected as well. If the wildlife in this alternate world is different from ours, it would make sense that the microorganisms would be as well.

The entire novel is a mystery that Lisey will have to decipher in order to survive and to bring her sister back to sanity. The story is one of Scott's "bools," a scavenger hunt that leads to a prize—in this case, a drink from the "pool" that will save her life. Scott apparently had foreknowledge of the things that would come to pass, knowledge that he must have found in Boo'ya Moon, and this enabled him to set up the bool for Lisey to discover. King allows his reader to play along with the heroine and figure out the puzzle in real time, so to speak. This raises the suspense, especially since solving the puzzle becomes a matter of life and death.

King also uses telephone calls to delay the answers to some questions. Just as Lisey is about to learn something or open another box that might contain information, she is interrupted by a phone call from one of her sisters. This delays the answers that readers are anticipating and, again, heightens suspense.

Since Scott has already died when the story begins, King brings him back to narrative life in a series of flashbacks that come as memories that Lisey reexperiences as she takes part in the bool. This allows Scott to posthumously become a character in the novel and reveal his backstory in his own words. Although Lisey plays the role of the protagonist and the story is "Lisey's story," Scott is the focal character through much of the novel. Furthermore, he is the character who writes Lisey's story.

Archetypes

Lisey's Story exemplifies the idea best expressed in the Dark Tower books that "there are other worlds than these." Whether Boo'ya Moon is part of the Dark Tower multiverse is open for discussion, but it is obviously part of an alternate universe where the walls between our two worlds are thin. This idea is based on several archetypes, including Alice in Wonderland and the Narnia stories of C.S. Lewis, both of which propose a magic doorway, and even the Martian Barsoom world of Edgar Rice Burroughs where the protagonist simply imagines his way to the fantastic world of Mars. It is worth noting that these three examples appeal to children and young adults, while King's narrative is distinctly an adult novel. Young people have an easier time shedding their disbelief. Scott Landon has managed to hang on to his childhood through his willingness to imagine and his ability to translate this imagination to his writing. And King is able to make the magical world beyond the thin walls of our universe so real and so detailed that it is believable to an adult reader as well.

Themes and Subtexts

Lisey's Story is one of the most complex of all of Stephen King's novels, both in structure and meaning. This narrative works at multiple levels. On the surface, it is a story about a widow who, after two years, still grieves for her husband whom she had loved deeply. Yet it is also a feminist narrative, depicting how the world views Lisey as nothing more than the wife of the famous Scott Landon. It is a story about families, both Lisey's relationships with her sisters and Scott's dysfunctional family. The narrative is rich with subtexts about writing and creativity as well and how the mind of a highly successful writer works. Finally, *Lisey's Story* suggests the "thinness" of the world ("there are more worlds than these") and the thinness of the line between sanity and madness.

While she was the wife of the famous Scott Landon, Lisey was willing to play the role of dutiful wife, at least publicly, and allow Scott to bask in the limelight. Critics, interviewers, and journalists seldom referred to her as anything but the wife of a famous writer except if she were asked to share a recipe. She is expected to stay in the background, applaud dutifully, and hold on to his plaques and awards while he gives speeches or performs his readings.

She accepts this role without complaint, but privately she plays a huge part in Scott's success. She provides the stable environment that her husband needs to be creative and successful. She is his therapist, helping and coaching him through difficult times. And in the ultimate act of courage, she saves his life from a crazed gunman. She receives no credit or acknowledgment for her heroism, of course, except from Scott himself. The accolades go to a security guard who, in effect, did nothing.

Once Scott dies, Lisey remains in the background for two years, becoming almost a recluse and refusing to deal with any decision-making. Inertia keeps her from taking care of her husband's estate and valuable papers or from moving on with her own life. Events come together to force her to take charge of things. First, there is the situation with Dooley, who has decided to kill her. Then there is her sister's mental illness, which must be addressed. Finally, there is Scott's bool hunt, the incentive that she needs to solve the puzzle that will resolve all these situations. Once she is triggered, Lisey becomes a force to be reckoned with. Rather than allow the law to take care of Dooley, she takes on the challenge herself and defeats him soundly. Since the mental health facilities are unable to help her sister, she also takes on Scott's challenge to solve the bool, journey to his secret world, and bring her sister back to reality. In the end, she is able to take the dangerous journey to Scott's world of Boo'ya Moon, understand and accept its reality, and do the things that must be done, both there and in the "real" world. The novel ends with her taking on the responsibilities that life demands—caring for her sister, handling Scott's legacy, and holding down the fort, so to speak. Lisey, the realist, can appreciate the world of Boo'ya Moon but, unlike Scott, has no need or desire to travel there again.

Lisey's Story brings up an interesting theme and observation about language, specifically private language and public language. Public language is the language we use when speaking to the world; it is the accepted language defined by dictionaries and rule books, and although it might be adapted to different audiences, it is remarkably standard. Then there is the private language used only within families and among loved ones. Each family has its own lexicon of words, sayings, and phrases that are known only to the intimate. This is even truer of lovers, who have their own pet names and code words that only they can understand and appreciate. King highlights this private language in the way that Scott and Lisey communicate and in the secret language of each family unit in the novel. The words "blood bool," for example, would make no sense to anyone besides Scott, his father, his brother, and once explained to her, Lisey. All families have secret languages of their own, code words, nicknames, and phrases that convey profound meaning with their linguistic shortcuts. King effectively conveys this idea in *Lisey's Story* by allowing the reader to be a part of the private language shared by these characters.

Writing and creativity play an important role in this novel, as is the case in so many of King's stories. Scott is the perfect model for what I call "the unicorn," an author who enjoys both critical and popular success. He has not only become incredibly wealthy from his writing but has earned prestigious awards, such as the National Book Award, and is praised by the critics to the point that major universities want his manuscripts for their library collections. Such a situation is rare in modern letters, where there is a chasm between literary and popular fiction.

This "unicorn" writer displays specific traits that make him successful. He has talent, of course (though King does say that talent is cheap and useless without effort) and has a childlike sense of creativity and belief. He easily accepts and embraces a "wonderland" type of alternate universe and is able to be open-minded enough to allow himself to travel to the world containing the word pool. He readily embraces games, like the bool, and uses his vivid imagination to create stunningly beautiful (and terrifying) worlds. Coupled with this imagination, though, is a serious work ethic.

Scott is a consummate professional who takes his writing seriously, treats it as a job, and works very hard at his craft. This proves to be a winning combination of traits, one that Stephen King himself possesses as a writer.

Last, King addresses the theme of mental health. Although not all creative people suffer from mental health issues, it does seem to be more prevalent among artistic types. Scott's traumatic childhood caused him to seek a means of escape from the real world, an escape that transported him to an alternate universe with a thin barrier that allowed him to cross. Scott was able to find a coping mechanism by escaping to Boo'ya Moon and by confiding in Lisey, who served not only as his wife but also as his therapist. Although Scott was able to function at a high level and live a productive and normal life, his childhood trauma and mental health issues did cause him great distress, which King is able to show in great detail. This theme points to the importance of mental health awareness and treatment and to the empathy that should be shown to those who suffer from these issues.

Human Universals

Lisey's Story addresses two very powerful human universals, grief and play. Both these affective emotions are an important part of being human, and readers can easily identify with them.

Grief is one of the strongest human emotions. Two years after her husband's death, Lisey is still suffering from Scott's loss. The grief is paralyzing, making it impossible for her to move forward with her life. She is unable to decide about what to do with Scott's manuscripts and other important papers, can't decide whether to move to a different location, and mostly just goes through life on a day-to-day basis without much motivation. This is made even more difficult for her by the fact that Scott was such a notable figure that she was shadowed in the background, at least publicly, as being the wife of a great writer rather than a person in her own right. Her love for Scott is genuine, though, and part of the reason she readily accepted this role. Now that this position has been taken away, however, she seems to be merely drifting along. It is not uncommon for marital partners who are this close to suffer greatly when one member of the pair dies. Often, especially in elderly couples, the remaining spouse also dies soon afterward. While Lisey doesn't die physically, she does suffer a metaphorical death by losing the role she has played for so many years. She is left with nothing to do except grieve and, thus, becomes a very sympathetic character.

Play appears to be a universal trait in many creatures and is an evolutionary adaptation that allows life-forms to adapt to their environments, practice life skills, and explore new habitats. This seeking instinct leads to curiosity and play beginning with infancy and continues into adulthood for most humans. Recreational activities account for billions of dollars in the economy, and once people's basic survival needs have been met, they seek pleasure and entertainment, as is evidenced by the popularity of books and films, video games, sporting events, and theme parks. Whereas many adults lose some of their sense of play as they grow older, Scott has not only retained this instinct but harnessed it into a career. Lisey is less playful as the story begins, but through her husband's coaching, she learns to play the most important game of her life, one that saves both her and her sister. Scott leaves behind one last bool for her to solve, and solving this puzzle is, indeed, Lisey's story. The reader's playful instincts are also hooked, as we follow along with the story and try to solve the mysteries of the bool ourselves. By engaging the reader's sense of play, King creates novels that are wildly entertaining and popular, something that serious "literary" fiction often fails to do.

Evaluation

Lisey's Story is, in my opinion, one of King's most "literary" works, yet it still manages to be interesting and entertaining for the casual reader. King considers it to be one of his best, and I concur. The book is multilayered and reflective in its language and subtexts and offers profound insights into the human condition.

Interesting Fact

The idea came to King in 2003 when upon returning home from the hospital after suffering from a serious case of pneumonia, he saw his books and possessions in boxes and imagined that was what his office would look like after his death.

Notable Quote

"Who would ever want to get close to another person if they knew how hard the letting-go part was?"

37

Blaze

Bachman Returns

Background

Blaze was originally written in 1972–73 after King had completed the rough draft of *Carrie* and was revised in the 1980s and then again in 2006 when the manuscript was rediscovered in King's collection at the University of Maine library. King considered it a "trunk novel" when it was published in 2007 under the Richard Bachman name, and King donated all the proceeds to the Haven Foundation, which he and Tabitha established to help freelance artists through difficult times.

Summary and Narrative Devices

Like the Bachman books that preceded it, *Blaze* is not a horror novel but falls into the thriller/mystery genre. The protagonist is a mentally challenged criminal who kidnaps a baby from a wealthy family, only to fall in love with the six-month-old infant. Clayton Blaisdell, Jr., nicknamed Blaze, measures in at six foot seven and over 300 pounds but has intellectual issues as a result of having been thrown down a flight of stairs by his abusive alcoholic father. He spent his childhood in an abusive orphanage, part of his teenage years in a reform school (after beating the sadistic headmaster of the foster home), and did some jail time for working scams with other con artists, including his friend George, who has died but still talks to Blaze through his subconscious mind. He is miraculously able to pull off the abduction of the baby, but things quickly go wrong, and the novel becomes a countdown to the main character's capture and death.

The novel is organized through alternating chapters set in the present, where Blaze plans and ultimately commits the kidnapping, and flashback chapters that detail the protagonist's life from infancy to the present time frame. Blaze's terrible background environment is slowly revealed in one plotline, while his descent into criminal behavior is revealed in the other. He has had the unfortunate bad luck to have not only suffered unspeakable abuse throughout his life but also to have hooked up with people who were on the wrong side of the law. Easily manipulated by anyone who shows him kindness, it is inevitable that Blaze will pursue a criminal lifestyle, and the novel masterfully documents this.

The major point of suspense in the book isn't whether Blaze will succeed in life or even survive—his destruction is inevitable from the very first page where he is able to steal a car by mere chance alone—but in the fate of the kidnapped baby. The infant, portrayed as completely innocent, cute, and endearing, is in real danger of being killed, through Blaze's incompetence, in a shootout with the police, or both. The baby is helpless but lovable, so much so that even Blaze is drawn to him and can't bear to give him back to his parents, not even for a million-dollar ransom. This suspense about the infant's fate is carried forth until the last pages of the novel, after Blaze has been violently killed by the police.

Archetypes

The character of Blaze is patterned after Lenny, the protagonist in Steinbeck's *Of Mice and Men*. Both characters are gigantic in stature but suffer from a lack of intellect, and both have been befriended by men who have taken care of them and helped them navigate the world. Both commit murder because of their enormous strength, and both are outcasts from society. Although Blaze is a criminal, he is a very sympathetic character because he is essentially a good person who has been ruined by an abusive society. He is the noble savage who has been corrupted and turned into a law breaker through no fault of his own. Fate turns against him time and time again, as, for example, when he is offered a place working on a blueberry farm owned by a kind man and the man is stricken down with a heart attack before Blaze can assume this position. Being subject to the whims of fate is a major theme in both the King and Steinbeck novels.

Themes and Subtexts

Fate plays a major role in *Blaze* and highlights a theme that runs through most of King's books—the fact that random events can result in life-changing consequences. The protagonist begins life with hope and promise. He is intelligent, loves to read, and has the potential to do great things. All this ends, however, when his abusive father throws him down the stairs, not once but three times in a row until the boy suffers brain damage. This event shapes his entire life, causing him to be put in an orphanage that treats him like an animal. His one chance to find a better life ends when a farmer who promised to take him in dies of a sudden heart attack, dooming Blaze to return to the orphanage and suffer more abuse. When his only friend dies from neglect and poor medical care, Blaze beats the headmaster, an action that sentences him to a life in reform schools and jails. Blaze is a victim of bad luck, bad parenting, and a damaged brain, which makes him a sympathetic character despite his flaws.

Abuse forms another important theme of the story, a theme that King returns to in so many of his novels. In this case, he takes a hard look at child abuse and its consequences. Blaze suffers lifelong damage, both physical and emotional, and this damage, in turn, has dire consequences for society as an otherwise promising boy turns into a criminal. Society, which is supposed to take care of those who can't take care of themselves, fails miserably, subjecting the child to further abuse and exploitation. Instead of providing help for Blaze, the state treats him as a throwaway to be used by others. He is treated as a slave when he is jobbed out to one family. The teachers in the orphanage fail to realize his intellectual deficiencies and punish him when he can't solve math problems. His only recourse is to cheat, and then he is punished again when he is caught. Instead of preparing him for some type of normal life, society sets him up for a life of failure and crime.

It is as obvious as the massive scar on his head that Blaze has suffered brain damage at the hands of his abusive father. Yet the mental health and child welfare systems are worse than useless in helping him. They offer no treatment, no therapy, no special education, and no comfort to the boy. This damning indictment of the system is a reminder of the importance of mental health and intervention. Blaze's condition doesn't just affect him but transfers to society at large. Because of his mistreatment, a grandmother and two police officers are dead, and the baby he has kidnapped almost dies. Innocents outside of Blaze's circle suffer for his condition. This theme demonstrates that mental health is a problem that affects everyone, not just the mentally ill.

Human Universals

Attraction to their young is a universal trait among mammals, and this is especially so in humans. Even Blaze, a brain-damaged male, finds himself unexplainably attracted to the baby he kidnaps, and he soon begins imagining a life with the child as his son. This attraction is so strong that the million-dollar ransom becomes irrelevant to him. He would rather keep the child than give him up for any amount of money.

Once Blaze is the subject of a police chase, he goes to great lengths to protect the baby, putting his own life at risk to do so. Even though the voice of George tells him to kill the child, he cannot bring himself to do so and, instead, falls in love with the infant. He might have been able to escape if he had left the child behind, but that wasn't an option for him once the two had bonded. The human universal emotion of needing to protect babies takes over, and this emotion becomes part of the reader's experience as well, as fear grows for the baby's safety. Although it becomes clear that things will not end well for Blaze, there is the hope that the child will be OK, and King delivers that happy ending that readers crave.

Evaluation

Blaze, while not a top-tier novel, holds up quite well and certainly shows King's mastery of fiction at a young age. Although technically a "trunk" novel, the book is worth reading, especially when put in the context of the Bachman books. Its theme of mental health, which perhaps is a bit didactic, is probably even more important now than it was when it was originally written.

Interesting Fact

King wrote the manuscript to *Blaze* on Tabitha's Olivetti typewriter while they were living in a rented mobile home.

Notable Quote

"It's a dirty world, and the longer you lived, the dirtier you got."

38

Duma Key
Art Therapy

Background

Duma Key was published in January 2008 by Scribner and rose to number one on the *New York Times* bestseller list. It is the first book King has set in Florida; after spending summers in the Sarasota area for several years, he claimed that he knew enough about the area to be able to write about it convincingly. King's accident and near-death experience also play a role in this novel as he convincingly describes the main character's recovery.

Summary and Narrative Devices

Edgar Freemantle, the protagonist of *Duma Key*, has suffered a horrible accident at a construction site, resulting in the loss of his right arm and traumatic head injuries. After the breakup of his marriage and severe depression, he decides to retire to a beach house on Duma Key, a small island in Florida. He employs a local college student, Jack Cantori, to run errands for him and help out where needed. He befriends wealthy Elizabeth Eastlake, an octogenarian, and her live-in attendant, Jerome Wireman, a former attorney, the only other residents of the island. Freemantle rediscovers his love for art and painting as a means of therapy and discovers that his art has enough merit to display and sell in one of the major galleries in Sarasota. He also discovers he has obtained the power to alter reality with his paintings. His artistic talent, however, is controlled by an evil force, Perse, who controls a ship of damned souls. Persephone, modeled on the Greek queen of the underworld, is using him for her own purposes so she can be awakened from her sleep and brought back to life.

Duma Key is written as a supernatural mystery, beginning as a normal, mundane novel about the recovery of Freemantle from his trauma, which is a compelling story in itself. It soon becomes apparent, however, that something is not right on the island, and so the discovery process begins. Much of the novel is spent unraveling this mystery. The last part of the book, of course, is the quest for Fremantle, Wireman, and Cantori to trap and subdue Perse and end her evil influences.

The novel is written in first person with Freemantle telling his story. He is a very reliable narrator who doesn't embellish the narrative or slant the story to make himself look good. He freely admits his mistakes, doesn't blame his divorce on others, and realizes that he has been difficult for his family to live with after his accident. He is also very honest about the pain he has endured, and his account is credible. His description of the phantom pain after losing his arm is haunting and believable. His acknowledgment of his artistic talents is realistic and not inflated. His descriptions of the joy he finds in creating artistic works are both authentic and poetic. The voice of Stephen King as an artistic creator of stories looms large in the background.

The novel opens with Freemantle briefly introducing himself and then immediately describing his accident and the aftermath in a chapter titled "My Other Life." Interspersed with Freemantle's story are chapters about "how to draw a picture," which refer to both the artistic process and to the paintings that the little girl created many years ago and that brought Perse and the ghost ship back to Duma Key. These chapters offer insight into the creative process and act as a sort of "intermission" from the linear plot of the novel.

Archetypes

The supernatural element is based on the Greek myth of Persephone, queen of the underworld, who was abducted by Hades and dwells in the land of the dead for half of the year, appearing on earth again in the spring to rejuvenate the earth and its crops. Although she is, in part, a fertility goddess associated with agriculture and grain, she is usually portrayed as the wife of Hades, often referred to as the "dreaded" Persephone whose name may not be spoken. As queen of the dead, she co-rules the underworld with her husband.

The legend of the ghost ship is an archetype for *Duma Key*. The ghost ship, best represented by the 18th-century story of the Flying Dutchman, is a legend where a ship commanded by the spirits of the dead is cursed to travel the seas forever with its dead crew. First reported in 1790, the legend of the haunted ship has endured over the centuries and has inspired a number of pieces of literature, including Coleridge's "The Rime of the Ancient Mariner," a trilogy of young adult novels by Brian Jacques (2001, 2003, and 2006), as well as a short story by Ward Moore in 1951 about a bomber that continues to fly over the ravaged earth after dropping its payload during a nuclear war.

Themes and Subtexts

Since *Duma Key* was written following Stephen King's near fatal accident, it is not surprising that the theme of survival from trauma should play an important role in the novel. It is worth noting that Freemantle's terrible injury is the catalyst leading to his retirement on the Florida coast. King effectively describes the pain and difficult recovery that faces the protagonist after his injury, including emotional problems, drug dependency, depression, mood changes, and family troubles. King depicts this trauma as being very complex and much more far-reaching than the physical pain and disability that it causes. This theme, I believe, is important in bringing to light the complicated issues that trauma survivors face both physically and emotionally and highlights the strength needed to achieve recovery.

This theme delivers the message of how important it is to keep on working at recovery, to never give up and become a "quitter." King has walked this walk himself, which makes this message more powerful. With his fame, fortune, and prestige, it would have been easy for King to go quietly into retirement and become a victim of depression and possibly addiction. But he fought against his injuries to return to the world and become as productive as ever. The protagonist of *Duma Key* embodies this grit and determination as he continues his fight for recovery, detailing the struggle in detail. The descriptions of the suffering he endures stem from the author's own experiences, and both Freemantle's and King's strength and success offer hope and inspiration to others who have experienced trauma and to those who care about them and assist in their recovery. This is an important theme with huge social implications, and since King's readership numbers in the millions, the novel ensures that the theme will reach a huge audience and help them to understand the complexities of trauma on the mind and the body.

Although Freemantle is not a writer, as are so many of King's characters, he is a creative character who manifests his talent through the medium of painting. The use of an artistic character brings to light two very important themes concerning art and creativity: art as therapy and the artist as a "god" creator who can create worlds and change reality.

King depicts art as a form of therapy that allows its creator to escape from the pain and problems of the mundane world, at least temporarily, and begin the healing process. When he is painting, Freemantle achieves a type of high that not even the painkilling drugs can provide. It is an out-of-body experience for him. He no longer inhabits a crippled body but is able to escape into a reality where he is whole and without pain. King has claimed on more than one occasion that he is "addicted" to writing, and Freemantle gives a first-person account of the high that comes with this addiction to creation. Just as King used his writing as a vehicle to help him recover from his injuries, so does the novel's protagonist, who can regain his strength and sense of purpose through the joy of practicing his art. The descriptions of the euphoria of this art accurately depict the feelings that creative individuals enjoy when they are in the zone. For Freemantle and other artists, it is true magic.

The magic of this creation goes further than just being emotional in this novel, though. It allows the artist to become a creator of worlds and actually change reality. This theme stands at the hub of the Dark Tower series of books, where the "death of the author" (as espoused by the critic Roland Barthes) is replaced by the concept of the author (or in this case, the artist) as a god, magically creating entire universes from words or pictures. Freemantle can use the magic of creation to change reality in his paintings which, even though a supernatural force, become reality. This magic (which is also a component of the Dark Tower series) can both create and destroy, as Freemantle first uses its power to return Perse to life and then to destroy, or at least banish, her. Painting it (or writing it) makes it so.

Metaphorically, this theme is not so far-fetched. Through their works, artists in all mediums have created worlds that have become a sort of reality in the real world: Oz, Narnia, Middle Earth, Castle Rock, and the Overlook Hotel are all iconic fictional places that have become part of the vocabulary of popular culture. Paintings such as "Starry Night," "The Scream," and "The Last Supper" are just a few examples of art redefining reality. These creations have spawned films, photos, music, and dance, among other artistic forms and are widely recognized as a realistic part of culture.

Finally, memory serves as an interesting subtext in the book. Freemantle's injuries result in his loss of memory and in his struggle to regain even simple things, like remembering a phone number. His traumatic brain injury has altered his memories, transforming his personality in the process. Freemantle's frustration with this struggle is evident in the book and reflects many of King's own memory loss problems after his accident.

Elizabeth Eastgate's Alzheimer's disease complements this theme of memory loss and brings home the true tragedy of this debilitating condition. Her loss of identity is depicted as heartbreaking, yet her decline is both steady and inevitable. Once again, the frustration of being unable to halt the progress of this disease colors the novel, making it painful to read in its realism. This memory loss spills over into the forgotten memories of childhood, forgotten memories that allow the reappearance of Perse and the renewal of her curse on the women of Duma Key.

Human Universals

According to Jaak Panksepp, play is a fundamental human emotion and is hardwired into our neural circuits. It seems to be an evolutionary survival skill among mammals, where the young engage in play to practice adult skills that they will need later in life. Lion cubs and house cats alike play at catching prey. Dogs love to fetch and tug, and dolphins are known to engage in playful activities just for the sheer fun of it. Playing is a child's reason for living, it seems, and as any parent knows, they would usually rather play their favorite games than eat, drink, or sleep. Indeed, the toy industry is a multibillion-dollar enterprise. Once we reach adulthood, play takes on a lesser role in our lives, though even most adults crave their weekend and vacation time when they can engage in leisure activities, and if they can't play the game themselves, they can always enjoy their favorite sporting event on television.

After devoting most of his life to work and securing his financial future, Freemantle's working life is interrupted by the horrible accident that changes things forever. As part of his recovery, he decides to move to the secluded island of Duma Key where he can, in effect, "play" at being an artist, a passion of his that he hasn't had the time to pursue. Play evokes creativity in humans, forcing them to imagine new worlds, to pretend, and to use whatever talents and skills we possess to just have fun. Freemantle begins his artistic journey with this in mind—to just enjoy painting the seascapes he can see from his balcony. It brings him pure joy, an emotion that any creative individual can relate to, whatever their creative medium might be. Freemantle doesn't expect his work to be commercial and is surprised when it is singled out by art critics as being worthwhile. But it is the happiness and peace that the act of painting brings to him that really drives him, not the fame or money that might come with it.

Stephen King is channeling his own delight in writing through the character of Freemantle—King has admitted that he is "addicted" to writing, and he no longer needs to write for money or fame, having achieved them both beyond his wildest dreams. It is the joy of creation that drives him. Readers of *Duma Key* can experience this "high" of creation through Freemantle as he describes the euphoria he experiences while painting. And any creative individual (indeed, most people and, I'd dare to say, all avid readers are creative individuals) understands this human universal emotion at a visceral level. *Duma Key* reminds readers of the adrenaline rush of creation and re-creates it within their own brains as they read the words on the page and create the world of the novel in their own imaginations.

Evaluation

The first time I read *Duma Key*, it was somewhat disappointing, but with each reread I find myself liking the book more. Although Freemantle's recovery is painful to read, I do enjoy the sense of hope that it inspires, and the book serves as a reminder of how fragile life really is, a lesson that King experienced firsthand with his accident. I'd rank the book in the lower end of the top third of King's works. The idea of the artist as a god is certainly fascinating, especially taken in the context of the Dark Tower books.

Interesting Fact

The inspiration for *Duma Key* was a sign that King saw by the side of the road that read, "Caution: Children." After seeing it, he imagined two dead girls holding hands.

Notable Quote

"Talent is a wonderful thing, but it won't carry a quitter."

39

Under the Dome
Ants Under a Magnifying Glass

Background

Under the Dome was published in 2009 by Scribner. It was developed into a television series that ran for three seasons from 2012 to 2015; the pilot of the show had over 13 million viewers, a record for a summer drama premiere. The novel is set in the small town of Chester's Mill, which is modeled after Bridgton, Maine. King originally started the book in the 1970s, then returned to it in 2006. The original draft was about a group of people trapped in an apartment. He scuttled the project, only to redo the work with the new idea of the invisible dome descending on a rural town.

Summary and Narrative Devices

The premise for *Under the Dome* is quite simple and, on the surface, almost silly: What would happen if a giant, invisible, impenetrable dome suddenly appeared and completely covered a small Maine town so nothing could get in or out? Spoiler alert: The dome over Chester's Mill is a plaything of some alien children who enjoy watching humans squirm, much like human children will burn ants in an anthill with a magnifying glass. According to King, the novel "deals with some of the same issues that *The Stand* does, but in a more allegorical way." The book really serves as a fictional experiment to see what might happen when people are isolated from the rest of the world and could, theoretically, be free from laws and control. In King's version, the town is taken over by a power-hungry two-bit politician who becomes a despot in true Orwellian fashion.

While the premise might seem difficult to accept, King's realism makes it easy to suspend disbelief, beginning with the very first chapter where the dome appears and, with it, immediate destruction of anyone or anything that was beneath it or had the misfortune to run into it. The novel begins with the microcosm; the dome suddenly appears and splits a woodchuck in half and then gradually pans out to affect larger things, people, an airplane, and eventually the macrocosm of the entire town. Much of the novel vacillates between this microcosm—how the dome affects specific individuals on a personal level—and the macrocosm—how Chester's Mill becomes its own universe. The tiny town is contrasted with its status as its very own world, totally divorced from any rules or government outside of the dome.

As in all his fiction, King uses specific foreshadowing techniques to build and maintain suspense. One of his strengths is his ability to create characters quickly, endow them with interesting personalities, and immediately put them in danger. Claudette Sanders and Chuck Thompson open the novel as a student and a flight instructor in a small airplane. They are developed just enough to be believable—and likable—and then King tells us that "their lives had another forty seconds to run," an obvious alert that something truly horrible is about to happen. He even personalizes an old, fat woodchuck before cutting the creature in half when the dome drops on him.

King uses a third-person omniscient point of view in this novel that allows us to selectively enter the minds of heroes and villains alike while still being attuned to a narrator who is not an inhabitant of Chester's Mill. This narrator provides us with a history and background of the town and is also able to leave the dome to observe characters outside of the confined area. This far-reaching viewpoint establishes multiple perspectives through which the events of the novel are presented and creates a seriousness that allows readers to suspend their disbelief concerning the impossible events of the story.

Archetypes

William Golding's *Lord of the Flies* is an obvious archetype for *Under the Dome* since both novels feature a group of characters that have become isolated from civilization and must fend for themselves to survive. Unlike the Golding novel, though, King's characters, while isolated, can be observed by the civilized world and, as we learn later, by alien children who are watching them to see what they do. In both novels, rules break down and the stronger alpha males take over the group and use their power to their own advantage.

Under the Dome also refers to the modern situation of "being in a goldfish bowl," a position that involves having all eyes on you as you go about life and being unable to draw the curtain of privacy, like a fish in a bowl. Not only can the outside world see in and judge, but so can the alien children who have set up the situation to resemble an ant farm. The image of children burning ants with sunlight intensified by a magnifying glass reoccurs in the novel several times, and the characters are, in effect, living in an ant farm.

To a lesser extent, *Under the Dome* may also owe some similarities to *Sand Kings*, the 1979 Nebula-award-winning novella by George R.R. Martin, where a scientist secretly raises insect-like creatures recovered from a Martian probe in his basement to see what they will do. The creatures turn to warfare when the food supply becomes short, then worship their human "god" before ultimately attacking and killing him.

Themes and Subtexts

The major theme of the novel involves addiction in three forms: power, drugs, and religion. Power is the main addictive force of the novel as epitomized by Rennie, a used car salesman and second selectman—in other words, a big fish in a tiny pond who suddenly has the opportunity to be a dictator once the dome descends on Chester's Mill. Rennie, like all petty tyrants, is seduced by the temptation of power. He recruits an army of true believers from the easily manipulated youth of the town, seduces them by granting them status and power, and allows them to do what they do best—intimidate and bully the townspeople. Rennie is a watered-down version of Randall Flagg from *The Stand*. Sadly enough, Rennie, with his charisma and oratory skills, could have been an effective leader had he used his abilities to actually help the town instead of corrupting it for his own purposes. Had he been an ethical and compassionate leader, he might have achieved the fame he so desperately sought by guiding Chester's Mill through the disaster and emerging as a hero once the dome came down. Instead, he chose the dark side, so to speak, once the possibility of absolute power was made available to him.

Rennie isn't atypical in both King's universe and the world at large; he is a personification of the phrase "power corrupts." This theme can be extrapolated to the real world where dictators like Vladimir Putin, Kim Jong-Il, Kim Jong-Un, and the ayatollahs of Iran seize power and use it to squelch human rights. It isn't surprising that Rennie's petty crimes quickly escalate to torture and murder. He has gained absolute power in the town and there is nothing to stop him. Once he believes that the dome will never come down, he is untouchable, a despot with no one to answer to. Under the dome, Chester's Mill becomes a tiny dystopia that is emblematic of what could occur in a country where power has no checks and balances and the story is a cautionary tale for us all. "Sometimes the sublimely wrong people can be in power at a time when you really need the right people," King said when interviewed about this theme.

The addiction to drugs comprises another theme in the novel. Rennie was able to build his wealth and power by manufacturing and selling drugs to dealers who transported them away from Chester's Mill and to other towns. His excuse that he was keeping drugs away from his town is lame and laughable, of course, since he has no remorse about what tragedies the drugs he makes might cause elsewhere. The desire for these drugs fuels his criminal enterprise, and he and others are all willing to exploit this addiction for their own ends.

Andrea Grinnell, the third selectman, is also a victim of drug addiction and personifies how the opioid crisis has developed. After suffering from chronic pain, she was given a legal prescription for the drugs, which led to a long-term dependency and addiction. Rennie and his sidekick Sanders, the pharmacist, were only too happy to supply her with the opioids since it made her a compliant member of the town council, willing to do whatever she was told. This theme is an important one for King, who has battled alcohol and drug addiction and who was also prescribed opioids after his accident and had to struggle to wean himself off them. His description of Grinnell's situation is sadly very accurate and very common.

Religion also represents an addiction in *Under the Dome*, though King portrays it as hypocritical in the novel. Those, like Rennie and Coggins, who flaunt their religion the most are the most corrupt and immoral of all, while those who have doubts, like Piper Libby, are actually the most moral characters. The "true believers" of the Holy Redeemer Church are willing to lie, cheat, steal, and even murder to achieve their goals, which they can justify by doing these things for God and country (i.e., Chester's Mill). They put themselves above the law and subvert the law for their own purposes. Under the influence of Rennie, the town becomes a despotic theocracy, a Taliban-like society where the corrupt church conscripts an army. Religion demands power in King's world (as it often does in our own); once the town is "under the dome," it achieves total control.

The novel also deals with the subversion of two of the basic rights of Americans as granted by the Constitution: freedom of the press and the right to bear arms. Julia Shumway, editor of the local newspaper, personifies the First Amendment's guarantee of freedom of the press. Once a despot is in place, the first action is to destroy this freedom, which Rennie does by silencing Julia and burning the newspaper office to the ground.

Copies of the paper exposing Rennie's crimes do manage to circulate, however; the truth has a way of being spread even in repressive regimes. The Second Amendment also comes under attack as Rennie confiscates all the town's guns except those held by his henchmen. Whereas Stephen King takes a bold stand for gun control in his online essay "Guns," he contradicts himself in his fiction. In *Under the Dome* and other novels (*The Stand, Cell, Doctor Sleep*, and *The Gunslinger*, to name a few), King shows the need to have an armed populace to stand up to criminals, terrorists, and tyrants. This novel shows what could happen when only storm troopers are armed and the citizenry cannot defend itself against a police state. Although one might argue the unlikelihood of the world being invaded by vampires or sanctioned off by a giant glass dome, more mundane catastrophes that can cause anarchy, such as Hurricane Katrina or a worldwide pandemic, are well within possibility and offer a rationale for allowing citizens to be able to defend themselves in the event of disaster. At an instinctive level, King, a country boy from rural Maine, understands this idea and portrays it in his fiction despite his public politically correct stand against guns.

Ecology and environmental concerns form an important theme in the novel, as King himself has said. The microcosm inside the dome becomes a fictional laboratory to study climate change, pollution, energy shortages, and resource management. The book shows how foolish, shortsighted decisions can become cataclysmic, resulting in fires, overheating, and food shortages that can be irreversible. The resources of Chester's Mill are limited, as are those of the earth itself. The world under the dome becomes a symbolic microcosm of our planet and how easily it could be ruined without proper stewardship of its resources.

Human Universals

Fear is the most basic emotion and is found in all mammals—perhaps, to some extent, in all living things. And fear of being trapped is one of the most fundamental fears of all creatures. Cleithrophobia, or the fear of being trapped, is an instinctual fear that biologists believe stems from an evolutionary aversion to being trapped in enclosed spaces where escape from predators is impossible. This desire for freedom of movement and action forms the rationale for democratic governments, the rationale for confining criminals in prison, and the cause for much stress and anxiety during the Covid-19 quarantine. It is human nature to avoid being confined against our will. The giant, invisible dome in this novel is the perfect metaphor to trigger a fear of captivity and causes the reader to be uneasy from the very start of the novel. The fact that the prison is as large as a small town does not ease the angst of being trapped.

Evaluation

I'd place *Under the Dome* in the lower half of King's novels mostly because, for this English professor at least, the characters seem rather stereotyped (and the film adaptation only enhances this fact). You have the hero, the corrupt politician, and the innocent children as the main players in the book; these characters, to me, are somewhat forgettable. This could be intentional, of course, since we are all just "ants" being watched by aliens. But it does weaken the book, in my opinion.

Interesting Fact

In season 2 of the television series, Stephen King made a cameo appearance as a customer in the diner requesting a refill of his coffee.

Notable Quote

"If you don't control your temper, it will control you."

40

11/22/63

Changing the Past

Background

11/22/63 was published in 2011 by Scribner and developed into an eight-episode series on Hulu in 2016. The novel was named one of the ten best books of the year by the *New York Times* in 2011.

King had been thinking about writing the book since 1971 and, in fact, refers to the idea of preventing the Kennedy assassination in several pieces of fiction, including *UR* and *Cell*. The momentous task of researching the story caused him to put it on the back burner. As an established novelist, King was able to hire a professional researcher to assist him with the book. The re-creation of the details of life in the 1950s–1960s brings back a sense of nostalgia to readers who have lived during that time and re-creates the culture and history of that time for younger readers, which is one of the attractions of the book.

Summary and Narrative Devices

One of the most beloved of King's novels, *11/22/63* is a fictional thought experiment that asks what might have happened if a time traveler could have killed Lee Harvey Oswald and prevented the assassination of John F. Kennedy in November 1963. The protagonist, Jake Epping, learns of a portal that will take him back to 1958 and is recruited to change history by carrying out a mission to kill Oswald in the Texas book depository just before he can shoot Kennedy. Jake encounters two major obstacles to his goal, however. First, "the past is obdurate," according to King, and presents obstacles to keep it from being changed. This means that Jake cannot kill Oswald too soon or else someone else may take on the assassin's role and the mechanisms of time will continue to throw barriers in

219

his way to prevent him from changing history. Furthermore, the "butterfly effect" ensures that if the past can be changed, even slightly, other unexpected and unwanted changes will occur.

Jake's second major difficulty lies in the nature of the time portal that will only allow him to enter the past at a specific date and time in 1958, which means he must live in the past for five years before he can confront Oswald. Jake's very presence in the past for this long threatens to change history, and despite his best efforts to not become involved and to remain undistinguished, he cannot help becoming a part of the past world that he inhabits. He falls in love, attempts to right wrongs, and finds it impossible to abandon his human feelings and desires. The real point of the novel, then, goes well beyond the thought experiment of changing the past and addresses the whole concept of humanity and how we are each such an integral part of the world, whether we wish to be or not.

Although some critics have accused the novel of being too long and too repetitive (it does weigh in at 842 pages), the length of the novel is, I believe, a necessary vehicle to create the nostalgia and re-create the culture of the late '50s and early '60s. It would be simple enough to recast the thought experiment as a short story, where any attempt to change the past has calamitous results (as many short stories have done, such as Bradbury's 1952 "A Sound of Thunder" that personified the butterfly effect). But King's time-travel story goes well beyond just a story with a plot twist and is really driven by character and setting.

King's re-creation of the past is remarkable in its detail and accuracy, from the food to the music, to the fashion. His details of the automobiles of the time evoke a sense of nostalgia before the days of high gas prices and economy cars. The vehicles of the time had style and were as artistic as they were functional. The pace of life is also depicted as being stylish and much more refined. The people of the past are shown as respectful, polite, and well mannered, especially in smaller towns. The lack of technology results in a slower pace, where people were able to know one another on a very personal level without interference from cell phones, social media, and constant cable news. The atmosphere is relaxing and evokes a sense of the past that invites reminiscence. True, it is an idealized version of the past in many ways, but it does induce a sense of longing for simpler times, a return to a more innocent time of eight-cent newspapers and root beer.

Although the narrator does idealize the past by avoiding references to racism, sexuality, and other social issues, he effectively portrays women during this time, especially concerning one of King's recurrent themes, domestic violence. The women of the 1950s were primarily confined to the home except for just a few career choices, such as nursing or teaching. Married women were ruled by their husbands, who could abuse them with impunity. And even though this theme is not the major focus of the novel, it does make a powerful statement about both the past and the present.

The novel is structured as a series of repetitions. Jake first returns to the past very briefly to experience the sensations of time travel. He then returns a second time to attempt to fix a wrong that happened to one of his students who suffered at the hands of an abusive father. This trip back in time is shorter than what will be required to stop Oswald and serves as a test run, or an experiment to see if the past can be changed. Whereas some readers may see this trial run as an unnecessary part of the book, King uses it effectively to establish the ground rules of time travel and to engage the reader in enjoying the nostalgia of the 1950s. It is also necessary for Jake to go through the time portal several times to set up the presence of the "yellow card man" who becomes an important part of the book.

The repetition is also a thematic element that shows the many layers of the past and the complexity of King's multiverse with its endless arrays of alternate realities. Each time Jake returns to the past, he not only relives his previous trip but also moves forward and closer to November 1963. He is also allowed to do things differently, which illustrates the idea of free will while also showing how destiny will shape itself to absorb our individual choices into the overall picture of history.

The interesting thing about *11/22/63* from a narrative structure perspective is that the ending is already written into the history books. Yet each time Jake travels to the past, he creates a new world in the multiverse, a world with different outcomes. In terms of our own world, however, the ending is known, and the plot elements contrive to make sure that this ending occurs regardless of what Jake does. His struggle with fate and a predetermined outcome drives the book and maintains the suspense.

Suspense is also built on a more personal level. Since the story is told in the first person, Jake's individual drama becomes a source of tension. To accomplish his goal, Jake must remain uninvolved in the past except for the one job he is there to do. Yet his frustration is evident. King effectively details the impossibility of not being emotionally involved in life for five years. As much as the protagonist tries to remain detached, he does become emotionally involved with the people of the past, falls in love, and suffers through the hardships and tragedies of that time. While the plot to kill Oswald might be the overall point of the book, its real power involves Jake's personal struggle against all of the human emotions that are a part of every human being.

Archetypes

The idea of a time traveler changing the past is an old one in science fiction, but perhaps no one has written a story in as much detail as King has in *11/22/63*. Ray Bradbury's 1952 short story "A Sound of Thunder" personifies what has come to be known as "the butterfly effect," the chaos theory concept that a tiny event in one place can have major effects on another, such as the flapping of a butterfly's wings in Africa causing a hurricane in the Caribbean. This leads to possible consequences that even a minuscule change in the past could create a vastly different present. Ward Moore's 1953 novel *Bring the Jubilee* is set in an alternate universe where the South was victorious at the Battle of Gettysburg, and a time traveler from this world changes history to bring about the present where the North won the war. Like every avid reader of speculative fiction, King is familiar with time travel and alternate-world stories, and this background certainly helped inspire and influence this novel.

The concept of falling in love with someone from a different era is another archetype for King's story and is best represented by Richard Matheson's 1975 novel *Bid Time Return*, which was adapted into the film *Somewhere in Time* and reprinted with that title. In this story, a man falls in love with the picture of a stage actress from the past and develops a way to travel back in time to meet her. Although they have never met, she seems to know him, and their love seems to transcend time.

Themes and Subtexts

One of the oldest and still unresolved philosophical debates is the question of destiny versus free will. Indeed, religious sects have been founded and still exist based on the interpretation of this subject. In *11/22/63*, King fictionally addresses this issue through the what-if motif of time travel as he asks whether our lives are predetermined by fate or if we are masters of our own futures.

The novel does not offer an easy answer to this question. At the micro level, Jake seems to be free to do whatever he wants with his life. He can make his own decisions, pursue his own interests, and even love whom he chooses, and the world doesn't seem to be changed much by it. Fate seems to readjust itself to accommodate these small acts of free will without changing the overall picture of history. "The past is obdurate," King says. It resists change. Yet Jake proves that it can be changed, both in small ways and in great ways. His successful mission in stopping Kennedy's assassination brings about a horrible new reality where civilization destroys itself.

His interference with smaller events brings about smaller but significant changes. As the yellow card man says, every time the past is changed, it creates a new alternate reality. Jake isn't really changing the past when he travels back in time; instead, each new passage creates a new universe based on the infinite possibilities of free will. Free will, then, theoretically gives each person the opportunity to create their own world. Unfortunately for those of us who don't have access to a time portal, once this reality is created, it becomes permanent and cannot be changed.

Another obvious theme is the thought exercise of whether we should alter the past if we could—the age-old question of killing Adolf Hitler in his cradle, were we to have the chance. The time-travel thought experiment, of course, is just an exercise in speculation since the chances of actually building a working time machine are slim to none (and slim has sneaked out the back door of the building). But the experience might have practical consequences if someone were convinced that a person might become the next Hitler and took it upon themselves to destroy him before any damage could be done. This is the premise for *The Dead Zone*, where the protagonist knows that a politician is going to bring about the apocalypse if elected and so tries to stop him. In the confused world that we live in, the prospect of someone holding a belief like this (psychic or not) is a distinct possibility and could be an excuse to assassinate someone. In fact, this type of belief may very well have been responsible for JFK's assassination, not to mention the deaths of RFK and Martin Luther King, Jr.

In *11/22/63*, King warns that trying to "do good" by performing an evil deed may backfire and create a world that is even worse than the one that would have resulted if things were left alone. The butterfly effect cuts both ways according to this idea, and there is no way of telling which way the cards will play out. We should accept our fate, then, and not worry about changing the past or doing things differently if we have the chance. The idea of regret, therefore, is a waste of effort. First, the past can't be changed—we don't get a mulligan to erase our mistakes. Second, even if we did, the results might not turn out the way we hoped, and things might be even worse.

Human Universals

Love is a human universal emotion that, according to evolutionary psychologists, developed to ensure long-term pair bonding needed to care for children for the extended period they need until they can support themselves. Although this definition may sound overly clinical, as anyone who has ever been in love knows, love is an extremely powerful force that shapes and even defines human lives. It is truly a human universal formed from the affective emotions that Panksepp labels as CARING combined with LUST.

When all the trappings of science fiction and thought exercises are removed from *11/22/63*, the novel is, in essence, a love story and a bittersweet one at that. The novel explores the universal human wish (and perhaps belief) that we each have a single soulmate in the universe, if we can only find and connect with that person. The tragedy of this novel is that Jake's soulmate was born too many years in the past for Jake to meet without the time-travel portal. In Jake's "present," she is an old woman. And although Jake wishes he could remain in the past with her, he knows that it would be too dangerous to create another alternate universe where things might go terribly wrong. The story is one of two true star-crossed lovers, separated by time rather than space, and who can never live out their preferred destiny.

Evaluation

11/22/63 is one of my favorite novels, definitely in the top ten ranking, in my opinion. Whereas some have criticized the book as being too long, I believe that the nostalgic details and multiple return trips to the past made the book more interesting. I've reread the novel several times, and it never seems to get old for me (pardon the pun). It's like reliving the past again each time. Furthermore, the theme of changing history continues to fascinate audiences to this day. King's fictionalizing this idea results in a beautiful thought experiment that resonates long after the book is finished.

Interesting Fact

King took the research for this novel seriously, and although he had toyed with the idea for decades, he didn't begin work on it until he knew he could manage to research Kennedy's assassination thoroughly. He hired a researcher to assist him and met with noted historian Doris Kearns Goodwin and interviewed her about some of the worst things that might have happened if Kennedy had lived.

Notable Quote

"We never know which lives we influence, or when, or why. Not until the future eats the present, anyway. We know when it's too late."

41

Joyland

Carny from Carny

Background

Joyland was published in 2013 by Hard Case Crime as a paperback and was nominated for an Edgar Award by the Mystery Writers of America for best original paperback. According to King, the idea for the novel originated as an image of a boy in a wheelchair flying a Jesus kite on a beach. The story is set in North Carolina but was inspired by the Canobie Lake Park amusement park in Salem, New Hampshire.

Summary and Narrative Devices

Although *Joyland* sells itself as a mystery/ghost story, it is really a coming-of-age story similar in some ways to King's earlier novella *The Body*. The story is set in a local amusement park named Joyland on the coast of North Carolina. The first-person narrator, Devin Jones, tells the story from the vantage point of a 61-year-old looking back 40 years to what he ironically refers to as "the most beautiful time of his life, and the unhappiest" time he spent working at the amusement park. The story opens with Devin's girlfriend, his first love, breaking up with him. He leaves his home in New Hampshire to take a summer job at Joyland and winds up postponing his return to college to stay on at the park after it closes for the season to do routine maintenance work. He learns that House of Horrors at Joyland was the scene of an unsolved murder some years ago and that the ghost of the dead girl supposedly still haunts the ride. Devin's fascination with solving the crime forms the mystery element of the plot.

Once the park has closed, he forms a friendship with a 10-year-old boy, Mike, who has a terminal illness, and his very attractive mother Annie, to whom Devin loses his virginity. Devin does figure out the identity of the murderer, a serial killer, who attempts to kill him as well. Mike and Annie save his life, with a little help from a ghost.

King's first-person narrator is an effective storyteller who often speaks directly to the reader. Devin, who dreamed of becoming a successful novelist, has instead carved out a good career as a writer and editor for trade journals. In telling the nostalgic story of his time at Joyland, he proves to be an adept storyteller who keeps the narrative suspenseful until the very end.

Joyland is a mystery story with Devin Jones, the college student, as the unlikely detective. The mystery is introduced early in the novel and forms a backdrop to Devin's "coming of age." There are several clues of misdirection, such as the Horror House operator habitually wearing gloves, perhaps to cover up an incriminating tattoo, but in the end, the real killer turns out to be an employee of the amusement park and an important character in the novel.

Psychic abilities work as a foreshadowing device to create suspense in the story. Joyland's resident fortune teller has just enough talent to predict some important events in Devin's life, as she warns him, "You are on the edge of great sorrow. And perhaps danger." She also tells him that he will meet two children in whose lives he will play a major role. He does save the life of a little girl choking on a hot dog and later meets Mike, the 10-year-old boy who will save his life. Mike also has some psychic ability and is able to put to rest the ghost of the murdered girl. But his skills, too, are limited and he has no idea who the murderer is. He does act as a conduit for another ghost, however, who warns him that Devin is in trouble.

King even builds suspense with minor details, such as "wearing the fur," the meaning of which is a mystery for scores of pages until he finally learns that it means putting on the mascot costume and entertaining children in the sweltering heat.

The setting of the amusement park is perhaps the most powerful narrative device in the story. Joyland becomes a character in and of itself as it invokes nostalgic memories for both the narrator and perhaps the reader who grew up with such local amusement parks. The reader soon learns the landscape of the park, which becomes as real as any imaginary place could be. The place even has a language of its own, "carny-talk," which adds to the rich detail of the setting. From a linguistic point of view, this theme illustrates the concept of language registers, different vocabularies that we use for different things. These registers include regional dialects, language we use only with family and friends, and registers that are unique to specific professions. A surgeon, for example, uses a different vocabulary in the operating room than at the dinner table. The worlds of carnivals and amusement parks have their own language among the workers, which allows them to converse in a "code" that the outside world wouldn't understand. At Joyland, "the talk" includes expressions like "dog top" for a Joyland cap, "mitts" for fortune tellers who read palms, and "chump hoister" for Ferris wheel. This unofficial language gives the park workers power over the uninitiated "rubes" (park patrons), and in the novel, this language creates a sense of authenticity that helps bring the fictional amusement park to life and immerses the reader in this world. King points out that he learned much of the carny-lingo from *The Dictionary of Carney, Circus, Sideshow & Vaudeville Lingo* by Wayne N. Keyser.

Archetypes

Joyland is built around the archetype of the bildungsroman, the coming-of-age story that is popular in literature. This archetype depicts the transformation of a young person into adulthood through experiences that usually occur over the course of a relatively short time, often a summer. Examples of this kind of story include James Joyce's *Portrait of the Artist as a Young Man*, J.D. Salinger's *Catcher in the Rye*, and Harper Lee's *To Kill a Mockingbird*, to name just a few of the best-known novels. King has used this device on several occasions, most notably in *The Body* and *It*. In *Joyland*, Devin grows up in several ways. He learns how to handle loss, both the loss of what he calls his "first love" and the loss of Mike when the boy succumbs to his disease. He learns that he is a heroic person, despite his self-deprecating tone, when he saves two lives and survives a near-death experience. And he also loses his virginity along the way, which marks his sexual maturity.

Devin's one-night affair with Annie also harkens back to *The Graduate*, the iconic 1967 film (based on a 1963 novel of the same title) about a 21-year-old losing his virginity to Mrs. Robinson, an older woman. Annie, of course, is not married and the affair is just a one-night liaison.

Joyland differs from a traditional archetypical mystery novel in the fact that the protagonist is a college student, not a detective or other law enforcement professional. Devin's unique perspective of working at Joyland and his interest in carnivals accounts for his ability to solve the murder with the help of Erin Cook's research skills.

Themes and Subtexts

In some ways, *Joyland* resembles King's previously published novel *11/22/63*. Both novels evoke nostalgia, and in both novels the protagonists have an opportunity to love someone who is not from their time and so must enjoy the memories of a brief affair. In *11/22/63*, the main character and his lover are off by decades, so they can only be together when he travels back in time. In *Joyland*, Annie is perhaps a dozen years older than Devin, and although their brief connection can work for a single night, their age difference makes a long-term relationship impossible except as a friendship. "That's not the world we live in," Annie tells Devin, reminding him that what they have is just a single moment that cannot last.

Joyland successfully re-creates the nostalgia of 1973, a time that many of King's readers (including myself) recall rather vividly (it was the year this English professor graduated from high school). More specifically, it re-creates the world of local, independent amusement parks and carnivals that were common in small cities along the East Coast. These amusement parks featured Ferris wheels, a kiddie land, a haunted house ride, a fortune teller, and a row of games that tested patrons' skill. Some of these features still exist in the annual state fairs, but the atmosphere of the amusement parks was unique and a part of the life of any kid who lived through this time. King's novel resurrects this part of America's past in rich detail that makes the story both believable and beloved.

The carnival, amusement park atmosphere is a perfect vehicle for themes involving reality and fantasy. Ray Bradbury explored this theme most effectively in *Something Wicked This Way Comes*, as did the fourth season of *American Horror Story* (2014), which was set in a carnival. King uses this setting to explore the difference between the real world of college and everyday life, and the fantasy-like world of Joyland. The carnival is smoke and mirrors, a place that sells fun and the illusion of happiness. It can make a terminally ill child happy for one day, just as Annie can make Devin forget about his lost girlfriend for just one night, but the next morning reality reappears with all of its heartaches. The illness hasn't been cured, the broken heart hasn't been mended, and the world's troubles are still there, looming larger than ever. The brief reprieve is sweet, but it is also cruel in its own way since it is so fleeting. Only the memories last, which explains why Devin's time at Joyland was both the most beautiful time of his life and the most unhappy.

Human Universals

According to evolutionary psychology, human love developed as a strategy to form pair bonds that would care for offspring for the extended time the latter required to mature and survive on their own. Depending on the time and culture, children need at least 12 years to reach this point—in the modern world, 18 to 21 is considered more realistic, and neurologists have determined that the human brain doesn't fully mature until the age of 25. Humans are among only 5 percent of mammals who are monogamous, and that, of course, is monogamy in theory and not always in practice. Still, the pair bond of love is one of the strongest emotions we can experience and can cause both ecstatic joy and terrible heartbreak.

Devin begins the novel experiencing heartbreak as the girl who he thinks of as the love of his life unceremoniously breaks up with him, dumping him for another college student who presumably is a better prospect with a higher income potential. Females of any species hold the cards in the mating game, according to biologists, since they are capable of producing just one egg at a time, hence, one child every nine months, while males can theoretically produce multitudes of children during that time. The female, therefore, is choosy about obtaining a mate that will provide the best chance for her child to grow and survive. This is why rich men and rock stars, no matter how ugly, often have young trophy wives and why, theoretically at least, Devin, the struggling college student, was destined to lose his girlfriend Wendy to a lacrosse player attending Dartmouth, a much more prestigious school than Devin's state college.

On the flip side of the coin, it isn't possible for Devin to plan a life with Annie, even though they obviously love each other. Their love must be tempered by age; if Devin were 12 years older, the relationship might have worked. But both evolution and culture do not approve of a younger man marrying an older woman. Biology suggests this is because a woman has a limited time in which to produce children, while a man can produce them well into old age. But whether because of biology, culture, or both, Annie is correct in telling Devin that this is not the world we live in.

As we have seen in previous chapters, altruism is a distinctly human universal trait that has helped our species to survive and thrive by forming cooperative bonds that have led to tribes, societies, and nations. Devin's altruism and special bond with Mike is a different sort, though, and also uniquely human. Unlike most animals in the wild, humans have a trait of caring for the weak and the sickly. This trait may have evolved as part of the instinct to care for children, who are born helpless and need the intense care of their parents to survive. Yet we also have an urge to care for the sick and those with mental and physical challenges. This characteristic is admired by society, as evidenced by the respect that is given to doctors, nurses, and first responders to emergencies.

One might wonder how this kind of altruism might stem from a survival mechanism in our ancestors. One theory, first proposed by Ronald Fisher in 1930, claims that "unfit" genes, like the ones that cause Mike's illness, survive in a population as a means of increasing the population's diversity and therefore its ability to adapt to changing environments. The sickle cell gene is a case in point in that it protects individuals from malaria in the hybrid state. Society now recognizes diversity in the population and goes to great lengths to care for its weakest members, who often have unique strengths and abilities. Indeed, some of our most productive individuals have suffered from mental and physical illnesses, such as astrophysicist Stephen Hawking, economist John Nash, and world champion chess player Bobby Fischer. In *Joyland*, Mike is endowed with a psychic power that he uses to save Devin's life and to release the ghost from her torment. Devin's good deeds—befriending Mike and saving Freddy Dean's life—produce karma that ultimately save him from being killed by Lane.

Evaluation

Joyland, I think, is the best of King's mystery novels and ranks as one of my personal favorites. The carnival atmosphere is compelling, and King has done an amazing job of making it seem so realistic that we might think that the amusement park actually exists. It also handles some very important themes, including terminal illness, religion, and language itself.

Interesting Fact

There is currently a real amusement park named Joyland in Lubbock, Texas, and there was another park with that name in Wichita, Kansas, that closed in 2006.

Notable Quote

"The first broken heart is always the most painful, the slowest to mend, and leaves the most visible scar."

42

Doctor Sleep

Danny Torrance Grows Up

Background

Doctor Sleep, King's sequel to *The Shining*, was published in 2013 by Scribner and made number one on the *New York Times* bestseller list both in print and e-book fiction. It won the 2013 Bram Stoker Award for best fiction and was adapted for film in 2019.

In 2009, King asked readers to vote on his next project, either the next Dark Tower book or a sequel to *The Shining*. With over 10,000 votes cast on the website, *Doctor Sleep* won by 49 votes. For years, King had been wondering what happened to Danny Torrance, so it was just a matter of time before he finished the novel.

Summary and Narrative Devices

Doctor Sleep picks up the story of Danny Torrance, the boy with "the shine" who survived the horrors of the Overlook Hotel. The adult Danny, like his father, is plagued by alcoholism and childhood trauma. The novel begins when he is eight years old, and the first of the ghosts from the Overlook begins to haunt him. Dick Hallorann instructs him on how to lock up these demons in a lockbox in his mind. But despite his coping skills, Danny is transformed into the adult Dan in the third chapter, and Dan has become a mean drunk. Finally, he reaches rock bottom and drifts into a small New Hampshire town where he gives up drinking and takes a job in a hospice where he uses "the shine" to assist terminally ill patients pass over with the help of the resident cat; Dan becomes known as "Doctor Sleep."

The conflict of the novel arises between a young girl and members of the True Knot, a group of vampires who feed on psychic energy (which

231

they refer to as "steam") of those who have the shine when they die in pain. The girl, Abra Stone, becomes a target of the True Knot when she psychically senses their presence and uncovers their use of sadistic torture and murder to feed their steam addiction. She establishes a telepathic bond with Dan and enlists his help in destroying Rose the Hat, their leader, and the rest of the group before they can capture and kill Abra.

Building suspense is one of King's greatest strengths, and he uses foreshadowing as a technique to accomplish this in *Doctor Sleep*. One excellent example of this occurs in the beginning of the novel, when Hallorann helps Danny face the reappearance of entities from the Overlook. He introduces the idea of the mental lockbox, which will certainly be used again. Then he warns Danny that even as he is being taught, he will someday become the teacher. Danny doesn't pay much attention to this, but later, when 12-year-old Abra appeals to him for help, he realizes that the wheel has come full circle and he will have to teach her and help her, just as Hallorann did with him.

In many of his novels, King uses the psychic ability of the characters as an interesting foreshadowing device. The psychic insight can create a hint at what is to come without giving away the entire mystery. In this novel, Dan "sees" a top hat years before it will come to be associated with Rose the Hat and the True Knot. He also writes down the name Abra in his journal when she is just two months old. Later, he shows this to Bill and John to offer proof of his psychic connection with the little girl.

Another interesting narrative technique is the movement through time in this novel. The first half of the book covers Danny's life from the time when he was still a child, not far removed from the Overlook Hotel debacle, to his adulthood as Dan, including his lowest points of alcoholism, his recovery, and his maturity into the beloved "Doctor Sleep" who eases the passing of hospice patients. The book also follows Abra from infancy until she is 13 years old. Yet the passing of these long intervals of time is handled skillfully, without becoming bogged down in meaningless, mundane details that aren't either part of the plot or character development. Then, once the real conflict appears in the middle of the story, time is condensed and moves much more quickly.

One of King's strengths is his ability to create interesting and believable villains. There is, of course, no such thing as pure evil. In good fiction, villains don't think of themselves as "bad" but have an understandable motive for behaving badly. In this case, cruelty is a matter of survival for the True Knot. While their desire for immortality might seem selfish, it is totally human. We might ask ourselves, what would we do to live forever? Humans are willing to subject themselves to cosmetic surgery, Botox, and all sorts of creams, gels, chemicals, and other tortures just to *look* younger.

If there were a cure for aging, my guess is that people would do almost anything to have it (a theme that is explored in William Barrett's 1963 novel *The Fools of Time*). So, while deploring the cruelty of the True Knot, readers must face the disturbing question of what crimes they might commit for the treasure of immortality. This question and the depiction of horrendous acts of violence make this book difficult to read, yet compelling at the same time. Although, as the True Knot say, "it's not personal," their actions are repulsive and unsettling, especially in light of the fact that they are plausible in terms of the cult members' survival and not merely the wild acts of comic book villains without any real motivation behind them except evil. As Snake says while dying, "We didn't choose to be what we are any more than you did. In our shoes, you'd do the same."

Rose the Hat is also notable for being a female villain when most of the notorious villains in literature are male. She is depicted as a strong leader whose concern is the well-being of her "family" and who has been an effective commander for hundreds of years. She has the respect of the cult members, and her orders are followed without question. She is powerful and deadly, a foe to be reckoned with for certain. Yet, despite her inhuman behavior, she is a sympathetic character in some ways. It is her fate to watch her family suffer from a lack of "food" and to grow weak with time. She does show love and compassion for those in the True Knot and genuinely thinks of herself as being a member of a different species than the "rubes" she feeds on. Humans are considered livestock, much like humans consider cattle and other meat products.

Interestingly enough, Rose the Hat is pitted against another female, the 13-year-old Abra who is her match when it comes to psychic power. She joins the ranks of Carrie and Charlie McGee from *Firestarter* as a girl with tremendous powers at her disposal. Although Dan may be the protagonist of *Doctor Sleep*, Abra is the character at the center of the conflict and the one who holds the most power and faces the most danger.

Archetypes

The Shining is the obvious inspiration for *Doctor Sleep* since it uses many of the same characters, the premise of "the shine," and the looming presence of the Overlook Hotel as a background setting. Yet unlike many sequels, this novel does explore different storylines and creates a most memorable villain in Rose the Hat.

The idea of psychic vampires can be traced back to the Satanic Church of Anton LaVey in the 1960s. LaVey used the term "psychic vampire" in *The Satanic Bible* to refer to a person who drains vital energy from others. The idea survives in contemporary culture as "energy vampires," needy people who just seem to drain the energy of their friends, colleagues, and family.

From a literary standpoint, one of the most notable works about psychic vampires is Dan Simmons's *Carrion Comfort*, published in 1989. This novel, which won the Stoker Award, among others, features psychic vampires who feed off violence and manipulate history to create violent events. Simmons, along with Brian Lumley and others, are part of the trend to modernize vampires, giving them a new backstory and a new premise about their powers. *Doctor Sleep* adds to this genre of "new-wave vampires" in an interesting way.

Themes and Subtexts

The major theme of *Doctor Sleep* revolves around the subtext of addiction on several levels. The obvious addiction concerns Dan's battle with alcoholism, a condition that King knows well from personal experience. King has managed to conquer his dependencies and his successful management of his alcohol and drug problem is reflected in the novel, which ends with Dan's 15 years of sobriety.

King's descriptions of the struggles of addiction are not only believable but form an integral part of the story itself. Dan is a flawed hero who battles his internal demons and has done some bad things in his life. His misdeeds, especially taking money from a woman and leaving her and her child destitute and helpless, haunt him and make him question his self-worth. The legacy of his father's alcohol dependency issues plagues him as well, though to his credit, he blames only himself for his situation, not his father or even the trauma he suffered at the Overlook Hotel. Dan's major conflict is an internal one, the classic "man against himself," even more so than his conflict with the True Knot. To defeat Rose the Hat, he must first conquer his own demons, beginning with being able to trap the haunting entities from the Overlook, and then the much more difficult task of managing his addiction. *Doctor Sleep* is really the story of Dan's being able to manage responsibilities and to learn to harness his "shine" for constructive purposes.

Rose the Hat and the True Knot also portray the theme of addiction on a symbolic level. They need "steam" to survive and have become so dependent on it that they will commit any type of atrocity to obtain it. This symbolizes addiction at a very elemental level: addicts will do anything and sacrifice anyone to secure their next fix. Morality and ethics become meaningless. Laws no longer exist for them. And loved ones will be dispensed with in favor of their drug of choice. Just as steam is a chemical dependency for the True Knot, addictive drugs also take over the physiology of addicts, hijacking their nervous systems along with their reason. Thus, the True Knot can be seen as victims of their own bodies, which accounts for their shocking behavior.

Science fiction stories have a long history of chronicling the downside of immortality, beginning perhaps with Mary Shelley's short story "The Mortal Immortal," written in 1833. Although immortality is seen as a desirable thing—hence the quest for the mythical fountain of youth—authors have shown it more realistically as a curse. Rose the Hat has achieved immortality, of sorts at least, but at a very dear price. The True Knot must remain on the run, must feed off the misery of others, and cannot lead true, productive lives. Although they think of themselves as a higher form of life than the "rubes," their lives are merely existence and not real living. They cannot settle down, cannot form relationships with anyone but each other, and cannot contribute anything meaningful to the world. It is a base existence at best and dominated by their need for their next steam fix. It is certainly not without stress as they are constantly forced to search for their next source of steam, be it a victim with the shine or an unthinkable tragedy like the September 11 terrorist attacks. There is little if any joy in their existence, only a common need to move on. Although they have accumulated power and wealth, they cannot enjoy it. Their amassing of these assets is strictly for survival, not for pleasure. They are a powerful symbol of addiction running one's life.

This curse of immortality has modern implications. As science and medicine come closer to solving the mysteries of aging, we may be faced with an ethical dilemma—just because we can achieve immortality, should we? A discovery like this would create layer upon layer of problems: social, religious, ecological, economic.... Would it be worth the price? And once discovered, such a technology could not be undiscovered. The curse of immortality depicted in *Doctor Sleep* may be metaphorical, but it isn't much of a stretch to see what serious dilemmas it could cause were it to become a reality.

Another theme that occurs, though a relatively minor one, is the disturbing concept of child predators. Members of the True Knot feed primarily on the psychic steam of children, which they obtain through sadistic torture of their victims. Regrettably, society has its share of nonsupernatural "vampires" who also feed off the suffering and torture of children. Whereas the members of the True Knot can be understood because of their need for steam for survival, real-life child predators are much more difficult to comprehend and are impossible to forgive.

Human Universals

Doctor Sleep taps into the universal fear of death. Although knowledge is the superpower of *Homo sapiens*, knowledge does come with its downside—the fact that we are probably the only creatures on the planet that understand their own mortality (perhaps the real forbidden fruit from Eden). We may comprehend death on an intellectual level, but we still have a difficult time understanding and accepting it on a personal level. We all, to some extent, perceive ourselves as immortal, especially in our youth. So when death does approach, we would yearn for a character like Doctor Sleep to ease our transition and to assure us that something exists after death.

The survival instinct causes all creatures to avoid what is perceived as danger and seek out that which gives life. But humans have the understanding to comprehend death at a higher level and can foresee more long-term results of actions or inactions. This insight has led to medicine and the cure and prevention of illnesses that might infect us. It also leads to the quest for a fountain of youth. Indeed, if aging and death can't be avoided, it can at least be disguised with cosmetics, surgery, and other antiaging schemes.

Another human universal is tragedy of the loss of a child. This universal fear is addressed in the metaphor of the True Knot, immoral creatures who take the life of children and suck out their essence. Since human offspring take many years to grow old enough to become self-sufficient, the death of a child affects us deeply. Putting Abra in unspeakable danger touches a nerve with the reader, escalating the stake to a much higher level than we would feel if Dan was the only one in trouble. And Dan, who also has the shine, is immediately drawn to Abra to help. We also learn that Dan is actually Abra's half brother, something he doesn't realize until the book nears its conclusion. One popular theory in evolutionary psychology claims that people are much more altruistic toward kin than they are toward strangers since they share many of the same "selfish genes." In King's novel, these selfish genes recognize one another, enabling Dan and Abra to connect on a more intimate level.

Evaluation

Doctor Sleep has, in my opinion, one of the most interesting and compelling villains in horror literature. King manages to make Rose the Hat despicable and sympathetic at the same time. Her actions, horrendous as they are, are realistically motivated and understandable. The character of

42. Doctor Sleep

Dan is also quite interesting; he begins the novel as a rather despicable character himself yet manages to overcome his addiction and turn into a heroic figure. *Doctor Sleep* is, in my view, one of King's best books (in some ways, I enjoy it even more than *The Shining*) and worthy of more detailed critical study.

INTERESTING FACT

Doctor Sleep was partially inspired by Oscar, the therapy cat who lived in the Steere House Nursing & Rehabilitation Center in Providence, Rhode Island, and who predicted the death of patients by sleeping with them in their final hours.

NOTABLE QUOTE

"Life was a wheel, its only job was to turn, and it always came back to where it started."

43

Mr. Mercedes
Enter, Holly Gibney

Background

Mr. Mercedes, the first book of the Hodges trilogy, which includes *Finders Keepers* (2015) and *End of Watch* (2016), was published in 2014 by Scribner. The novel is a true detective story and won the Edgar Award from the Mystery Writers of America. Originally intended as a short story, the book was inspired by a real-life event when a woman drove her car into a McDonald's restaurant. Regrettably, terrorists have used vehicles as weapons to kill innocent people on more than one occasion since the novel's publication. The book was adapted into a television series that ran from 2017 to 2019 on Audience, a pay TV network.

Summary and Narrative Devices

Mr. Mercedes introduces two iconic characters: Bill Hodges, a retired detective, and Holly Gibney, who is also a supporting character in *The Outsider* (2018), *Holly* (2023), and the novella *If It Bleeds* (2020). Holly, an offbeat but lovable individual, is one of King's favorite characters.

The novel begins where 2,000 applicants are waiting in line at a job fair and are mowed down by a psycho in a Mercedes who drives into them and then escapes after killing eight innocents and injuring others. The story then picks up a couple of years later when Bill Hodges, the lead detective on this unsolved case, is contacted and taunted by the "Mercedes killer." Hodges decides to pursue the case on his own. Brady, the Mercedes killer, plans to up the ante and blow himself up at a pop concert filled with teenage girls. Hodges and his friends, Holly, a 40-something-year-old who suffers from mental illness, and Jerome, a high school senior, are the only ones who can stop the terrorist act in time to save thousands of lives. The story then turns from a mystery into a thriller with a literal countdown until the explosion hits.

In a Stephen King novel, no one's life is certain. This fact is established at the outset of the novel when he creates three likable innocent characters, a single mom and her baby, and a man who shows true kindness to them; the characters are then brutally murdered by the Mercedes killer. This raises the suspense level concerning the welfare of the lead characters, Hodges and Jerome, and later Janey and Holly, as they are introduced. And sure enough, Janey, who has become Hodges's love interest, is blown to pieces in an explosion engineered by Brady.

Another interesting technique in this novel is the reader's knowledge of who the killer is. The mystery, then, isn't finding him—he is identified early in the narrative—but how Hodges will discover his identity. King uses irony to show that Brady, the local ice-cream man, is hiding in plain sight right under the noses of the main characters.

Suspense is also created when Brady launches plans to kill Jerome's sister's dog. Every dog-loving reader dreads what is sure to happen and is relieved when the plan backfires and Brady kills his own very unlikable mother with the poison meat instead.

King, always the master of creating suspense, interjects powerful tidbits of foreshadowing in the middle of mundane events. For example, the crowd of job seekers watch as the janitor passes by, presumably to open the building, and one of the men in line, Keith Frias, makes a wisecrack. King then states that this character's left arm would soon be "torn from his body." Foreshadowing also appears when a neighbor makes the statement that "they walk among us," referring to the aliens she imagines in her mind, and then casually mentions that the ice-cream truck has been around the neighborhood more often than usual.

Throughout the novel, the main characters are put in imminent danger. This culminates in the final concert scene. Once Brady's plans to take a suicide bomb into a teenage concert are revealed, King ramps up the suspense by having Jerome's sister and mother attend the event and initiating a "countdown" until the terrorist act is committed. This gives Hodges a deadline to both solve the crime and prevent it. And like in all good thrillers, the team comes through just in the nick of time.

Finally, King uses narrative tense in an interesting way in *Mr. Mercedes*. The opening scene is written in past tense. Then, when Hodges is introduced, most of the novel is written in present tense, with the events unfolding in real time. This technique transports the reader ahead in time from the Mercedes incident to the retired Bill Hodges leading his life of quiet desperation, even considering suicide.

Archetypes

Like most of King's novels, *Mr. Mercedes* employs the classic hero's journey motif. As the novel opens, Hodges is not inclined to do anything except watch mundane television shows and contemplate the uselessness of his life now that he has retired. He avoids the call to action initially, but the Mercedes killer's taunting letter is too strong to avoid, and Hodges takes on the quest of finding the criminal who has caused so much mayhem and death himself, rather than turning it over to the police.

Mr. Mercedes is based on the trope of the "hard-boiled" detective genre espoused by such fictional detectives as Philip Marlowe, Mike Hammer, and Sam Spade, who are known for their toughness and grit. Although Bill Hodges is an aged and overweight version of these pulp fiction detectives, he does show his toughness when he beats up three bullies who were harassing a young boy. After Janey hires him to work on the Mercedes killer case for her, he imagines he could be a Philip Marlowe after all, and the much younger Janey does fall for him and even buys him a detective's fedora.

The idea of the retired cop becoming a private eye isn't anything new in the mystery genre. Sue Grafton's Alphabet Mysteries feature Kinsey Millhone as a former cop turned private detective. Jeffery Deaver's Lincoln Rhyme comes out of retirement to solve crimes. Jack Reacher, created by Lee Child, is a former officer in the military police who retires and becomes a private detective.

The hard-boiled detective novel has become a well-known trope, but King does change the formula in this novel. Hodges is in his sixties, overweight and has heart issues, and has a much softer side than the traditional pulp detectives. Suffering from depression and some self-esteem issues, he is a very realistic character. His motivations are different as well. He truly seeks justice for the crime he couldn't solve when he was on duty and feels a real sense of compassion toward the victims. The crime is not simply a puzzle to be solved but a wrong that needs to be made right. He is also sympathetic toward others, especially weaker characters like the little boy who was attacked by bullies, and Holly Gibney, whom most people consider a misfit.

Themes and Subtexts

The economy certainly plays a role in *Mr. Mercedes* as the victims of the Mercedes killer wait in line for a job fair to open, knowing that there are far more applicants than available jobs. These people are shown as desperate and willing to take any kind of a job just to pay the bills. In 2009, the year that the book opens, Wall Street suffered a collapse, and the unemployment rate rose to 10 percent, resulting in a great recession that affected most Americans. The novel shows the hardships that average people faced, including foreclosures, the loss of pensions, and widespread bankruptcy. Even Brady, the killer, is affected and must work two low-paying jobs to make ends meet, a situation that fuels his mental illness.

After September 11, 2001, the threat of terrorism became a part of life in America. Although terrorist acts are considered the domain of radical Islamic fanatics, domestic terrorism is a far more likely scenario. It is difficult to understand how someone like Timothy McVeigh, the Oklahoma City bomber, thinks about the world and what could drive someone to do such a heinous act. King tries to imagine the mind of a deranged killer in this novel, setting up the theme of mental illness as a cause. The product of an abusive father, an alcoholic mother, and just plain bad luck, Brady Hartsfield cannot experience empathy toward others. He is a high-functioning sociopath in that he can hold down a job and interact with others by pretending to have feelings, but his real thrill comes from killing. He is extremely intelligent, and if things had worked out differently, he might have had a successful career in the computer industry. Instead, he uses his technical skills to feed his ego and to hurt others.

Brady is an interesting villain because his motives, while appalling, make sense in the context of his mental illness. As a sociopath, he has no empathy for others, so he cannot feel remorse or regret or relate to human suffering. He has murdered at a young age, which has made him even more unfeeling. His environment only added to his issues, living with abusive parents and deprived of any real education. Brady has come to look upon all of humanity as "sheep" who exist only for his enjoyment. He carries an enormous chip on his shoulder, and nothing short of harming others makes life worthwhile for him. Since his life is misery, he feels that it is only fair to spread the wealth and inflict pain on others.

This theme of mental illness is common in King's novels and helps to explain the violence that occurs in the world and serves as a warning as well. Had some intervention occurred in Brady's life when he was a child, tragedy could have been averted. This theme is true in so many real-life events, where untreated mental illness results in mass shootings and other unspeakable acts. In the case of the Mercedes killer, economic issues also played a major role in the tragedy. Brady's mother's alcoholism is a direct result of financial troubles and an indifference from society as to the fate of the less fortunate, who often fall into difficulty through no fault of their own. The father's death and the brother's brain trauma were the result of sheer bad luck and nothing more. Yet these things had a profound ripple effect on the family and society.

Human Universals

The quest for justice is a human universal trait that has served the species and society well for thousands of years. This trait forms the basis for the entire mystery genre, which remains as popular as ever. There is a strong desire for people to see wrongdoing punished and altruism rewarded. Evolutionary psychologists believe that this goes back to times when Paleolithic tribes had to rely on cooperation to survive, putting the needs of the tribe above the desires of any individual within the group. Those outliers who were dangerous to the group had to be either discouraged from committing crimes against other members of the tribe or punished if they did. This led to the enactment of laws, which were probably more informal at first and then codified once civilizations emerged.

Unfortunately, justice is not always realized. Although society harbors a strong urge to punish crimes, evildoers sometimes escape. In the crime novel, the detective becomes the hero who will solve the crime and ensure that offenders are caught and punished. In the most satisfying crime stories, the villain receives a punishment that fits the crime. The horrible crimes of the Mercedes killer require more than just a prison term or even a long stint on death row, and the novel delivers. Holly Gibney not only disarms Brady's suicide bomb but delivers a punishing blow with the "Happy Slapper" that effectively turns him into a vegetable, a fate that most people would consider to be worse than death. She beats him senseless, calling it "therapy," and it is—both for her and for the Constant Reader, who feels great gratification that the Mercedes killer has suffered at the hands of the heroic Gibney.

Mr. Mercedes also addresses the human need to have meaning and importance in the world. This human desire fuels much of what people do. It drives them in their careers, in their quest to reproduce and raise children who will live on after they are gone, to produce art and culture, and to be productive. Unfortunately, people who look forward to retirement sometimes suffer depression and a loss of self-importance once they leave their careers. This is the case with Bill Hodges, whose life has been defined by his job. Once he hangs up his badge, he finds himself living life without a purpose. He is divorced, his daughter is absent, and he has no real friends except former colleagues, who have lives of their own, and Jerome, who, at the start of the novel at least, is just a high school kid who does odd jobs for him. His unsolved cases haunt him, especially the case of the Mercedes killer, and his only recreation is mundane and meaningless television shows that he doesn't even really like. When the novel opens, Hodges is borderline suicidal.

The taunting letter from the Mercedes killer, which is meant to drive him to take his own life, has the opposite effect and recharges Hodges with a new purpose—to solve the mystery despite his retired status. Rather than turn the case over to his former partner in the police department, he takes on the challenge himself. Once he has a renewed sense of purpose, his depression disappears, the gun he'd thought of as a suicide weapon goes into storage, and the banal television shows are turned off. Hodges is reborn once he has a reason for living.

Psychologists advise retired people to keep active as a way of warding off depression and dementia. Retirees are counseled to pursue a hobby, engage in an exercise program, take part in social activities, and continue to engage their brains by learning new things. When Hodges takes on the case once again, it results in his doing all these things and he once again embraces life. He makes new friends, loses weight, and makes a major contribution to society by identifying and helping to stop Brady Hartsfield's final terrorist act.

Evaluation

King's more recent fiction seems to be getting even better. No longer tethered exclusively to the horror genre, he has been free to write whatever book he chooses at an age where most writers would be comfortably retired. *Mr. Mercedes* is a perfect example of King's more recent work. He has embraced the mystery genre, which he loves, and has created a most memorable character in Holly Gibney, whose reappearance in later works is most welcome by this English professor. She is not the stereotyped detective but a realistic woman with real flaws and an admirable heroic streak. *Mr. Mercedes* ranks in the top third of King's novels.

Interesting Fact

King began the novel before the Boston Marathon terrorist attacks but claims the novel's premise and the real-life events were "too creepily close for comfort."

Notable Quote

"Most people are sheep and sheep don't eat meat."

44

Revival

Reanimation and Revelation

Background

Revival was written between April and December 2013, and published in 2014 by Scribner. The book is a return for King to the horror genre, specifically to the cosmic horror of H.P. Lovecraft but, as King has said, with more modern and less inflated language.

Summary and Narrative Devices

The basic plot of *Revival* hinges on the relationship of the protagonist, Jamie Morton, and Charles Jacobs, a Methodist minister who takes over the parsonage of the rural Maine church when Jamie is a child. Jacobs, who is interested in science and electricity, makes an immediate impression on the boy, and when Jamie's brother Conrad (Con) is injured and loses the ability to speak, the reverend cures him with a gadget that channels electricity. Not long afterward, Jacobs's wife and toddler son are killed in a horrible car accident, and the minister loses his faith, shocking the congregation with his terrible sermon that denounces God and religion. Jacobs leaves town, and Jamie doesn't see him until many years later when Jamie has become a professional musician and a heroin addict. At the lowest point of his life, Jamie encounters the reverend at a county fair where he is creating portraits using electricity. Jacobs uses his knowledge of what he calls "secret electricity" to rid Jamie of his addiction, nurse him back to health, and set him up with a job at a recording studio in Colorado. They part ways once again.

After some time, Jamie learns that Jacobs is once again touting himself as a reverend and has reinvented himself as a faith healer and is raking in millions of dollars curing people of their ills with his secret electricity, which he markets as a miracle of God. After doing some research, however, Jamie learns that these "miracles" have disastrous side effects, causing many of their recipients to go insane and commit suicide, sometimes killing others as well. In a final encounter with the minister, Jamie, against his better judgment, is cajoled into helping Jacobs with one final experiment in return for curing Jamie's teenage sweetheart of terminal cancer. This experiment involves the reanimation of a dead woman with the object of seeing into the afterlife. Jacobs dies in the process and Jamie catches a glimpse of the Lovecraftian world that awaits us all after death.

The idea behind *Revival* is the sharing of forbidden and astonishing knowledge with a reader who must, in the context of the novel at least, accept the impossible as truth. King accomplishes this through the character of Jamie, who is presented as being totally reliable throughout the narrative. Although it might be thought that Jamie might be suffering from mental illness—he, of course, was a recipient of the reverend's cure— King is careful to present the protagonist as being totally sane, rational, and truthful. The story is told in first person and Jamie makes no attempt to embellish the story in any way. "I didn't sit down at my computer to put on rose-colored glasses," he says. He reveals his innermost thoughts and weaknesses, never making excuses for his drug addiction or his mistakes. He takes ownership of his life, both the positive and the negative, and the telling of his story is more an unburdening of his soul than anything else. "What a relief in the telling," he says and, addressing the audience directly, urges the reader to check out the verifiable facts on the internet. Even his therapist, who is highly skeptical of his story, is "given pause" by some of Jamie's concrete details. Jamie admits that part of the reason he agreed to help Jacobs was his curiosity, and he says that although the telling of the story is difficult, he must share it as a cautionary tale to stop others from traveling down the road that the reverend has taken. This use of a highly reliable narrator conveys ideas that are difficult to comprehend and believe.

Archetypes

On the dedication page of *Revival*, King acknowledges Arthur Machen's novella *The Great God Pan* (1894), which "has haunted me all my life." The Machen story recounts an experiment by a scientist to induce his wife to experience travel to a higher plane of existence by having electricity shocked into her brain. The scientist believes he will then see what exists after death. Unfortunately, his experiment destroys the woman, leaving her in a vegetative state because of the horrors she has seen on the other side. This narrative is the core of *Revival*, where forbidden knowledge causes those who have experienced it to become insane and suicidal.

Mary Shelley's *Frankenstein* remains the archetype for all reanimation stories and has inspired numerous other tales over the years, including H.P. Lovecraft's "Herbert West: Reanimator" and countless Hollywood films of varying quality. King uses this reanimation motif to enable his protagonist to gain a brief but horrible glimpse of the afterlife, a terrible existence inspired by Lovecraft's Cthulhu Mythos, which created an entire pantheon of elder gods and other monstrosities that lurk just beyond the fringes of our perceived reality. The mythos plays a role in King's overall multiverse theme that underlies much of his fiction, most notably *It* and the Dark Tower books. This idea of cosmic horror, introduced by Lovecraft, has expanded into a subgenre of horror fiction and offers a terrifying view of the world based on science rather than the supernatural.

Themes and Subtexts

Religion forms a major theme in this novel and in no other book is King harsher in his criticism of it. His thoughts on religion are complex, ranging from the fondness he shows toward God-fearing characters such as Mother Abigail in *The Stand* to criticism leveled at fanatical believers such as Carrie's mother and the corrupt reverend in *Under the Dome*. *Revival* goes so far as to denounce religion entirely, though, by showing that heaven is nothing but a wishful fantasy and that we are all doomed to an afterlife worse than hell regardless of how we behave (or misbehave) during our lifetimes.

On the more microcosmic level, *Revival* compares organized religion to a con game. Jacobs admits that he was taught how to trick people in divinity school under the guise of "kindling the faith." He equates preaching to working in a carnival, admitting that there is no difference—"they're both just a matter of convincing the rubes."

Addiction forms another subtext in the novel and is a thread in much of King's work. In this case, Jamie suffers from a heroin addiction which began after his being prescribed opioids after a painful accident, reminiscent of King's own near-fatal accident. As in other post-trauma novels, King eloquently describes the suffering that comes with addiction and withdrawal. In Jamie's case, it takes one of Jacobs's "miracles" to cure him of the condition.

Finally, *Revival* introduces the idea of cosmic horror, horror that is based on science rather than the supernatural. In this case, the horror comes from the realization that our reality is just one small part of the multiverse and that human beings are merely a tiny, insignificant race of helpless beings inside an immense and powerful universe. This theme, introduced by H.P. Lovecraft, reminds us that the earth and everything in it is nothing more than a speck of dust in an infinite cosmos composed of beings that would consider us lower than fleas in the overall scheme of things. Whereas religion claims that humans are favored by God and made in His divine image, *Revival* depicts *Homo sapiens* as nothing more than suffering slaves of insects, who, in turn, are slaves to more powerful, merciless creatures. This hierarchy of the multiverse, also alluded to in *It*, leaves humanity at the very bottom of the cosmic food chain, so to speak, in a place called "The Null." It is a frightening thought that might indeed drive one to madness were it to be proven true.

Forbidden knowledge also forms a subtext in the novel. This theme, a natural consequence of cosmic horror, is a warning not to look at things that should remain hidden. This idea traces back to the forbidden fruit eaten by Adam and Eve in the Garden of Eden, fruit that granted them knowledge that God did not want them to have. The modern form of forbidden knowledge is scientific rather than mythic and has revealed itself in discoveries such as the atomic bomb, germ warfare, and Darwin's theories of natural selection, which have been denounced by various religions even to the present day. But once the paint has been spilled, it cannot be put back in the bucket, so "unknowing" something is not possible.

The interesting part of our nature, however, is the human compulsion to share that which should not be shared. People gossip, can't help but look at automobile wrecks on the highway, and are quick to dig into areas that could be dangerous. Jacobs cannot help but explore the ancient texts that refer to secret electricity and cannot help pursuing his experiments to the point where ethics and morality are left flying in the wind. Furthermore, even Jamie, who detests such things, is driven by curiosity to take part, and as much as he claims to keep the knowledge secret, he does share his story with his therapist and, as an added irony, writes it down for the unsuspecting audience to read. Although he claims this is a warning to prevent others from pursuing the knowledge, realistically it would more likely cause others to rediscover the secret and use it for their own purposes.

Human Universals

One of the primeval affective emotions of the human species is what Panksepp terms the SEEKING instinct, which evidences itself as curiosity. While this impulse may have proverbially "killed the cat," it exists in most mammals as a survival mechanism that allows them to move to new ecosystems and adapt to changes in the old ones. It is the hallmark of human beings, especially creative ones. As King says, "Curiosity is a terrible thing, but it's human. So Human."

Curiosity about the afterlife is a normal human urge, one that has given rise to myths and religions since the time of our Stone Age ancestors. So-called magicians and psychics have attempted to communicate with the dead since time immemorial (with no success, of course). Charlatans have made fortunes by conning people into thinking they have such power. But if there were a way of knowing what lies beyond the grave, the lure of such knowledge would be impossible to resist for many, if not most, people. Whereas religion is accepted on faith, modern Americans, for the most part, trust in science. Readers of *Revival*, then, are treated to a firsthand account of what the afterlife might be like, at least in a fictional sense. This quest to know drives readers to experience the novel and inspire fear that the unlikely but terrible scenario just might be true.

In *Frankenstein*, Mary Shelley envisioned a case where we might cheat death and bring the deceased back to life. Her novel has become part of the collective unconsciousness because of the human instinct to survive. As far as we know, humans are the only creatures who are aware of the certainty of their own death. The quest for a fountain of youth is an old one, made modern using cosmetic surgery, Botox, and drugs that claim to rejuvenate just about every part of the body. Jesus was said to be able to raise the dead, and Christianity promises that after death we will be resurrected and born again into eternal life.

This human universal desire to cheat death underlines *Revival* as Jacobs performs his miracle cures on the terminally ill and the infirm. The idea is an appealing one to us mortals who want to believe in an afterlife but often lack the complete faith to do so. A character such as Jacobs appeals to the reader's desire for immortality, even if it is only in a fictional setting. But as King reminds us, any attempt to cheat death has dire consequences.

Evaluation

As a Lovecraft fan and scholar, I love the way King has taken cosmic horror out of the Victorian age and thrust it into the modern world with *Revival*. I find his exploration of religion, the afterlife, and philosophy in general compelling. Speculative fiction, in my view, is the most effective way (perhaps the *only* way) to delve into these topics, which makes it difficult for me to understand the scorn that some critics have for genre fiction that dares to investigate these matters. *Revival* is one of my favorite King novels and, from a critical standpoint, one of his best.

Interesting Fact

Charles Jacobs hones his huckstering skills in an amusement park named Joyland, the setting of the previous Stephen King novel with that title.

Notable Quote

"Curiosity is a terrible thing, but it's human. So Human."

45

Finders Keepers

The Problem with Buried Treasure

Background

Finders Keepers, the second book of the Hodges trilogy, was published in 2015 by Scribner. Although some of the characters remain the same throughout the trilogy, the City Center Massacre is the unifying element of the series, as it follows different characters and the aftermath of that attack through different narrative threads.

Summary and Narrative Devices

The main character is a boy named Pete Saubers, whose father suffered a debilitating injury at the hands of the Mercedes killer. When he was 13 years old, Pete was exploring the vacant woods behind his house and discovered a suitcase containing over $22,000 in cash and the handwritten private notebooks of John Rothstein, a famous reclusive writer who was murdered by Morris Bellamy, who stole and buried the journals in the woods and is serving a life sentence in prison for a different crime. Bellamy, Rothstein's "number one fan," has killed the writer in the break-in and because of his anger at the author for the way he ended the final Jimmy Gold novel. The cache of priceless notebooks contains, among other things, two unpublished Gold novels that would complete a five-book series. Bellamy's real goal is to read and keep the unpublished manuscripts for himself, and he dreams of returning to them once he is paroled from prison.

Over the course of several years, Pete anonymously doles out the cash to his parents, who are suffering financial and marital problems because of the injuries Dad has suffered. Believing the money is coming from an anonymous charity, they never suspect their son is behind the windfall,

45. Finders Keepers   251

which arrives every month. But when the money runs out, Pete (who as a Rothstein fan himself discovered the value of the dead author's journals), decides he must sell the notebooks to help his family, who has come to depend on the money. Around this time, Bellamy is paroled from prison and returns to collect his buried treasure.

The trio of Bill Hodges, Holly Gibney, and Jerome Robinson, heroes of *Mr. Mercedes*, don't appear until page 157 when Jerome's sister (and Pete's sister's friend) realizes that Pete is in trouble and asks for help. Even then, they play a minor role as the metaphorical cavalry and come to the rescue at the very last minute.

Always the master of hooking a reader and building suspense, *Finders Keepers* opens with a very realistic home invasion scene where an aging but iconic author is beaten, tortured, and then brutally murdered, an especially horrible scene for anyone who enjoys books! The character of Morris Bellamy is created and developed, and like Anton Chekhov's archetypal gun that appears in scene one, the villain is allowed to ferment throughout much of the book as Pete is introduced, and the novel flips back and forth in time to introduce the City Center Massacre and its influence on the Saubers family and shifts point-of-view characters as Pete and Bellamy ride paths that are certain to converge. The more likable Pete becomes, the more unsavory Bellamy grows and the danger increases. The climax builds into inevitable violence.

The chapters that alternate between 1978 and the narrative present effectively develop the Saubers family backstory, making Pete's motivation to keep the money and the notebooks understandable, all the while maintaining suspense. This backstory allows readers unfamiliar with *Mr. Mercedes* to enjoy the novel and reminds readers familiar with the book about the events but from a different perspective. Since Hodges and his team are not introduced until page 157, the story is about a likable young man rather than a retired detective, which also increases the suspense because Pete is quite defenseless against the hardened killer who will confront him. Finally, when we reach the narrative present, the story tense subtly shifts from past to present tense to remind readers that the story is now unfolding in real time.

Archetypes

King's Bill Hodges trilogy, and all detective fiction, for that matter, is built on the mystery stories of Edgar Allan Poe, who invented the genre. In the case of *Finders Keepers*, Poe's story "The Gold Bug" was the first American "buried treasure" story. King has modernized the buried treasure in his novel from the typical pirate booty of *Treasure Island* (serialized in 1881–82) to the idea of a criminal concealing his plunder in a hole in the New England woods, but the concept remains the same. The difference here lies in the moral and ethical questions that Pete face when he discovers the money. It is a question readers would ask themselves—what would they do if they found such a treasure?

The novel also explores the thriller motif of putting loved ones in danger and having to save them. This is a common enough trope and forms the last section of the novel where Pete's sister is taken by Bellamy and held hostage as he demands that Pete turn over the notebooks. This plot device is used in scores of contemporary films, including the *Taken* movies starring Liam Neeson.

Finally, and perhaps most important, King rides the motif of creating psychotic killers that are shown both as victims and as monsters. Bellamy is the product of an unhappy childhood: an absent father and a coldhearted mother. Although this does not excuse his behavior, it does help to explain it, making him more than just a cardboard cutout villain.

Themes and Subtexts

While writing and other creative endeavors form a reoccurring theme in King's works, *Finders Keepers* examines authorship from a different perspective, that of the creative and legal rights of the author. As in *Misery*, Rothstein is at the mercy of his fans, who demand that he write stories the way they want them written and not according to the wishes of the author. In fact, Bellamy kills him because he believes he has "sold out" the character of Jimmy Gold, mainstreaming him into the mundane world rather than keeping up his persona as a radical and a rebel. Ironically, Rothstein's character returned to his nonconformist ways in the last two unpublished novels, which Bellamy never had the opportunity to read. Why Rothstein refused to publish these last two books and stipulated in his will that they be burned after his death is not clear. According to Pete, a young but astute critic of his works, they were the best novels in the series and their nonconformist statement would have been a powerful defense of Rothstein's own eccentric ways. But the author had his wish after all; the manuscripts perish in flames.

Finders Keepers also poses the question of the ownership of literary works. Legally, they belong to the author and, after his death, to the author's estate until the copyright expires and they become part of the public domain. Yet the reading public feels that it is a distinguished author's obligation to publish everything he or she has written. This theme appeared in *Lisey's Story* as scholars demanded that every scrap of Scott

Landon's writings be preserved for future scholars to examine. Landon willingly gave most of his works to a university library, and even though reluctant, his wife Lisey eventually donates whatever is left. In the case of Rothstein, however, the unpublished works are destined to be destroyed after his death.

One might wonder why Rothstein keeps the journals in the first place if he never intends to publish their contents. Deep down, he finds it impossible to destroy his work while he lives. In *Misery*, Annie Wilkes forces Paul Sheldon to burn the only copy of his new unpublished novel, an act that he finds unthinkable. And Rothstein himself lacks the courage to burn his writings while he is alive. To an author, a book is like a child and destroying it amounts to infanticide.

Rothstein is styled after the reclusive J.D. Salinger who, after publishing the highly successful and acclaimed *Catcher in the Rye* and *Nine Stories*, hid himself away in Cornish, New Hampshire, virtually disappearing from the literary world and publishing only a few scattered works until his death at the age of 91. According to Salinger's estate, his unpublished work will eventually be released. Perhaps Rothstein expected that his wishes would not be followed and that his remaining books would be published after his death. Otherwise, why not destroy them when he had the chance?

The theme of the economy and how it affects middle-class working families is carried over from *Mr. Mercedes* into the second novel of the series. Pete's family suffers from the financial crisis of the late 1970s in a very long-term way since his father is crippled by the Mercedes killer while standing in line at a job fair. The economics of this crisis has been blamed on greed, corruption, and fraud. King, never one to hide his politics, specifically faults the Republican Party for failing to control less-than-ethical bankers, junk bond traders, and Wall Street. In this case, the issue is personalized when the Sauberses find themselves in financial trouble because Tom has lost his job, through no fault of his own. This leads to a cascade of problems, including trouble in his marriage and to his being nearly killed in the City Center Massacre. The economic effects are shown as far-reaching and multilayered and leading to effects that would not have been imagined. Unemployment is depicted as not just a financial issue but a mental health challenge as well, leading to depression, anxiety, alcoholism, and even possible suicidal behavior.

Human Universals

Care for one's family is a human universal emotion and, according to Dawkins's "selfish gene" theory, represents an evolutionary benefit to specific genes in our DNA. According to this idea, natural selection occurs at the genome level rather than the organism level and accounts for human altruism beginning with kinfolk, or as the popular saying goes, "charity begins at home." In this respect, readers can empathize with Pete's behavior, first in keeping the money he has found for his needy family instead of turning it in to authorities and, second, for risking his own life to save his sister, who shares a large part of his genetic makeup. Even in the most horrible fairy tales of wicked stepmothers and stepsisters, true siblings are bonded in blood. And despite the idea of sibling rivalry, most siblings will defend each other against outsiders. It is only natural, then, that Pete puts his life on the line for his sister, especially since he believes himself to be the cause of her danger. His sister's predicament causes anxiety in the reader, who is rooting for Pete to save her.

The quest for justice is another human universal desire. People want bad behavior to be punished and punished severely. Although we may understand some of the motivation behind Bellamy's actions, his painful, brutal death is satisfying. As in so many of King's novels, evil is purged by fire.

Evaluation

For my taste, *Finders Keepers* is the weakest book in the Hodges trilogy because, for me at least, the trio of detectives isn't really necessary and arrive at the last minute in what English professors term a deus ex machina ending—the cavalry arrive just in the nick of time to save the day. For me, the plot would have been more interesting had Pete taken care of his problem without external help. Therefore, I'd rank this novel in the lower third of King's works, though it does pose some interesting questions about literary rights.

Interesting Fact

The character of John Rothstein is based on an amalgamation of three writers: John Updike (and his "rabbit novels"), Philip Roth, and the reclusive J.D. Salinger.

Notable Quote

"Even the greatest storms begin as gentle breezes."

46

End of Watch
To Be or Not to Be

Background

End of Watch, the third book in the Bill Hodges trilogy, was published in 2016 by Scribner. Whereas the first two books fell easily within the mystery genre, this novel returns to the supernatural horror genre that made King so famous. Reminiscent of *Carrie* and *The Dead Zone*, the novel explores psychic phenomenon, only this time practiced by an evil serial killer.

Summary and Narrative Devices

The Mercedes killer from the first book in the trilogy wakes up from his coma and develops telekinetic powers that enable him to make people kill themselves. In this novel, Bill Hodges and Holly Gibney, now proprietors of the "Finders Keepers" detective agency, become involved in the case of learning Hartsfield's secret and stopping him before he can initiate a mass suicide event through a video game that has been altered and distributed to teenage girls in the city. To complicate the plot, Bill Hodges is diagnosed with cancer and must begin treatment immediately.

Like the two previous books in the Hodges series, *End of Watch* opens with a flashback to the Mercedes massacre, with the story told this time by two first responders driving an ambulance. This not only gives a new perspective on the tragedy and introduces another victim, a woman who becomes a paraplegic as a result of the terrorist act, but also the backstory allows readers not familiar with the first two books to enjoy this novel as a stand-alone story.

The novel also begins with Hodges in the doctor's office and some hints that all is not well with his health. Although readers expect the worst, the truth isn't revealed until Hodges becomes involved in the mysterious suicides, and then once his cancer diagnosis is revealed, a countdown is initiated. Holly gives him three days to solve the mystery and then he agrees to sign himself up for treatments that will prevent him from working on the case. As the novel progresses, the stakes are raised, and by the end of the novel, thousands of lives are at risk. Because of this technique, the novel maintains a brisk pace and the consequences become more compelling.

The title *End of Watch* is itself a foreshadowing device; the expression is used to signal a police officer's retirement, his last "watch," so to speak, or his death. Since Hodges is already retired and is diagnosed with terminal cancer, this title signals the latter. It is only fitting that the expression is engraved on his headstone at the story's conclusion.

Archetypes

End of Watch is a zombie story in disguise and actually references the Haitian zombie myths as told by William Seabrook in his nonfiction travel story *The Magic Island* (1929), where plantation owners used powerful drugs to create a workforce of "walking dead" to harvest their crops and work as slave labor. This idea was continued in the film *The White Zombie* (1932), where a sorcerer turned people into zombies to exploit them, including the female star whom he tried to turn into a sex slave. The idea of flesh-eating zombies came much later with George Romero's *Night of the Living Dead*.

End of Watch also builds on the idea King first used in *The Dead Zone*, which has a character developing psychic powers while in an extended coma. Johnny Smith used his powers for good; Brady Hartsfield turned his toward the dark side. In the King universe, the comatose mind develops extraordinary powers.

Themes and Subtexts

The obvious theme of teen suicide runs throughout this novel. Since suicide is such a troubling issue in our society, King addresses it in a very realistic but compassionate manner, making sure that readers understand that taking one's own life is not the answer to life's problems. *Mr. Mercedes*, the first book in the trilogy, finds Hodges contemplating suicide. However, the detective finds new meaning in his life and saves thousands of innocent lives through his actions. By the time we reach *End of Watch*,

46. End of Watch 257

Hodges has a terminal illness, but he never considers suicide even when he knows his treatment will be painful and probably not work. On the contrary, he shows a love for life and treasures the little things, special moments, and friendships. Hodges clings to life for as long as he can.

In contrast, several characters are shown to be suicidal, especially after Hartsfield infects their brains with his pink fish video game. Characters like Barbara Robinson, who have everything to live for, are driven to the brink of suicide. Once she is rid of Hartsfield's trance, Barbara realizes what a terrible mistake she almost made.

Hartsfield can infiltrate characters' minds and prey on their very human weaknesses. Virtually every human being on the planet has, at one time or another, been plagued by depression, a sense of unworthiness, and a feeling of not being wanted. For most people, this feeling is temporary, and they recover. Unfortunately, far too many give in to this terrible feeling, which can be especially strong in young people whose frontal cortexes, which regulate decision-making and are the last part of the brain to mature, haven't quite caught up with their emotions. This accounts for the high incidence of suicides among young people. *End of Watch* serves as a warning to readers about how dangerous this can be. In both the text of the novel and in the author's note at the end of the book, King shares the suicide hotline phone number as a public service to anyone reading the novel who might be considering harming themselves. The theme of suicide is a real horror in our world, and addressing it in a realistic but fictional way may help to bring understanding to the issue and may, in fact, save lives.

The addiction theme, so common in King's work, appears in this novel in a slightly different form, the addiction to electronics and video games. *Cell* explored the concept of mobile phones turning people into zombies. *End of Watch* expands this idea into video games. The letter Z, used throughout the novel, is a reminder of the zombielike state that the Zappit video game induces. Researchers have shown that video games can cause a hypnotic effect in players, which sometimes lasts even after the game is turned off. This phenomenon, called "the Tetris effect" by psychologists, lingers in the mind of players both in the real world and in their dreams. The fears that some parents may have about video games are reflected in *End of Watch*, where the electronic device exacts the ultimate price by luring young people into committing suicide. The book is a cautionary tale about how electronics can influence people and may even be developed to the point where they can control people's minds. The concept may be science fiction today but presents a plausible reality in the future.

Finally, King addresses the mental illness theme once again, not just in the exploration of suicidal behavior but as it relates to people like

Holly Gibney who register on the Autism spectrum. In the first book of the trilogy, Holly is introduced as a misfit who can't fit in with society. Her mother treats her as a helpless child, even though she is a woman. Hodges sees something in her from the beginning, though, and in each of the three books she becomes more independent and competent until by *End of Watch*, she is quite functional in almost every situation. The novel serves as a reminder of the value of people who may be different. Holly is a genius in some areas, as her insight proves to be most valuable, and she is very heroic, putting her life on the line for others on many occasions. This theme of valuing those who might seem weak occurs throughout the King canon (most notably perhaps in *The Stand*) and tells a poignant truth about the risks of dismissing those who may seem to be different in some way. Holly has become such an interesting character to King that he uses her again in *The Outsider*, *If It Bleeds*, and *Holly* (2023).

Human Universals

End of Watch references several human universal emotions. First, there is the human universal need for survival at any cost. This can be evidenced in Brady Hartsfield's struggle to stay alive and regain a sense of being no matter what. Humans are, as far as we know, the only species where individuals can realize that they are mortal and will die. The base instinct to preserve life at any cost is turned around when Hartsfield coaxes people into taking their lives. This goes against our natural impulses, yet evolutionary psychologists predict that suicide will exist in the population. According to evolutionary psychiatrist C.A. Soper, humans are the only creature capable of committing suicide. This leaves the possibility that this latent trait could be manipulated by a powerful force like Hartsfield and his video game.

Hartsfield's video game hijacks the human emotion of playfulness to do its nefarious work. All mammals engage in play, most likely as a way of practicing for real-life events. Thus, dogs and cats chase toys (imaginary prey), birds may gather and play with shiny things (nest building), and even pet mice will run on wheels. Humans, however, have taken play to the next level with the invention of toys, games, and elaborate electronic devices. Americans spend fortunes on toys and games, and as the saying goes, "the only difference between the toys of an adult and those of a child is how much they cost." We are attracted to things that amuse us—that is how we evolved. Those ancestors who could practice their hunting skills with contests and games became better hunters and outsurvived those who didn't. This might explain why sports such as archery, javelin

46. *End of Watch* 259

throwing, and running are Olympic sports even today. And it explains why video games involving hunting and shooting are bestsellers. The Zappit latches on to this idea with its fishing hole game, which entrances players to the point of being susceptible to mind control.

The idea of altruism is also present in *End of Watch*. Hodges, Holly, and Jerome are all willing to put themselves in harm's way to save each other and to protect innocent lives. Altruism toward family and friends is elicited by the affective emotion of caring; saving a loved one from danger or death is one of the most common plotlines in all of fiction. Saving innocent lives from evil is equally as common in literature. Heroes who put themselves at risk for others are honored in every culture. Readers enjoy being able to be a part of this emotion vicariously through the characters in narratives.

Evaluation

End of Watch is my favorite of the Hodges novels, probably because it melds the genres of horror and suspense together. The clever turn of the zombie theme with video games exerting mind control over teenagers speaks to the modern problem of artificial intelligence and social media. The theme of terminal illness appears again as well and adds to the book's meaning. Finally, Holly Gibney's character is developed further, preparing her for her role as the lead character in later King stories. I'd rank *End of Watch* in the top third.

Interesting Fact

End of Watch was originally titled *The Suicide Prince*.

Notable Quote

"Everyone casts a shadow."

47

The Outsider
The Doppelgänger Effect

Background

The Outsider, published in 2018 by Scribner, combines the mystery and horror genres and was adapted into a 10-episode miniseries on HBO in 2020. An excerpt of the novel was released in *Entertainment Weekly* on May 25, 2018. This story features the reappearance of Holly Gibney.

Summary and Narrative Devices

The Outsider is a mystery novel with a supernatural twist based on the legend of El Cuco, the shapeshifting monster that preys on children. The novel opens with a horrendous brutalization and murder of a boy, and all evidence points to Terry Maitland, a local high school English teacher and beloved Little League coach, who is publicly arrested, humiliated, and charged with the crime. However, conflicting evidence places him at a teachers' conference hours away from the crime and with an undeniable alibi. The conclusion, that he was at two places at the same time, makes no sense and yet is the only explanation.

Maitland is killed at his indictment, leaving his attorney and Ralph Anderson, the guilt-ridden police detective who had him arrested, to clear his name. They call in Holly Gibney, who now runs the "Finders Keepers" detective agency to help. Piecing the evidence together, she discovers that the murder (and others) was committed by an "outsider," a shapeshifting predator that feeds on children to stay alive. Holly and the others verify the theory and hunt the outsider down and destroy it.

The opening section of the novel combines the narrative of the arrest of Terry Maitland with transcripts of interviews done with witnesses who place him at or near the crime scene. This device, reminiscent of the patchwork of narrative and "evidence" presented in *Carrie*, gives the novel a level of verisimilitude similar to true crime stories. It also sets up the ironclad case against Maitland, convincing the reader of his guilt until the conflicting evidence begins to appear. In fact, we aren't even immediately introduced to Maitland but see him only through this evidence and through the eyes of others, which also makes it easy to believe in his guilt. This lays the groundwork for the justice theme that pervades the book—innocent until proven guilty, in theory, but in practice, the law, the media, and the public jump to immediate conclusions.

The first-person interviews heighten suspense in their own way, as each witness seems to take forever to get to the point. They digress, go off on tangents, and engage in irrelevant small talk, all the while complaining that they are pressed for time and have things to do. The irony is humorous yet rather faithful to the way that people tell stories, dragging them out for effect and to maintain control of the dialogue.

Although Maitland appears to be one of the central characters in the story, he is killed rather early, turning the story over to Ralph as the main character. Since Ralph was originally presented as the "enemy" in the story, opting to have Maitland arrested, and then doing just about everything wrong, the entire perspective of the novel changes, just as Ralph's perspectives and beliefs must do a complete turnaround. Holly Gibney, the ongoing heroine of King's recent crime fiction, doesn't even enter the narrative until the halfway point of the novel. Her role is to unearth the supernatural elements of the crime (she can believe in such things after her experiences in *End of Watch*) and then convince the others, especially the pragmatic Ralph, of the truth so they can destroy it. The district attorney, Maitland's attorney, and the other characters who join the quest are expendable, the "red shirts" of *Star Trek* fame who probably won't survive very long once the real action begins.

The novel contains the usual assortment of foreshadowing. King judiciously places a rattlesnake in a sniper's nest, and the snake does reappear at a very opportune time, for example. Other clues are also planted, leading to the discovery of the supernatural elements of the story. The reader is one step ahead of the investigators, of course, having been conditioned to believe the impossible can occur in a Stephen King novel.

Archetypes

The Outsider is an obvious hero's quest tale, with Ralph as the disbeliever/reluctant hero who is enlightened to the truth and destroys the evil being. It is the classic three-part horror tale: "(1) something weird is going on here, (2) we think we know what it might be, and (3) it's a shapeshifter, let's kill it." Although this trope is common to so many horror films and stories, it remains effective and entertaining in the hands of a master like King, who creates interesting characters and realistic details.

The evil twin motif is also a relatively common subject for horror, one that King used in *The Dark Half*, where his own doppelgänger tried to take over his body. The novel is also similar to Harlan Ellison's short story "Shatterday," where the protagonist spawned a double who slowly took over his life. The original doppelgänger story is Edgar Allan Poe's "William Wilson," which King refers to in *The Outsider*.

Themes and Subtexts

King explores the concept of the "outsider" as a source of fear in several of his novels, including *It*, *The Dark Half*, *Bag of Bones*, and *The Regulators*, among others. From the earliest childhood terror of the boogeyman, humans are conditioned to fear that which doesn't belong and can't be explained. Once a ghost, vampire, werewolf, or other supernatural horror is identified, it can be named, understood, and destroyed. But nameless things hold a special kind of terror and metaphorically make the blood run cold. Serial killers, whose psychology is beyond the comprehension of normal people, are particularly feared. Coupling this with an unknown supernatural being accelerates the terror.

On a more practical level, *The Outsider* exploits our terror of identity theft, a very real concern in our society that can destroy people's lives in many ways. Not only can this crime ruin someone's finances, but thieves have used stolen identities to even steal people's homes by taking over property deeds. Untangling oneself from such a crime is complicated at best, and the justified fear of someone hijacking our persona is evidence in the lucrative business of identity theft protection companies. The thought of someone committing a horrendous and disgusting crime, such as raping and murdering a child, brings this fear to new levels, forcing readers to put themselves in the shoes of Terry Maitland, a truly good person who is systematically destroyed by an evil entity that steals his self. The novel paints this scenario in a realistic and concrete way that engages the imagination of readers who would never think about committing violent crimes.

King claims that *The Outsider* is about seeing only the ugly side of life and how this can be especially true in small towns where gossip and rumor sometimes rule. But the theme is more universal and applies to the way society sees justice as a whole. Although the United States Constitution is grounded on the premise of innocence until proven guilty, this concept is seldom followed outside of the strict confines of the court system (and often, not even there). The media, in particular, seems obsessed with taking sides in criminal cases, especially high-profile ones, offering opinions and judgments and releasing evidence and hearsay that prejudice the public and potential jurors, often judging the defendant guilty before the trial even begins. Trials seem to be treated like sporting events, with commentators and pundits weighing in on every aspect of the case. In the small town of Flint City, Oklahoma, the assumed guilt scenario is played out at every level. First, Ralph Anderson, who knows Terry personally, assumes his guilt without bothering to check all the facts, including the whereabouts of the suspect when the crime occurred. The district attorney, anxious to close the case and get a win, pushes forward as well, and Terry is arrested in a very public setting that ensures he will be seen as guilty. Even when new evidence is brought to bear on the case, the law refuses to acknowledge it and goes so far as to make Terry's arraignment a public spectacle, where his safety is compromised and he is killed by the dead boy's brother, who is convinced of his guilt. The media has, of course, run with the story and has surrounded Terry's home, harassed his wife and children, and incited public hatred toward the man who is supposedly presumed innocent. This fictional account reflects real life and is played out on network news, Court TV, and on the internet.

Human Universals

Humans are one of the few species on earth that have a sense of the core SELF, a concept that continues to perplex neuroscientists. Whereas recent studies have shown that rats and other invertebrates may have a primitive sense of self, according to Thomas Hill, one of the lead researchers, this sense "falls far short of the kind of self-awareness commonly attributed to humans." People have a very clear idea of their own identity, their self, even their "soul," if you will, and much of human motivation seems to be geared toward enhancing our self-image and the way others see us. To have this "self" stolen by an outsider grates at the core of our being. This is, perhaps, the underlying fear behind zombie narratives, that we will be taken over and used by an outside force. In *The Outsider*, victims are not literally taken over, but their self is stolen and used by the outsider for its own evil purposes, then discarded, leaving the original victim to face the consequences of the outsider's actions. This form of horror touches the human universal sense of self and self-awareness, forcing the reader to empathize with the characters whose selves have been hijacked.

The human universal desire for justice is also explored in this novel.

In defense of the law enforcement offices of Flint City, there is a universal need to find wrongdoers and punish them quickly and, when the crime warrants harsh measures, severely. Justice reinforces the human desire to feel safe from law breakers and to send a clear message to those who would commit crimes. In the case of crimes against children, outrage is heightened and the desire for vengeance is triggered. This explains the rage felt against Maitland and the vengeance enacted on him at his arraignment. The reader, who now strongly suspects his innocence, understands the violence of the crowd, which is not privy to all of the inside information that has been revealed in the story. If readers thought that Maitland had committed the crime he was accused of, they would have felt great satisfaction in his death. However, knowing that the real killer is still at large activates the desire for justice and that the remainder of the novel seeks to satisfy.

Finally, the novel triggers the human universal emotion of grief, especially at the death of a child. King has explored this emotion in multiple novels, such as *Cujo* and *Pet Sematary*. In this story, it explains the behavior of the Peterson family; the mother dies from a heart attack brought on by stress and grief, the father commits suicide, and the brother who murders Terry is killed by police in the encounter. Readers can empathize with the tragedy this family has suffered and understand the consequences.

Evaluation

King uses the horror motif to explore some interesting social issues in *The Outsider*, especially problems with the justice system. For me, though, the book is too long for what it is and too reminiscent of *Desperation* in its ending. Even though it has its good moments, I'd rank this novel in the middle of the King canon.

Interesting Fact

After the novel was published, it took just 20 days for the rights to *The Outsider* to be acquired and for a TV show to move into development.

Notable Quote

"Reality is thin ice, but most people skate on it their entire lives and never fall through until the very end."

48

Elevation

King's Feel-Good Book

Background

Elevation is a 146-page novella that was published by Scribner in 2018 as a stand-alone book. The novel has been described as a "feel-good" book, perhaps a gift to America that the country desperately needed in 2018 (and may still need). Although it won the Goodreads award for best horror novel, it is not a horror novel in the traditional sense—more of a fantasy, as in a holiday story to lift people's spirits. The novel is set in the infamous town of Castle Rock, yet this Castle Rock, despite its prejudices, is a milder version of the place of horrors that appears in other novels.

Summary and Narrative Devices

Scott Carey, the protagonist of the story, has a problem; he is consistently losing weight, only he, impossibly, isn't losing mass, and the trend continues until he is essentially weightless even though he inhabits a body that still has a mass of 240 pounds. The phenomenon is not explained. Indeed, King makes no attempt to explain it, either through science or the supernatural. Carey doesn't suffer from any illness. He isn't the victim of a curse or a poison or a magic spell. He simply loses weight at an accelerating rate.

As a parallel plot element, Carey also has an issue with his neighbors, a lesbian couple, Deirdre and Missy, whose dogs have been defecating in his yard. When he confronts them, Deirdre accuses him of targeting them because of their same-sex marriage, which Carey vehemently denies. Yet when he takes time to think about it, he realizes that he hasn't taken time to meet them or eat at the new restaurant they have opened and that the town of Castle Rock is openly hostile to them because of their lifestyle.

Even as he realizes that his weight loss will kill him, he tries to make amends and befriend the couple. Deirdre resists, however, until Carey enters a 12K charity race and in the home stretch helps her to her feet when she falls, enabling her to win the race. The photo goes viral, and the couple are accepted by the town, their restaurant thrives, and bigotry seems to have been defeated, at least in one small rural town.

Shortly afterward, he confesses his secret, his "elevation," as he calls it, to the couple. Knowing that he will no longer be able to live a normal life once he becomes completely weightless, he enlists his friends to help him die a good death and float away to the stars in the end. The novel is bittersweet and, despite its tragic end, an uplifting story (pardon the pun).

Elevation is a countdown story, similar to *Thinner* and *The Running Man*, where we begin with a number, in this case the protagonist's weight, and count down until zero, when all of his weight will be gone. The suspense comes in wondering exactly what will happen once the weightless stage is reached. The obvious conclusion is that it will kill him in some way, but the manner of his death remains to be seen until the end of the novel.

Archetypes

This work is reminiscent of *The Karman Line*, a 2015 short film (24 minutes) about a mother who begins to rise from the ground at a slow rate and the story of how her family deals with the certainty of losing her as the strange illness accelerates with time, lifting her higher and higher as the days go by until she is floating high in the atmosphere, bundled up in warm clothing and wearing an oxygen mask while her loved ones communicate with her with a cell phone.

Themes and Subtexts

Elevation is Stephen King's effort to explore the biases and intolerance directed at same-sex marriage by conservative members of the population. Since King's daughter Naomi identifies as a lesbian, this issue has special importance to him. This theme is made obvious not by Scott's bias toward the lesbian couple (he claims to have none, and his denial is believable) but in his lack of awareness about the feelings of the rest of Castle Rock which, with just a few exceptions, harbor negative feelings about Deirdre and Missy. Scott's enlightenment comes when he begins to pay attention to the mindset of the town, overhearing comments and noticing discrimination toward the women and their restaurant. This message is perhaps the most poignant one of the novel—that a lack of awareness only empowers prejudice.

Many readers, including this English professor, found the book too didactic, with the political message interfering with the plot. Yes, even though we should all embrace diversity, tolerance, and civil and social rights for the LGBTQ+ community, *Elevation*, in my opinion, simplified the issue too much. The acceptance of the same-sex couple by the town came too easily, and the characters were too predictable. The novel preaches directly to the choir, so to speak, who, for the most part, already believe in equality. Regretfully, this little book, charming and uplifting as it might be, is unlikely to change any closed minds who show intolerance toward anything but a traditional definition of marriage. Of course, the ultraconservative are unlikely to read Stephen King's books anyway.

The term "elevation" serves as a symbol for dying, especially for terminal illness. Once Scott realizes that his lifespan is being quickly counted down, he experiences an "elevation," both physical and mental. Terminally ill patients routinely report a sense of well-being once they have accepted their own imminent death. *Tuesdays with Morrie* by Mitch Albom, for example, recounts the author's visits with his terminally ill sociology professor (Morrie) and the insights into life that the professor shared with him after accepting his fate. Among other things, Morrie expressed a new appreciation for the small things in life, his ability to live in and enjoy the moment, and to feel more love and compassion for others. Scott Carey finds himself experiencing these same traits and paradoxically is happier than he has ever been. This "elevation" allows him to be more understanding, to help to spread more love and joy, and to see the good aspects of life rather than the bad. Although it's difficult to know for sure, King himself may have experienced an elevated sense of the beauty of life after his near-fatal accident.

Human Universals

Human beings naturally form social groups; this trait allowed ancient peoples to work together to survive by bringing down large prey, pooling resources, and diversifying the gene pool through marriage. According to evolutionary psychology, cooperative groups will outperform noncooperative groups in the long run, and successful groups will insulate themselves by forming in-groups and out-groups. The regretful by-product of this trait is a bias against those who are not like us and are not part of our in-group. This results in racism, wars, and even genocide.

The natives of Castle Rock form an in-group, and those in the LGBTQ+ community are members of an out-group. Although this doesn't justify bad behavior, it does explain it. People are very slow to include outsiders in their group. Civilization has eliminated some of the relics of human evolution, which were a valuable adaptation in the distant past, but unfortunately, many of these vestigial characteristics remain. We still desire belonging to an exclusive group; hence, terrorist organizations and criminal gangs still flourish. We also exclude those considered to be "different" from our in-groups. This human universal trait is the subject of *Elevation*, as is the hope that groups might expand their parameters and be more inclusive without the necessity of rules and laws that force them to do so.

Evaluation

Although I may agree with King's sentiments regarding inclusion and acceptance of the LGBTQ+ community (and of all people, for that matter), I think *Elevation* is too political and too didactic to be successful as fiction, so I'd rank it near the bottom of his list. Everyone is entitled to express political opinions and ideas, but they can weaken a good story. King, regrettably, has allowed his politics to creep more deeply into his later works at the expense of the story itself. And since he is, for the most part, preaching to the choir, his political opinions aren't really reaching the book banners, the intolerant, and the conservative crowd anyway. *Elevation* is successful as a "feel-good" book—and is perhaps exactly what we needed during the Covid-19 pandemic—but as lasting literature, it falls short.

Notable Quote

"Perhaps in their time of dying, everyone rises."

49

The Institute
Suffer the Children

Background

The Institute was published in 2019 by Scribner. The book has been optioned for a limited television miniseries but has not been produced at the time of this writing. According to an interview in the *New York Times*, King originally had the idea for the story back in the 1990s and envisioned it as a school with kids who had supernatural powers.

Summary and Narrative Devices

The novel begins by following the character of Tim Jamieson, an unemployed police officer who settles in a small town in South Carolina. After a few chapters of establishing his character, the book picks up the story of 12-year-old Luke Ellis, a genius child who is kidnapped because he has demonstrated telekinetic powers. He is taken to The Institute, a secret facility in the Maine woods where psychic children from all over America have been brought against their will. Those who run The Institute subject the children to torture and unethical experiments to evaluate and develop their talents. Once they pass an initial period, they are sent into a back area where they are put to work assassinating people whom The Institute sees as dangerous to the world. Their minds are used up in this process, and they are sent into another area where they become, essentially, a hive mind and die a miserable death.

Luke manages to escape his prison with the help of his friends and one terminally ill employee of The Institute whose conscience makes her do the right thing. Purely by chance, Luke winds up running into Jamieson in South Carolina, and Jamieson returns with him to destroy The Institute.

King's use of the omniscient point of view allows him to jump back and forth between characters in this novel, moving effortlessly from South Carolina to Maine, especially in the later chapters when multiple crises are occurring in both places at the same time. This builds suspense as he shifts from one emergency to another, from the shootout with Tim and the goons from The Institute to the kids in Maine taking control of things and preparing for an attack of poison gas.

One of King's most interesting uses of foreshadowing occurs early in the novel when Sherriff John asks Jamieson to consider a job with the police department once one of his officers retires. "He did. And he was still thinking of it when all hell broke loose on a hot night later that summer," the text reads. That "hot night" doesn't occur for nearly 400 pages, but King has planted the seed of suspense as we leave the character of Tim behind and enter Luke's story in the next chapter. Tim is essentially written out of the story until he and Luke meet up on page 350, a meeting that seems purely random but could just as easily be considered as fate.

Archetypes

The Institute is reminiscent of King's *Firestarter*, the story of a child who can start fires with her mind and what might have happened to her had she not escaped the clutches of "The Shop." Whereas The Shop is a symbolic rendition of the CIA and other government agencies, the secret organization of The Institute is a worldwide agency, and even though its motive might be good (saving the world), its methods are barbaric and immoral.

The novel was partially inspired by *Tom Brown's School Days*, written in 1857 by Thomas Hughes, where the main character is bullied. This book influenced the British school novels genre in the 19th century and, with its cricket and rugby matches, has parallels with the Harry Potter series. King adapted the boarding school concept to that of a school run by what he calls "privately funded zealots."

Themes and Subtexts

The issue of missing and exploited children is obvious in *The Institute*. Although King is not seriously blaming governments or organizations for this problem, the novel does call attention to the fact that children do go missing and are never found. This fact is referenced in the epigraph at the beginning of the novel, which cites statistics from the National Center for Missing & Exploited Children that approximately 800,000 children go missing each year and thousands are never found. Some are probably victims of human trafficking and others are victims of pedophiles.

Utilitarianism, the philosophy of sacrificing the few for the good of the many, runs through this novel as well. This idea, popularized by John Stuart Mill in the 1860s, hinges on the concept that moral actions should bring the greatest amount of happiness to the greatest numbers and the least amount of pain to the fewest. The Institute uses this concept to justify torturing a few children to bring about the safety and well-being of the many. And although this idea of the welfare of the many may have its merits, King points out the horrors of such a philosophy if taken to the extreme. To further complicate matters, it is unclear whether the methods developed at The Institute actually work. True, the world has not been destroyed, but there is no real evidence to show that the enslaved children had anything to do with preventing the apocalypse or whether the wrinkles of time would have worked things out anyway. However, the novel does raise the question of what lengths we would be willing to go to if the destruction of the world were at stake.

Another theme King explores in this novel is the contrast between fate and randomness, predetermination versus chaos theory, if you will. The various facets of this duplicity were examined in *Insomnia*, which proposes that both forces are somehow at work. In this case, however, The Institute believes it can foresee the course of future events and manipulate them directly. *11/22/63* considered the difficulty of changing events in the past and speculated on a multiverse where all options occurred. *The Institute* projects this notion into the future; presumably, a new future is created by changing events in the present, which would result in a different multiverse because of these changes. Once again, the novel only suggests this possibility, while the argument still holds that the assassinations that were committed by The Institute had no effect on the future and were either irrelevant or predetermined themselves. Whether there are hinges or pivot points on which the door of human extinction may turn remains an open question for readers to ponder.

Human Universals

As "Smith," the representative of The Institute, tells Tim toward the end of the novel, "primitive human emotions hold sway over rational thought." This idea is one of the tenets of evolutionary psychology and explains many things about human behavior, such as why we crave sugar and fats, why men favor youthful, attractive women and women prefer successful men, and why violence still exists in the world. *The Institute* does look at the dark side of human behavior and how, given enough power, humans can become sadistic and cruel. The famous Stanford prison experiment conducted by Philip Zimbardo in 1971 documents this concept clearly in a clinical setting. In this experiment, college student volunteers were randomly divided into two groups, prisoners and guards, and left to run the experimental prison on their own. Although both groups came from the same pool of volunteers and those assigned the prisoner role committed no crimes, it didn't take long before the "guards" began showing aggressive and abusive behavior and the prisoners began to experience emotional issues and anxiety.

Another experiment conducted by Stanley Milgram at Yale studied the amount of punishment a volunteer would inflict on another person if ordered to do so by an authority figure. In this case, volunteers were assigned the role of "teacher" and told to administer an electric shock to a "learner" (an accomplice in the experiment) whenever he made a mistake. The voltage was increased from a slight shock to a dangerous severe shock (though, in actuality, no shock was given, and the confederate faked a reaction). All the "teachers" were willing to administer 300 volts, and 65 percent of the volunteers administered the full 450 volts when ordered to do so by the researcher. The results showed that the average person will exhibit sadistic behavior when ordered to do so, which helps to explain inhuman behavior in prisons ranging from Auschwitz to Abu Ghraib. And this, of course, is exactly what happens at The Institute.

While "Smith" tried to justify the existence of The Institute based on the premise that "primitive human emotions hold sway over rational thought," the methods that the organization used harnessed these primitive emotions, which resulted in the torture and murder of innocent children. Reminiscent of Nazi Germany, those with power had no remorse about their actions, and most even relished in the torture of the kids. It wasn't rational thought that guided them—the belief that the project was for the greater good was not part of their day-to-day behavior—but their lust for power over the weak controlled their actions. In the end, they might believe they were following orders, but the enthusiasm they showed in administering punishment went above and beyond the call of duty. All sense of compassion was lost at The Institute, and the employees reverted to the state of savage animals, not rational beings.

Evaluation

With its interplay of plots involving Luke and Tim, *The Institute* makes for an exciting read. As a literary novel, I'd place the book high in the rankings, with its complex themes of destiny and chaos. The exploration of ethical questions is also compelling in this work, making the reader think deeply about the lengths that should be taken to keep the world safe. *The Institute* is a favorite of mine, and I especially enjoy its realistic characterization of children.

Interesting Fact

King originally planned to use "The Shop" as the organization that ran The Institute but decided on a privately run institution instead.

Notable Quote

"Great events turn on small hinges."

50

Later

I See Dead People

Background

Later was published in March 2012 as a paperback original by Hard Case Crime, which also published *Joyland* and *The Colorado Kid*. This novel is a cross-genre book, a mystery and a horror story combined into one.

Summary and Narrative Devices

Later is a first-person narrative featuring Jamie Conklin, a boy who can see and talk to dead people. The dead are only visible for several days after they perish, then they disappear and they must truthfully answer any questions Jamie asks them. The novel is told from the point of view of Jamie at 22 years old as he looks back over the events of his life, beginning when he was six years old and saw a dead man who had been run over by a taxi. The event upset him badly but convinced his mother that he did have a special ability, one that he must keep a secret. The ability is useful, as he helps his neighbor find his dead wife's lost wedding rings, but the boy soon finds that it is a curse.

His mother, a literary agent, finds herself in financial trouble when her top client, a best-selling author, dies unexpectedly after receiving a hefty advance but with his book unfinished. She enlists Jamie to talk to the dead author, who dictates the remainder of the novel's plot, which Jamie's mother is able to finish, thereby solving their financial worries. Later, his mother's lover, Liz, a police detective, recruits him to find a bomb that a serial killer had hidden in a busy grocery market before shooting himself in the head. The serial bomber reluctantly tells Jamie the secret but, while doing so, is infected by a demonic entity that refuses to go away and haunts Jamie for some time. With the help of his neighbor, a retired professor whom he'd helped find his wife's jewelry, Jamie learns how to neutralize the demon and, in fact, put him at his command should he choose to summon him. At the novel's conclusion, Liz, now disgraced after she'd been caught peddling drugs, kidnaps Jamie and forces him to interrogate a drug warlord whom she had killed in order to locate what she thinks is a huge stash of drugs. Jamie summons the demon, which kills Liz; he then banishes the entity for good.

The novel crosses genres from a mystery to a horror novel; in fact, the protagonist says several times that it is "a horror story." It delves into the ghost story, as Jamie speaks to the dead, but moves beyond the realm of harmless spirits and into the domain of a serial killer and a malevolent demon that possesses the killer once he is dead. The suspense is also enhanced by the threat of Liz, who murders two men, one in cold blood while Jamie watches, and who has become unhinged due to her drug addiction. This leads to the real danger that Jamie could be killed by his mother's ex-lover, who fears him as a witness to her crimes.

Like many of King's first-person narrators, Jamie addresses the reader directly on more than one occasion. The protagonist has an attitude, which he displays when he tells the reader, "If you don't [understand], you're an idiot," and when he essentially tells the reader that he doesn't really care how he is viewed. Jamie also addressed the fact that his narrative is written and that he is not merely the protagonist but the author. This textual code, or metafiction, addresses the idea of writing about writing, especially when Jamie remarks that his writing "got better as I went along." Jamie has proven to be well-read, excelling in literature and having grown up in a literary environment with books well above his grade level.

King employs the usual foreshadowing and flashback devices, beginning the book with a prologue of sorts that announces that the story has been written down by the narrator and that it occurred in the past. Foreshadowing occurs often as well, as, for example, when Jamie says that the next time he will see the professor, he will be dead. These devices quicken the pace of the story and build suspense.

Archetypes

One of the more popular stories involving characters that speak to the dead is Brian Lumley's *Necroscope* series, now consisting of 18 books, the first of which was published in 1986 and the last in 2013. In this series, Harry Keogh can speak with the dead, and since he treats them as equals, the "teaming masses" befriend him, assisting him and granting him secrets, such as the ability to teleport using a Möbius Continuum, an ability he learned from a dead mathematician. Keogh used his abilities to combat an alien race of vampires and to solve mysteries and engage in espionage.

The fictional concept of communicating with the dead was popularized in the 1999 film *The Sixth Sense*, which contained the iconic line "I see dead people." The film, which also featured a child protagonist, is referenced in *Later*.

The novel is a classic example of a bildungsroman, a coming-of-age novel where the protagonist grows from a boy to a man. Jamie is traumatized the first time he sees a dead person, the bicyclist who was hit by a vehicle. The scene would be unnerving to anyone since the man's death was violent and bloody, and Jamie, just six years old at the time, acts as would be expected, becoming violently ill and experiencing terror. As time goes on, however, he adjusts to the sight of the dead, and if they haven't been disfigured or maimed, he isn't rattled by them at all. He holds a conversation with the dead professor's wife, even becoming irritated that she insults his drawing. Although unnerved by the situation, he can speak with Mr. Thomas, his mother's best-selling client, and is able to convey the plot of the last Roanoke novel in detail to his mother so she can complete the manuscript. The meeting with Therriault, the serial bomber, is more difficult, but even here, Jamie gets used to the horrible sight. And once he is stalked by the demon inhabiting Therriault's dead body, he gets used to this as well, even to the point of being able to engage in a physical battle with the entity and defeat it. This gives him the confidence he needs to survive later when he is kidnapped. Seeing the shocking side of life and death has forced Jamie to grow up much faster than a normal child would.

Jamie not only grows in terms of his confidence and his comfort with his supernatural ability, but he also matures as a person. Among other things, he learns to distinguish truth from lies. As he says, "I know more now, but I believe less." He has learned that people lie and that not everyone is good, lessons taught by Therriault and, perhaps even more so, by Liz, who showed that even those claiming to enforce the law can be corrupt.

Themes and Subtexts

Truth and falsehood form a major theme of *Later*. Jamie's first encounter with truth occurs when he discovers that he can see the dead, and they can see him. This is an obvious truth to him, yet he knows that others will not easily accept it. He convinces his grudging mother that he has this ability, but even she is unwilling to address it and, instead,

50. *Later* 277

discourages him from talking about it. She hopes that by avoiding the subject, this uncomfortable truth will simply go away once and for all. Jamie obliges, keeping his ability a secret from everyone and pretending it doesn't exist. He does feel betrayed when his mother shares this secret with Liz, who also doesn't believe him until he has proven it directly by relating the details to the final Roanoke novel directly from the words of its dead author. Professor Burkett is also skeptical, and Jamie is never fully convinced that the old man believes him, even after he has disclosed overwhelming evidence. His power is a secret that he must maintain at all costs, especially after he finds out how it can be used against him by Liz and others who might profit from it.

One interesting sidenote is that Jamie does write down his story in a manuscript that is preserved as the novel itself. This demonstrates how difficult secrets are to keep. "Forbidden knowledge" seems to never be kept hidden but usually finds a way out in a horror novel. Narrators, from those of Poe and Lovecraft to those of Stephen King, have an almost pathological desire to spill everything, knowing full well that doing so is a bad idea. Poe's killers confess to crimes they might have gotten away with; Lovecraft's narrators refuse to burn ancient tomes containing dangerous knowledge; and King's narrators, the protagonist of *Revival*, for example, simply must not only tell their story but also preserve it in writing. This theme of truth telling at all costs says something about the human condition.

Jamie comes to learn more mundane truths as well. He learns about sex from reading the Roanoke novels from his mother's client and extrapolates that to his mother's relationship with Liz. He also learns the truth about Liz, who has kept secrets of her own that come to light at the novel's conclusion, when she shows herself to be not just corrupt but also capable of cold-blooded murder. Jamie has seen through some of her facade, even as a child, but didn't really understand how deep her immorality ran until he saw her in action, torturing and killing a drug lord. Learning this truth is part of Jamie's maturation process and provides a lesson he will never forget.

Finally, Jamie learns the truth about himself and how he was the product of incest. Although he is certainly capable of extracting all the torrid details from his father, who, once dead, must answer any question truthfully, yet he chooses not to do so, instead piecing together a plausible story that softens the harshness of the truth. Sometimes it is better not to know, and in this case, Jamie avoids the temptation to learn everything; once his father's ghost has passed on, that particular truth will be lost forever.

Jamie also puts off the search for the truth about whether he will suffer from the early-onset dementia of his father. That is knowledge he will pursue "later," he says. Once again, not knowing seems to be the most comfortable course of action, though with genetic testing an easy alternative, it seems likely that Jamie will, at some point, seek the answer to this question.

In terms of truth and deception, only the dead tell the truth and, even then, only in response to a direct question. His mother lies about his father, even if the lies are mostly by omission. And Jamie himself lies to the police about his powers and what transpired at the drug lord's house. He is truthful in the story he writes—a classic example of a reliable narrator—but he never discloses how his written narrative will be used. We can only speculate on whether it will be published as a memoir, a piece of fiction under a pen name (Stephen King, perhaps?), or never.

Human Universals

Incest seems to be a human universal taboo, occurring in virtually all societies and cultures, from ancient to contemporary. Sociologists have long speculated on the nature of this taboo. The logical reason, of course, is the likelihood that genetic diseases will be transmitted to children of sibling incest (15 times more likely, according to genetic researchers). Yet cultures that lack the knowledge of genetic transference seem to have an almost instinctual prohibition against incest, which is considered taboo and even outlawed in most societies. And the case can be made that rare recessive positive attributes are also more likely to be transmitted to children whose parents are siblings. This could account for Jamie's rare ability to see the dead.

The relationship between Jamie's mother and her brother appeared to be consensual, probably occurring in a moment of mutual weakness, as Jamie suspects, since his mother harbors no ill will toward "Uncle Harry," takes care of him even when he cannot take care of himself, and genuinely seems to love him. And for whatever reason, abortion was not considered an option. Yet the taboo is so strong that Jamie can only learn this truth from "Uncle Harry" once he is dead and is compelled to answer questions truthfully.

Evaluation

Later is an entertaining book, but I'd rank it somewhere in the middle of the pack—not one of the novels I'd teach in my Stephen King course.

50. *Later*

INTERESTING FACT

Jamie says, "Books are a uniquely portable magic. I read that somewhere." The "somewhere" is Stephen King's nonfiction book *On Writing*, which Jamie has obviously read and which, presumably, has helped him become a better writer.

NOTABLE QUOTE

"You get used to marvelous things. You take them for granted. You can try not to but you do. There's too much wonder, that's all. It's everywhere."

51

Billy Summers
The Moral Assassin

Background

Billy Summers was published on August 3, 2021, by Scribner. The book deviates from King's usual horror novels and, although billed as a mystery, lives more comfortably in the thriller category. Originally, the book was to be set in 2020, but to preserve realism, King had to move the story back in time due to the Covid-19 pandemic.

Summary and Narrative Devices

Billy Summers has an interesting and ironic premise: a professional assassin who is a "nice guy" who only kills bad people. A former Marine sniper, he is extraordinarily good at what he does, and since he only kills people he considers evil, he has no moral issues with his profession. In this novel, he is tasked with shooting Joel Allan, a murderer who is turning state's evidence. Billy plans to make this hit his last job and then he will retire comfortably and become anonymous.

In many ways, this novel resembles *11/22/63* where the protagonist has to wait for a certain event to occur before he can act. In this case, Billy can't complete his job until his intended target arrives at his location. The first part of the book, then, involves all the preparations that Billy makes to successfully complete the hit. He is Oswald-like in his approach, shooting his target from an office window with a high-power sniper rifle. This section of the book creates suspense as he waits for and anticipates the big day when the assassination will occur. In the hands of a less skillful writer, this plot would have comprised the entire novel, with Billy accomplishing the task and escaping. In this first section, Billy must kill time (no pun intended) as he waits for the appointed day when the assassination happens. King allows Billy to fill in his own backstory under the guise of writing a piece of biographical fiction as part of his cover story of being a writer.

The bulk of the book, however, involves the aftermath of the assassination and how after successfully evading the law Billy must escape from the criminals who hired him and are now trying to kill him. The novel turns from a story of escape into a revenge novel, and readers love revenge stories.

King also uses tenses in a creative way in this novel. While the bulk of the book is written in present tense (which is uncommon in fiction), Billy also writes about his past to fill in his backstory, and these metafictional accounts are in past tense. This device helps to keep the reader oriented in time and clearly shows which parts of the story are told by a narrator and which are written by Billy himself as part of his fictional autobiography.

Perhaps the most successful narrative device in this novel is King's rich use of detail about the assassination plot itself. King's character is believable, as is the operation he carries out. While King's details enrich all his stories, he is out of his element here, writing about an assassin rather than a teacher or a professional writer. His meticulous descriptions of the rifle, the plans for his office setting and for his escape, how to account for distance and wind in zeroing in on the shot, and his intricate backstory, which explains so much about Billy's character, make this story compelling and put the reader into the mind of a professional killer.

Archetypes

One archetype for *Billy Summers* is the series of thriller novels by Stephen Hunter featuring Bob Lee Swagger, a retired Marine sniper who assassinates bad people. Unlike Billy Summers, he works for the government and other "good" people and organizations. Although Billy only kills targets he believes are "bad," he has no issues with working for criminals, and his killings are not sanctioned by anyone. Otherwise, the characters are similar as they must complete the assassination and escape with their lives.

King also leans heavily on the structure of an earlier novel, *11/22/63*, where the protagonists took on the task of going back in time to prevent the assassination of John F. Kennedy. The point of view of the earlier book focuses on the character who would stop the assassination rather than the assassin himself. Billy is more closely associated with an Oswald-type character in this novel since he plays the role of the sniper shooting his target from the window of a tall building. The parallels between Billy and

Oswald are clear: both plan the attack carefully, both use high-power rifles from a tall vantage point, and both take advantage of the chaos after the shooting to make their escape. Billy, the professional assassin, succeeds in his escape while Oswald, the fanatical amateur, is caught.

Finally, King makes references to *The Things They Carried* by Tim O'Brien, a realistic piece of fiction set during the Vietnam War, and quotes O'Brien's observation about fiction being a way to the truth. This idea forms the basis for Billy's fictional autobiography and is the philosophy behind King's writing as well. "Fiction is the truth inside the lie," King has famously said. *Billy Summers* serves as King's truth about writing and employs O'Brien's technique of using very specific, concrete details to create that truth in a very precise, visual way.

Themes and Subtexts

Billy Summers has been called King's "love affair with writing" because it celebrates the act of writing and creation for its own sake rather than as a profession or a path to fortune and fame. Billy begins writing his story as a way of keeping up the facade of his cover story, a writer who is working on a novel. Before long, though, he becomes caught up in the act, and by chapter 3, he is already looking forward to "picking up the thread" of the story. He thinks that maybe he is a writer after all.

Although Billy is an assassin by trade, it is not a stretch to see him as an author. He is extremely well read and references books of all types, from the classics to modern fiction. He is familiar with the heritage of English and American literature and follows one of King's own rules from *On Writing*: to be successful, a writer must read. The second rule, of course, is that a writer must write. Billy shows amazing discipline at this task, sitting down in front of the keyboard every day that he can. Even though he considers himself an amateur, he emulates the professional writer with his work ethic, transforming himself from a "wannabe" to a "real writer" over the course of the novel.

Billy displays another trait of the successful writer by allowing himself to just play with words and have fun with what he is doing. He allows himself to regress into childhood, channeling Faulkner's technique with the mentally challenged character of Benji in *The Sound and the Fury* and adopting the informal "dumbed down" point of view of the character he pretends to be, a somewhat slow-witted assassin who reads comic books and doesn't think too much. This character, like that of Benji, can convey valuable insights about the world that a more cultured, sophisticated, and cerebral character would not be able to express without sounding pompous and unlikable. Billy's ability to adopt this persona offers him good camouflage for his role as an assassin and an interesting point of view for his story.

Billy Summers explores the definitions of "good" and "bad" and poses the moral dilemma of whether it is acceptable to kill an evil person. King has also toyed with this question in *The Green Mile*, where he looks at the death penalty, and in *11/22/63*, where he questions whether it would have been ethical to kill Adolf Hitler in the crib, or in this case, Lee Harvey Oswald. As forensic science becomes more sophisticated in the areas of genetics, neuroscience, and psychology, this question turns from a mind experiment to a practical question of ethics, as we may soon be able to predict violent criminal behavior before it occurs. Billy feels more than justified in killing pedophiles and violent criminals, and he enacts vigilante justice on Alice's rapists in a scene that would have audiences cheering in a movie theater.

The question then becomes, is Billy a good person or a bad person? Although he is a cold-blooded killer, he displays compassion and altruism, loves pets and kids, and seems to be a "nice guy" were it not for his profession. Couple that with the idea that not all "good" people in the King multiverse really are good (especially preachers, it seems), and we have a moral dilemma fit for an ethics class. King seems to weigh in on the side of Billy, while denouncing some of the men of God, such as Charles Jacobs, the minister from *Revival*, and of course, the seemingly squeaky-clean college boys who gang-rape Alice.

Once again, King turns to the question of abuse in this novel, creating the character of Alice who is slipped a date-rape drug and violently raped by a gang of college students. Male violence against women and children runs deep in King's multiverse: spousal abuse in *Dolores Claiborne* and *Rose Madder* (among others), child abuse in *The Body* and *Lisey's Story*, and violence against women in "The Big Driver" and "A Good Marriage," to name just a few examples. King portrays these abusive characters as the worst possible specimens of humanity, and the reader is rewarded when revenge is painfully administered by their abusers.

Human Universals

A social society tends to select for the trait of altruism among its members. No place is this more obvious than in the hive societies of insects and bees, where the individual will sacrifice her life for the benefit of the colony. While humans are not as self-sacrificing as bees, our species does exhibit altruistic behavior, especially from men toward women and children. This trait is demonstrated in *Billy Summers*, as the protagonist knowingly risks his own safety to help Alice, who has been raped and left for dead by the side of the road in front of his house. Billy has pulled off a successful escape and it's clear that he can disappear if he chooses. Instead, he risks everything for a stranger. This shows that Billy really is a "good guy" despite his profession. But it also portrays a universal human desire to help someone in trouble.

Alice is female, but she is also a child, at least to Billy, who is much older than her. This compelling need to help children is almost baked into the human psyche. Once he is faced with this dilemma, Billy really has no choice but to rescue the girl. If he fails to do so, he will no longer be considered a sympathetic character, and readers will no longer care what happens to him. He will be no better than the criminals he works for. Readers expect him to help, just as they would likely do if they were in his situation, and Billy does not disappoint.

King also wisely avoids the very unrealistic trope of a sexual relationship between an older man and a girl young enough to be his daughter, a cliché that occurs far too often in Hollywood productions (and in this professor's humble opinion, caters to the egos of aging actors). It would be extremely unlikely for the victim of a gang rape to be attracted to anyone right after her ordeal, and King's maintaining a platonic relationship between the characters makes narrative sense.

Humans also have a universal need to seek justice, both for themselves and for society. Billy's assassination of "bad guys" is one way of administering justice, and his revenge against Alice's rapists is another. A pushback against order in society is one of the triggers that, according to R. Douglas Fields, makes us "snap." This justifies Billy's violence against the rapists and satisfies society's need for criminals to pay the price. Another trigger involves resources: when someone takes something that belongs to you, a rage response is triggered. This justifies Billy's pursuit of and violence against his employers, who have cheated him out of what was rightfully his. Readers can empathize with this reaction and have absolutely no remorse for what Billy does to his employers.

Evaluation

The idea of an ethical assassin is an intriguing concept and King uses it to create a memorable character in *Billy Summers*. I see this novel as almost a companion narrative to *11/22/63* since it is the flip side of that story in many ways. This book, for me, ranks somewhere in the

51. *Billy Summers*

middle range of the canon—very entertaining and with some provocative themes—but not of the same level as his best stories.

Interesting Fact

Because of Covid-19, King changed the setting of the novel from 2020 to 2019 to avoid the authenticity problems of quarantines and other shutdowns during the pandemic.

Notable Quote

"When things go wrong, they don't waste time."

52

Fairy Tale

Once Upon a Time

Background

Fairy Tale was written from late November 2020 until February 2022 during the worst of the Covid-19 pandemic; the gray blight on the fantasy world of Empis reflects the horror of this awful period and the hope that emerges from it at the story's end, with its fairy-tale happy ending. King says that this novel came about during the time of the lockdown when he asked himself what he could write that would make him happy during the dark times of the pandemic. Therefore, he turned away from traditional horror and entered the world of fantasy, where fairy tales come to life.

Summary and Narrative Devices

The protagonist of the story, Charlie Reade, is a 17-year-old high school student who befriends a grumpy old man living in a "spooky" house in the neighborhood when he saves the old man's life after he falls from a ladder while cleaning out his gutters. Charlie takes care of the elderly man's dog, Radar, and discovers that Mr. Bowditch's shed is sitting on top of a well that leads to a fairy-tale world that is waiting for a prince to arrive and save the day. This secret world contains giants, a huge telepathic cricket, and enormous treasures of gold, not to mention a giant sundial that can turn back time and make one younger. When the old man dies, Charlie inherits both his wealth and his secrets and takes up the quest to bring the aging, dying Radar back to the magical world and renew the canine's life on the giant sundial. This quest, however, turns into an epic journey where Charlie is tasked with saving the entire world of Empis from the curse of an evil rogue king that has poisoned the land and its people.

Although King's hero is just a 17-year-old boy, the story is told as a retrospective tale by the 26-year-old Charlie who has grown up, graduated from college, and become a writer and a professor (specializing in mythology and fairy tales, of course). This allows King to put an adult perspective on a childhood quest and allows him to use more sophisticated language in the narrative.

In true fairy-tale form, the reader is assured that the story will have a happy ending (though there may be tragedies along the way) because the older Charlie obviously survives the adventure and is able to tell the tale in the first-person point of view.

Still, the suspense occurs when Charlie proposes a story that "no one will believe" and addresses the reader directly, in a challenge to read on and discover the mystery of this fantastic story. The novel only hints at magic and the supernatural for the first 163 pages until the existence of the other world is revealed when Charlie says, "This is where your disbelief begins." Until then, the story is set in the "mundane" world of high school, chores, hospitals, and a cranky recluse who slowly comes to trust Charlie with his enormous secret.

The first section of the story does pose questions, such as where Bowditch came by a king's ransom in gold and what is making a racket in the shed, but these questions could easily enough have rational answers without the need to descend into an alternate world. Once Charlie descends into the well, however, everything changes, and the narrative becomes a fantasy novel.

King does create some fascinating characters in the novel by taking classic fairy-tale characters like the old woman who lived in a shoe, the goose girl, and Jiminy Cricket and skewing them to make them interesting and original. The evil characters are rather stock and stereotyped, though King does pay homage to the horror master H.P. Lovecraft by making the Flight Killer a Cthulhu-inspired monster.

Archetypes

Fairy Tale adheres to the hero's quest model with a hero who embarks on an adventure into a fantasy world. He leaves his comfortable, mundane home to venture into an unknown world with the mission of saving the beloved dog Radar, only to find himself caught in a much larger role as a reluctant "Disney prince" who is called on to save the world. He receives magical help from some of the inhabitants of that world, including Leah, the exiled princess who has been maimed by the Flight Killer who has poisoned the world with his evil curse. Charlie achieves the first leg of his journey, saving Radar, but is captured, imprisoned in the dungeon ("the belly of the whale"), and forced to fight the other prisoners, like gladiators in *The Hunger Games*. With the help of a magic cricket, he is able to escape, destroy the evil, and save the princess. Unlike the traditional "Disney prince," however, he doesn't marry the princess but returns to his own world with a healed dog and a treasure.

Another archetype, of course, lies in the fairy tale itself, especially an inverted form of "Jack and the Beanstalk." Instead of climbing a beanstalk into the clouds, Charlie descends into a well and moves through a tunnel to enter the enchanted world, sort of like Alice in Wonderland entering the rabbit hole. The giant in the story—in this case, a giantess—guards an enormous hoard of gold and a huge sundial that can turn back the years and make one younger. This is the object of Charlie's original quest, returning Radar to a younger state to save the dying dog's life.

The novel also pays homage to Ray Bradbury's *Something Wicked This Way Comes*, a story that contains a Ferris wheel that can reverse the process of aging. The twisted carnival-like atmosphere of an evil funhouse is also reminiscent of the Bradbury novel. References are also made to *The Wizard of Oz* and H.P. Lovecraft's Cthulhu Mythos stories. Finally, King's reference to there being "other worlds than these" calls attention to much of his other fiction, including the Dark Tower books, *Lisey's Story* with Boo'ya Moon, *Revelation* and its Cthulhu-inspired nightmare world, and even the short story "Cookie Jar," where an old man who has lived well beyond his allotted years tells his great-great-grandson about an alternate universe of warring armies that exists at the bottom of an heirloom cookie jar.

Themes and Subtexts

Since *Fairy Tale* was written during the worst part of the Covid-19 pandemic, it is not surprising that the novel is rich with images of suffering, plague, and disease. The inhabitants of Empis have been cursed with a plague that turns them gray and consumes them slowly, eating away at their lives. The dethroned royalty has been cursed by losing parts of their senses, being rendered unable to speak, see, or hear by having their sense organs grown over with skin and sealed shut. The disfiguring curse is painful and disabling. Leah's mouth has closed up so drastically that she is forced to eat through a straw in a painful hole in her lips just to gain enough nourishment to keep her alive. She has learned to speak by throwing her voice into the mouths of other creatures, a painful and difficult process at best.

This evil curse is obviously symbolic of the coronavirus that has brought about so much pain and suffering. The disease has destroyed the fairy-tale society; the closed shops and empty streets of the capital cities are emblematic of the quarantine that people endured during the height of the pandemic. And although King supported the idea of wearing masks and isolation, this novel shows the distress it caused. The only way to escape the situation was to fight back and destroy the evil at its root. It might be a stretch, but Charlie and his band of heroes could be compared to the researchers and scientists who developed Covid-19 vaccine and kept the invasion of the virus from spreading any further.

This novel also addresses the theme of immortality, the fountain of youth that humans have been seeking since the beginning of history. The giant sundial holds the key to this magic, and anyone who rotates this wheel counterclockwise will have their years turned back, making them younger. This works perfectly fine for Radar, since he is a dog and cannot really comprehend the implications of what has happened to him. But for a human, this reversal of time has dire consequences. It turns Mr. Bowditch into a sullen recluse, making him sterile both physically and emotionally. Someone who is evil by nature would become obsessive about the wheel. One cannot help but think of those who have become addicted to plastic surgery and who maim themselves in an effort to look younger.

The novel also explores myths and storytelling and seems to say that there are universal stories that transcend culture and may even transfer into other worlds. This idea of monomyths was popularized by Joseph Campbell and Carl Jung, who claimed that there are certain narratives that are universal and are part of the collective unconscious. Vladimir Propp and other structuralist literary critics studied fairy tales in particular and have attempted to catalog them almost as mathematical formulas. The Brothers Grimm were linguists who collected tales from the oral traditions of Eastern Europe and wrote them down for posterity. King's novel is building on this basic idea of the fairy tale and modernizing it for contemporary readers.

The idea that "there are other worlds than these" forms the bedrock of most of King's stories, most notably the Dark Tower series, which establishes the model of the multiverse. *Fairy Tale* completes another piece of this puzzle by creating another world that is very close to ours in the fabric of space-time. According to his fictional idea, portals exist in unlikely places where one may travel to other worlds (as in *Revelation*), alternate universes ("UR"), or other times in our own universe (*11/22/63*). These portals allow the characters in the Dark Tower books to move through space and time as well. *Fairy Tale* connects to our universe and is connected to another deeper universe as well. All these universes may well be cogs in the Dark Tower wheel.

Human Universals

Grief and loss are human universal emotions that everyone experiences at some time in their life. Charlie has lost his mother and grieves for her. His father also suffers and self-medicates with alcohol, causing Charlie more grief. He has, in effect, lost both parents until his father cleans up his act. Then, when Charlie befriends Mr. Bowditch, he suffers another loss with the old man's death. The protagonist is a character worthy of our sympathy. When Charlie inherits Radar, he finds himself about to lose a beloved pet. The avoidance of still more grief fuels his quest to rejuvenate the dog and save the pet's life.

Dogs have been faithful companions to *Homo sapiens* for some 14,000 years, according to the most recent scientific theories. They have become so bonded to humans that they are considered family. This human universal love for dogs propels *Fairy Tale*. We are sad to hear that Charlie's mother has died, and we are sad over the death of Mr. Bowditch. But when it is revealed that the dog has a terminal illness, that triggers an emotional response in almost any reader. Charlie must do whatever he can to save Radar, and his sacrifices and risks are never questioned. Readers can see themselves also doing whatever it would take to save a beloved pet.

Evaluation

Even though I enjoyed *Fairy Tale* very much and appreciate its upbeat tone and happy ending, it remains in the middle ranks of King's novels, in my opinion. His fantasy works are interesting and even refreshing, but his best works (other than the Dark Tower books) seem to be set in the real world. The first part of *Fairy Tale* seems to me the most compelling as it explores the relationship between Charlie, Radar, and Mr. Bowditch. The characters in the fairy-tale world, for me, aren't as captivating as those of Charlie's mundane world.

Interesting Fact

Charlie's father references a quote, "Long days and pleasant nights," that he read "in some book." King fans will recognize that quote as being from *The Gunslinger*, the first book in the Dark Tower series.

Notable Quote

"You never know where the trapdoors are in your life, do you?"

53

Holly

A Journal of the Covid-19 Years

Background

Holly was released on September 5, 2023, by Scribner and showcases the character of Holly Gibney, who is now the proprietor of the Finders Keepers detective agency. Set during the height of the Covid-19 pandemic, the story came to King when he imagined Holly attending her mother's funeral on Zoom. He coupled this with an image he found in a newspaper article about a "sweet old couple" burying bodies in the backyard.

Summary and Narrative Devices

Holly finds itself purely in the mystery/suspense genre rather than horror and is what King calls a "whydunit" rather than a "whodunit." The novel opens with the abduction of a poet in 2012 by a pair of retired professors who imprison him in their basement before killing him. As the novel progresses, we learn that this duo believe that consuming human flesh will cure their ailments and keep them healthy. Their 2012 victim is just their first.

Holly Gibney becomes involved when she is contacted by the distraught mother of a missing young lady and asked to help find her daughter. Holly, who has just lost her mother to Covid-19, isn't really in the market for work but reluctantly agrees to take the case. The novel then follows the story as she discovers that she is investigating in a serial murder case involving what seems like two 80-year-old professors.

The novel is structured by chapters that are organized by dates and oscillates back and forth from the past and the kidnapping and murder of victims to the present storyline with Holly digging up clues to the mystery. The reader knows what is happening, so the plot isn't to solve the crime but to watch Holly solve it.

The strength of this novel rests, I think, in the development of the character of Holly Gibney, who has been featured in King's work since her introduction in *Mr. Mercedes*. Holly, who began her fictional life as a mousy, socially inept individual with self-esteem issues and who was completely controlled by her mother, has, over the course of several books, transformed into a strong, competent self-sufficient woman who has proven herself to be a true hero. Although she still finds social interactions difficult, she has effectively managed her issues. She is multifaceted and very realistic, a well-developed character who comes to life on the page and does her own thing, so to speak, rather than being manipulated by an author lurking in the background.

Archetypes

Holly can be considered a mystery novel in the subgenre of the "whydunit," a type of story where the reader knows who the criminals are but doesn't know why they are committing the crime, at least not right away. Jessica Brody, in her book *Save the Cat! Writes a Novel*, defines this genre: "a mystery must be solved by a hero during which something shocking is revealed about the dark side of human nature." For the detective, in this case Holly Gibney, the mystery is also to find "whodunit" as well. The reader, being privy to information that Holly doesn't have, reads along to find out first the why and then to discover how the detective will solve the crime. The plot is driven by questions and mysteries revolving around the mechanisms and motives of the crime, more so than the revelation of the criminal to the reader. This type of story often takes the protagonist down a dark path and forces her to work alone, which usually leads to trouble. In the case of this novel, Holly recognizes that she is metaphorically going toward the chain saws instead of escaping in the running car, as she refers to a popular television commercial about people making poor decisions in horror movies. This path does nearly lead to her death.

Classic films such as *Chinatown*, *Silence of the Lambs*, and *L.A. Confidential* employ a similar motif. Dan Brown's *The Da Vinci Code*, Daphne du Maurier's *Rebecca*, and Stieg Larsson's *The Girl with the Dragon Tattoo* are whydunit novels.

Themes and Subtexts

It would be impossible to read *Holly* without recognizing the influence of Covid-19, which was deeply affecting the world during the time

53. Holly

King was writing the book. In fact, the novel may in future generations be looked at as a chronicle of the pandemic years. Although some readers and critics may complain about King's inserting his opinions on this matter into the story, it would, in my opinion, be impossible to write about this time in America without either pretending that Covid-19 did not exist or making its controversies part of the narrative.

King makes his beliefs about the pandemic known through the persona of Holly Gibney. An outspoken critic of the anti-vaxxers and anti-maskers, King's protagonist echoes his conviction about the senselessness of those who refused to take these precautions. Holly's mother, an avid "Trumpster" who refuses to be vaccinated or wear a mask, is killed by the virus, and those who echo conspiracy theory beliefs are depicted as being ignorant. In perhaps the ultimate irony, Emily Harris and her husband don't believe that masks or vaccines work, yet they subscribe to the totally insane idea that eating human flesh will cure their ailments and prolong their lives. Totally out of touch with reality, their world is completely turned upside down.

King also exposes the subtext of politics and divisiveness that was so prevalent during the time he wrote this story. He makes no bones about his distaste for Donald Trump and uses his celebrity status to disparage the former president often by using his characters as mouthpieces and depicting Trump supporters as ignorant and cultish. Once again, King has been criticized for airing his opinions, which, I'll agree, become heavy-handed at times; however, divisive politics has formed the fabric of the Trump and post–Trump years, and anyone living during this time has a strong opinion on the subject, one way or another. It is a sad fact that these political debates destroyed friendships and even caused dissension and hatred within families.

Both the Covid-19 and political subtexts are, in my opinion, part of a larger subject that expresses the theme of appearance versus reality. The anti-vaxxers and Trumpsters are shown to be living in an alternate reality where fiction replaces truth. This is most evident in the characters of Rodney and Emily Harris, two retired professors who seem weak and harmless while leading double lives as serial killers who cannibalize their victims. Even Holly, an astute detective, falls for their deception, thinking that at best, they must be accessories to a crime committed by someone younger, healthier, and stronger. As King says in the Author's Note, their characters were inspired by a newspaper headline: "Everyone thought they were a sweet old couple until bodies began turning up in the back yard."

This "sweet old couple" also manages to conceal their racism and homophobia from the world and from their academic colleagues, yet they express it in private. This theme is a symbolic manifestation of intolerance, which often exists beneath the surface and is not openly acknowledged.

Human Universals

Holly exploits one of the most widespread and abhorrent universal taboos, the prohibition against cannibalism. Even under the direst circumstances, such as the 1972 Andes plane crash where survivors were forced to consume their dead in order to survive, it is considered unthinkable. Those killers who have engaged in the practice, such as Jeffrey Dahmer, are considered to be the most extreme psychopaths. Portraying a pair of highly educated octogenarians as cannibals is the ultimate horror. Their behavior violates all codes of conduct and morality, and ironically, they justify their actions with pseudoscience. It is only natural that the reader feels revulsion for these villains and takes great delight at their ultimate defeat at the hands of Holly, who shows herself as anything but meek in the endgame.

As I have said in previous chapters, altruism is a human universal trait that has enabled humans to survive and thrive in cooperative groups. The cannibalistic professors use the human desire to be helpful as a way of trapping their victims. Playing the part of weak, disabled old people, they entice their victims into helping them, and the ruse works every time. Indeed, Constant Readers can imagine themselves doing exactly what the victims do. King uses this device to garner sympathy for the victims and loathing for the killers. In this novel, no good deed goes unpunished.

The human instinct for survival at any cost is also evident in this narrative, especially when King puts us into the minds of the victims who wake up to find themselves in a basement prison and forced to eat raw liver. This survival instinct reaches its climax when Holly, a character we have grown to adore and admire, is captured. Unlike the other victims, she finds a way to fight for her survival even when all seems lost.

Evaluation

I must admit, when I learned that King's newest book was about Holly Gibney, I was a little disappointed. Even though I like Holly just fine, I was thinking maybe this is too much of a good thing. However, when I read the book, I was happily surprised at how much I enjoyed it, and Holly's character has, in fact, grown on me. I do think that Holly Gibney is one of King's best-drawn characters, one who has developed in so many ways

53. Holly

since her first appearance in *Mr. Mercedes*. In *Holly*, she has earned her place among famous fictional detectives. And King has proven that he can, indeed, create realistic, believable female characters.

Interesting Fact

When King introduced Holly Gibney in *Mr. Mercedes*, he considered her a "walk-off" character, but she took on a life of her own and, as King says, "grows beyond herself."

Notable Quote

"Sometimes the universe throws you a rope."

Conclusion
The English Professor and Constant Reader

Full disclosure: I wasn't an early adopter of Stephen King's work. In fact, I recall seeing his novels on the book rack in Ann & Hope, a local independent department store like the kind that existed before Walmart and other megastore chains gobbled them up. His works were mixed in with tacky romances, bestsellers by the likes of Jackie Collins and Harold Robbins, a zillion translations of the Bible, along with lots of self-help books. My first thought was, how can this stuff be any good? I had graduated from college with my BA in English in 1977, and my ultimate goal in life was to publish a short story, and at the time, my chosen genre was heroic fantasy in the tradition of Robert E. Howard's Conan the Barbarian stories. So now that I was freed from reading the classics for classes, I dived into every fantasy short story I could get my hands on. And there were plenty of them at the time.

As a fan of science fiction, I also began reading short stories in that genre, including the Lester del Rey "Best of" collections and of course H.P. Lovecraft and other practitioners of the "weird tale." King's works were quite far down on my reading list at the time. Then, in 1978 or so, I decided to try out his short story collection *Nightshift*, which was available in paperback, figuring, why not? Maybe I can learn something even if it's how *not* to write a story. And I was hooked. I raced through *The Shining*, *'Salem's Lot*, and *Carrie* and then was fully engaged when *The Stand* was released.

By 1979, I had made my first professional sale, an Egyptian fantasy piece to Andrew J. Offutt's *Swords against Darkness V* anthology, and I attended the World Fantasy Convention in my hometown of Providence, Rhode Island, chaired by my dear college friend Bob Booth, and where Stephen King was the guest of honor. I was able to meet the King briefly, he signed my copy of *The Dead Zone*, and I was even asked to autograph a few copies of *Swords against Darkness V*, which had just been released. Never in my wildest dreams did I think I'd ever become a bona fide English professor with a PhD and several book-length critical studies to my credit. At the time, I was a member of the United Steelworkers of America, working in a place that repaired and manufactured textile machinery.

So, the bottom line is that I discovered Stephen King as a reader, not a critic, and very quickly entered the realm of "Constant Reader," eagerly anticipating anything new that he would write. And when I did enter graduate school a few years later, doing any serious critical work on King was the furthest thing from my mind. I wrote about Ray Bradbury for my MA thesis and H.P. Lovecraft for my PhD dissertation. It was difficult enough getting an academic committee to approve those authors as suitable for study, never mind a living best-selling author. And I still considered myself primarily a writer of fiction, along with feature stories for newspapers and magazines that actually paid real money as opposed to contributor's copies.

So why did I decide to study King seriously? Simple. The man sold a bazillion books and I wanted to figure out why. My naive self thought that there must be a secret, and if I could "discover" it, I could copy it and sell a bazillion books too. Hey, I may be an English professor, but I'm also an unashamed capitalist. So I began writing a few short critical studies, things for *Studies in Weird Fiction* and I presented papers at academic conferences (by then, I'd been hired by Johnson & Wales University as an assistant professor and I was looking to be promoted up the ranks to eventually become full professor, with all of the honors and privileges that rank held). I was also able to publish my Bradbury and Lovecraft critical studies with Wildside Press, so I had some credibility with both the horror and academic communities. At this point, I thought I might actually find a publisher for a book-length study on King, which had become a cottage industry, if you will. My first two books on King were quite academic, appealing to scholars rather than the general public (but that's how academia works). My goal was to prove that King, although a best-selling author and a brand name, also had literary merit. I'd like to think I succeeded in that endeavor.

So did I learn the secret to King's success? Well, yes and no. I was able to discover many of his tricks and techniques as well as his appeal to human universal emotions that have been hardwired into us (the subject of my second book, *Excavating Stephen King*). I was able to decode his secrets of simple but very descriptive prose that engaged a reader, his ability to create characters that have become icons of popular culture, and his uncanny ability to generate and maintain suspense, even in books that are the size of doorstops. But was I able to duplicate these things into my own

Conclusion 299

fiction? The answer, sadly, is no. I am a much better critic than a fiction writer and have, in fact, had more success with poetry than with novels or short stories. So it goes, as Vonnegut famously said.

So here I am with another book on Stephen King, and once again, I am tasked with making some conclusions about his work in general, after having made lots of conclusions about each of his 53 (to date) novels. So what can I say that hasn't already been said? I'm not sure, but if you've actually put out good money for the book you're now holding in your hands, I owe it to you to give you something. And after doing critical studies on King and now analyzing each of his novels individually, I wouldn't be an English professor (albeit a retired one) if I didn't have some conclusions to share besides just that "he's good and he sells a lot of books." So here goes.

First, King is one of the very few authors who has enjoyed both critical and popular success. The popular success speaks for itself, with over 60 books still in print, each of them an international bestseller. In fact, the only book in King's canon not in print is *Rage*, which he demanded be taken out of circulation after several horrific school shootings. As one of the top-selling authors of all time, King is able to command huge book advances, his novels are optioned by Hollywood almost before the ink is dry on the books, and he has become an icon of popular culture, with associated T-shirts, King souvenirs, and even a Stephen King "Funko" figure (number 43 of the Pop Icons, in case you're interested). He's turned clowns into objects of terror, turned the senior prom into a horror show, and even made classic cars seem creepy. There is no debating the impact he has made on popular culture.

His literary merit, though, is another thing. The late Harold Bloom (may he rest in peace) has accused him of "dumbing down" American letters and took particular exception to his being awarded the National Book Foundation's annual medal for distinguished contribution to American letters in 2003. Other writers of literary fiction have dismissed him as well, even though he has won an O'Henry Award for short fiction and his works have appeared in "literary" publications, including *The Atlantic*, the *New Yorker*, and the *Virginia Quarterly Review*. Let's face it, Stephen King doesn't need me to defend him. But there are some reasons I think that he has been discredited.

First, jealousy. Frankly, what author wouldn't love to trade royalty checks with Stephen King? I'm not too proud to admit that I would. So why doesn't my work sell as well as his? Obviously, because "I'm a better writer who tells stories that are deep, meaningful, and incredibly insightful, but that the American public is too stupid to understand." So I criticize King as a hack because it makes me feel better about my own poor sales figures. Yeah, I believe there's quite a bit of that going on out there in the literary world by writers who take themselves much too seriously and whose works appear to such a small, snobby section of the reading public that they will never sell more than a handful of copies.

Snobbery. "I'm too smart, erudite, sophisticated, and downright good to read anything by Stephen King. James Joyce's *Finnegan's Wake* is my kind of story, even if no one in the known world has any clue what it means or why it is still studied in snobby graduate school literature classes. The snobs from the Ivy Leagues praise it, so it's got to be good. And these same snobs snub King, so his work can't possibly be worth reading. Besides, anyone who sells that many books must be appealing to the unwashed masses, and I'm too good for that."

Genre fiction. "Stephen King writes horror! Yuck! And sometimes mystery. And science fiction. And fantasy. Everyone knows that genre fiction is crap. Oh, Edgar Allan Poe wrote mystery and horror? No. Poe was a writer who just happened to write some horror and mystery stories. He wasn't a genre writer. Horror stories don't deserve to be considered literature, so King's work can't be any good."

So how is one to respond to those critics? First, we can ignore them. They aren't going to make a difference to King or his work, nor will readers stop reading his fiction just because some critic tells them to. And I think we can all see some of the underlying motives here. But I believe a case can be made for Stephen King based on logic rather than emotion. First, let me make a distinction between "liking" a piece of work and its overall literary worth. I like lots of things that are pure, unadulterated crap. Sometimes, after a stressful day, I just want to sit back and enjoy films where things blow up, for example. Many of the current television shows fall into that category—an hour of police chases, gunfights, an explosion or two, and the bad guy gets shot or arrested. Do these shows have any literary merit? No. But I like them anyway. And for that matter, since I watch films solely to be entertained, I'm not fond of the high-brow type of film, and I seldom watch anything that has been nominated for an Oscar unless, by some miracle, it's fantasy or science fiction. My film-viewing tastes don't usually include complicated themes or messages about social justice. Like I said, I enjoy watching things explode.

By the same token, I can appreciate the artistry of things I really don't like. I once had the occasion to attend the opera, for example, as the guest of my university's chancellor, as a reward for obtaining a high-profile government grant for the institution. It was one of the most agonizing experiences of my life, pretending to love something that made me want to run for the exits. But with that said, I can freely admit that those people sure can sing! The voices were amazing. But the music? I didn't like it. Some

Conclusion 301

literature is like that. Milton's *Paradise Lost*. Brilliant poem. Do I enjoy reading it? No. I've had to read it and analyze it as part of my literature studies but was very happy to move on from that chapter of my life. So, to simplify, liking something doesn't make it any good. And hating it doesn't make it bad. It all comes down to taste. And sometimes the two converge and we actually like things that have artistic merit.

If we really want to judge a work's value, we need to apply some measurable criteria. In my field, this is based on literary theory, which English professors study as a matter of course. That's how I know that Milton is a genius, even if he isn't my cup of tea. There are specific things we can look at when studying a narrative; among them are influence, substance, style, technique, and characterization.

Let me take the easiest one first, what I call the low-hanging fruit: King's influence on literature. There are certain iconic writers who have changed the very nature of writing. Whitman turned poetry from the archaic verse of Longfellow into the democratic free verse that we love today. Hemingway got rid of the purple prose and favored nouns and verbs. Mary Shelley invented science fiction. Langston Hughes, Jane Austen, Allen Ginsberg, William Faulkner, Toni Morrison—all these practitioners, and too many more to name, changed the face of literature with their works, and some, like Harriet Beecher Stowe, even changed the world. So, does Stephen King fit into this category? Well, to a degree, yes, though we won't really know until a few more decades have passed and we see what happens.

So how has King influenced literature?

First, he has made it acceptable to write horror novels. Horror was at least partially accepted in the short story form, probably because classic writers like Poe, Hawthorne, and others dabbled in it. But the horror novel has been a different animal and usually had a possible mundane explanation for the horror (i.e., Henry James). King, an English teacher with a real background in literature, changed all that by unabatingly writing horror novels and almost single-handedly creating a section for horror on bookstore shelves. For better or worse, this spawned a horror boom in the 1980s that continues to this day, and although most of the novels produced during this time are forgettable (but often very entertaining, like those TV shows I enjoy where things blow up), some incredibly talented horror writers did emerge: Peter Straub, Brian Lumley, Dan Simmons, Anne Rice, and Caitlín R. Kiernan come to mind, along with many others. And with horror, science fiction and fantasy also became more respectable and popular.

King's influence on the horror genre is immeasurable not only in terms of encouraging new practitioners but in the way he treated horror itself. H.P. Lovecraft was a major influence on the genre with his invention of "cosmic horror," which combined elements of both science fiction and horror to create a form of terror based on science rather than the supernatural. King's influence was in taking horror out of the dreary haunted house and bringing it to Main Street (Maine Street, if you will pardon the pun). His very first novel, *Carrie*, turned senior prom into a terror-ridden nightmare (perhaps verbalizing the fear that most teens experience when confronted with the prospects of prom night). *'Salem's Lot* brought vampires to small-town America, and *The Shining* turned a luxury resort hotel into a horror show. Even the characters were normal, mundane people, not some snobby scholar searching for the meaning of life in old, dusty books. A teenage girl, an ordinary writer, and an English teacher populate these three novels. While elements of the Gothic may still exist in King's work, they have been taken out of the shadows and placed in the light of day. And the horror novel was changed forever.

Although some traditional academics might question the subjects that King writes about (horror, science fiction, mystery), his genre is really just the canvas on which he builds deeper meanings. In many ways, horror and speculative fiction allow authors to handle subjects that would be impossible to address in more traditional forms. Dystopian governments, for example, would be impossible to describe without the what-if element of speculative fiction, a fact that George Orwell and Aldous Huxley certainly understood. By expanding the imagination of what is possible, authors can explore all sorts of themes that are outside the realm of the traditional. King uses speculative fiction to dive deeply into many of these important ideas.

The danger of governments having too much power is one common theme that runs throughout the King canon. His creation of the entity known as "The Shop" serves as an example of what could happen were the CIA and other federal organizations given free rein to do whatever they pleased. Individual rights are destroyed in *Firestarter*, where an innocent but exceptional girl is exploited by the government in the name of national security. In science fiction dystopias like *The Long Walk*, *The Running Man*, and *The Institute*, big government abuses its people for its own ends. In *The Green Mile*, a racist government puts an innocent man to death. In *Roadwork*, the state takes a man's property simply for profit. A corrupt government takes charge in *Under the Dome*, turning a small town into a fascist state. The military goes overboard in *Dreamcatcher*. For Americans, the loss of freedom and democracy is a major concern (now more than ever after the events of January 6, 2021), and King's works remind us to be ever vigilant and maintain a healthy distrust of the government.

Justice is a familiar theme in King's novels, and it is often found lacking in modern society. *The Green Mile*, *The Outsider*, and *Rita Hayworth*

Conclusion 303

and the Shawshank Redemption are three examples of misguided justice. In two of these narratives, an innocent man dies, and in *Shawshank* the protagonist serves decades for a crime he did not commit. All three novels end with justice ultimately prevailing, but this justice occurs outside the purview of the law.

King's fiction delves into some deep questions of philosophy. The theme of fate versus free will occurs repeatedly in his books and is examined from different angles. *The Dead Zone* and *The Institute* speculate on the possibility of changing future events if we knew what would happen beforehand. *11/22/63* questions the prospect of changing the past. *Insomnia* proposes an entire mythology that governs fate and chaos. And a common thread running throughout all his fiction is the existence of a multiverse where all possible outcomes can exist. King says that "great events turn on small hinges," which sheds light on how seemingly tiny, insignificant events can open up all kinds of consequences. Sometimes these events seem almost random, as when the characters in *The Institute* converge on a small town, which leads to outcomes that could conceivably change the world. Whether these events are truly random or a product of fate is a subject for debate.

Life and death are also subjects of study in King's world. The ever-present struggle against death is, of course, the underlying point of any horror story. But King does take this to a deeper level. *Pet Sematary* shows that there are worse things than death and warns against trying to defeat death, which is the natural fate of all living things. *End of Watch* draws attention to the extremes of death: people facing terminal illness and others contemplating suicide. *Elevation*, *Joyland*, and *Doctor Sleep* also examine end-of-life issues. *The Green Mile* questions capital punishment, *Lisey's Story* looks at the grieving process, and *Revival*, *Insomnia*, and *Later* speculate on what comes after death. Other stories, such as *The Girl Who Loved Tom Gordon*, *Gerald's Game*, and *Cujo*, push the limits of what people will do to survive.

King has been an outspoken advocate for the rights of women, children, and traditionally repressed people and his fiction reflects this theme. Child abuse and bullying is frequently referred to, most notably in *Carrie*, *It*, *Dolores Claiborne*, and *The Institute*. The abuse of women is a subject for *Rose Madder*, *Gerald's Game*, and *Billy Summers*, among others. Racism rears its ugly head in *The Green Mile* and *Bag of Bones*, and LGBTQ+ rights are highlighted in *Elevation*.

Mental health has come to the forefront in America in recent times, but King's works have been addressing this topic since the publication of *Carrie*. *Rage* attempts to get inside the mind of a teenage school shooter; *Roadwork* looks at depression; *End of Watch* explores suicide; and *Rose*

Madder enters the mind of a woman escaping from years of domestic violence. Substance abuse is addressed in many of King's books: *The Shining* and *Doctor Sleep* highlight it as a major theme.

Religion plays a major role in many of King's novels as well. In some cases, such as *The Stand*, faith is a powerful force for good. In others, like *Revival*, it is a sham. And in still others, like *Carrie*, it is destructive and abusive.

King's works also question the place of technology in the modern world. It leads to apocalypse in both *The Stand* and *Cell*. In the hands of alien beings, it can be terrifying, as is the case with *The Tommyknockers* and *Under the Dome*. And psychic phenomenon, technology's secret cousin, can be a curse rather than a blessing, as seen in *Carrie*, *The Dead Zone*, *Firestarter*, and *The Institute*.

Finally, most of King's works address the idea of creativity in general and writing in particular. So many of King's characters are writers that it would be exhaustive to list them all. And many of those who are not writers still work in the creative realm as artists, musicians, or teachers. These characters express universal truths about the creative process, even to the point of explaining how great writing works (*Misery*, *The Dark Half*, and *Billy Summers* are obvious examples of this). And although King's fiction does appeal to writers, it also has a more universal appeal because just about every human being on the planet longs to be creative in some way.

All of the themes and subtexts in King's fiction could be (and often are) addressed in essays, op-eds, and nonfiction books. But these types of nonfiction works usually preach to the choir, to use a true but worn-out phrase, and are often overly didactic. Only those who believe in diversity and inclusion will read a book about extending rights to those who have been denied them. Such works fail to change hearts and minds since people tend to hold on to their confirmational biases. Fiction, on the other hand, works in a more subtle manner. By actually experiencing the thoughts and emotions of a Rose Madder, for example, a reader can empathize, understand, and help initiate change.

Finally, universal human emotions form the bedrock of King's fiction, and this is one of the reasons that he is so popular. He has managed to expose the basic things that make us human: fear, rage, love and caring, grief, a sense of play, a sense of seeking adventure, and basic survival. His fiction taps into these human universals at the neurological level, causing readers to experience what King's characters experience at a biological level. One might wonder how he is able to do this so successfully. The answer, I believe, lies in his style and techniques.

King's style is unique, and although it has been criticized as being "homey," it is this trait that makes him so accessible and so popular. One trademark of King is his extensive (some critics have called it excessive) use of brand names. This deliberate way of using concrete, descriptive nouns creates a specific and vivid picture in readers' minds. It is easier to visualize a Big Mac than it is a hamburger, and the specific detail puts the reader in the scene and immediately paints a realistic picture. America is a brand-name consumer society (a theme King acknowledges in *Needful Things*), and the products and services that appear in the stories are instantly recognizable. Furthermore, brand names are an efficient tool for character creation since people are essentially what they eat, so to speak. We can immediately evaluate the differences in a character who wears a Rolex watch from one sporting a Timex, for example. And if a cotton farmer just happens to be wearing a Rolex, that certainly says something about that character as well.

Some have criticized the use of brand names as dating King's work, and this may very well be true. He has been publishing fiction for over 50 years, and some of those early brand names no longer exist. But even this is effective in that it sets a time and place for the fiction, serving as a reminder that the story occurs in the 1970s, for example. For younger readers, it is a slice of history and culture. And for those of us who have been around for a while, it creates a neat sense of nostalgia.

Another trait found in King's style is his creation of first-person narrators and dialogue that is realistic and believable. When the narrator of *Needful Things*, for example, welcomes the reader to town—and into the story—we see this character as a real narrator with an interesting story to tell. Dolores Claiborne tells her story in her own way, and it comes off as authentic with the words coming right from her lips rather than from a distant author. The narrators of *Later*, *Billy Summers*, and *The Green Mile* all appear as complex, complicated people who tell their story in their own individual way.

When the narrative is told in third person, King makes things realistic with authentic dialogue. His children speak and think in age-appropriate language (*The Institute*, *The Girl Who Loved Tom Gordon*, and the characters in *It* and *The Body*); his educated characters come off as educated without being snobbish; and King is quite comfortable allowing all his characters to speak in the vernacular of their time and place.

Another component of King's style is his ability to create memorable characters that have become icons of popular culture. Although readers can relate to heroes like Holly Gibney and Danny in *Doctor Sleep*, it is King's villains that are the most interesting. Rose the Hat, the Trashcan Man, Pennywise the Clown, Annie Wilkes, Cujo, the Man in Black, the Mercedes massacre killer—these villains are realistic, no matter how fantastic their premise. Furthermore, they all have very realistic reasons for doing the horrendous things they do. Rose the Hat, despicable as her actions may be, is merely trying to survive—the fact that she must inflict pain and suffering to do so isn't her fault. The Trashcan Man and other antiheroes suffer from mental illness and cannot help their actions. In some ways, the villains invoke a certain amount of sympathy. This is especially evident in the case of Cujo, the poor dog who wanted to be good but was infected with rabies. King's villains aren't cardboard cutouts but are real characters who symbolize the complexity of morality and ethics.

Despite King's "homespun" style, the man is quite capable of turning a beautiful phrase, as I have demonstrated by the inclusion of a notable quote from each of his novels. Often, I had to choose a single quote from among many that appeared in a novel, any of which would be worthy of inclusion in a quotation dictionary. "Great events turn on small hinges," for example, says so much with so few words, and I have often found myself remembering this quote when eventful things happened in my life. This quote also forces me to evaluate so many of the things I do and the decisions I make and examine the possible long-term and perhaps unanticipated benefits and consequences of what may seem like simple decisions. This has (hopefully) helped make me be a better person and avoid inflicting pain on others without becoming obsessive or paranoid. Other King quotes speak to readers in different ways, but they all make us stop and think.

King's style and technique are often difficult to distinguish, but there is no question that he has mastery over the art and science of writing a compelling novel. As a former English teacher and student of literature, King has read all the classics as well as the modern masters and has often referenced them in his works, either overtly or more subtly. His horror stories have been built on the solid foundations of Edgar Allan Poe, H.P. Lovecraft, Arthur Machen, Shirley Jackson, Mary Shelley, Bram Stoker, Robert Bloch, and too many others to name. His novels contain allusions to nonhorror classics as well, including Thornton Wilder (*'Salem's Lot*), L. Frank Baum's *Oz* books, and Evelyn Waugh (*Misery*). He is, of course, well versed in the styles of virtually every accomplished classic writer, and King's advice to would-be writers is simple: read and write.

Liberal and skillful use of narrative devices, point of view, foreshadowing, flashbacks, and other techniques make his novels highly readable and loaded with conflict and suspense. He often uses the hero's quest structure, a highly successful method of telling stories that has been around from the time of the ancient Mesopotamian story of Gilgamesh to modern Hollywood blockbusters such as *Star Wars*. Although many postmodern critics scorn the idea of plot, King's pronouncement that "story is boss" has proven true for millennia. Readers like stories where things happen—it is as simple as that—and no amount of criticism will change this fact. It is woven into human nature, as evolutionary psychologists claim.

Finally, the devil is in the details, and in this technique, King doesn't disappoint. I have already mentioned how his use of brand names creates details that result in a believable reality. But his use of specific, concrete details goes well beyond that. Some of King's places, for example, are so rich in detail that they seem more like real places than fictional settings. Castle Rock, Derry, the Overlook Hotel, and Jerusalem's Lot have become iconic places in popular culture, each with a rich history and fictional present that rival Faulkner's Yoknapatawpha County in its veracity. King's fiction paints a very concrete, three-dimensional picture (which makes it rather easy for Hollywood to adapt into films). Because of this attention to detail, readers become immersed in the story and keep turning pages until the end (and wind up wanting even more). In stories like *11/22/63*, King re-creates the past, and in novels like *It* and *Insomnia*, he invents alternate worlds and populates the multiverse. It is one of the secrets of his success, easy to explain but difficult to duplicate.

So the question remains, will Stephen King be celebrated as a great writer or dismissed as a hack? As a Constant Reader, I am biased, of course. But as an English professor with a background in both literary theory and literary history, I would predict that King will be read and studied by future generations and at some point be admitted into the literary canon. Some of his works are already over 50 years old and are still being read, written about, and readapted into film. And in many ways, King has only gotten better as time has gone on. Yes, not all his fiction is brilliant (then again, Ernest Hemingway, recipient of both the Pulitzer and Nobel Prizes, published *Over the River and into the Trees*, which has generally been panned by critics, then and now), but all of it is memorable, and some of it is, in the opinion of this English professor, absolute genius. Novels like *The Stand* will (pardon the pun) stand the test of time. *Lisey's Story* has a psychological depth that will be studied by future scholars. And *The Green Mile* (perhaps my personal favorite, though it is so hard to choose just one) is highly successful both as a book and as a film. King's "mainstream" works *Rita Hayworth and the Shawshank Redemption* and *The Body* rival anything being written by any contemporary American author, in my opinion. And his Dark Tower series (which merits an entire critical study of its own) may very well be the American version of epic literature that has been missing from the canon since the time of Herman Melville. So, yes, I believe that King will not only survive and endure but will also be elevated in the canon despite the petty jealousies of snobby critics (most of whom, I venture to say, have read very little, if any, of his works). Critical studies are being written by academics and not just "fans," and his works have been the studies of MA theses and PhD dissertations in prestigious universities. An ever-growing library of these studies exists (see appendix 2).

So with that, I will wrap up this study and move on. There's a new Stephen King book about to be released (isn't there always!) and I'm dying to read it (King can produce them faster than I can write about them, it seems). I'd like to thank you, Constant Reader, for sticking with this for so long. I hope that you've gained some insights into Stephen King's novels, insights that, I truly hope, will enhance your enjoyment of the stories.

APPENDIX 1

Theoretical Works Consulted

Barthes, Roland. "The Death of the Author." In *Image, Music, Text*. Hill and Wang, 1978.

———. *S/Z*. Hill and Wang, 1974.

Bloom, Harold. "Dumbing Down American Readers." *The Boston Globe*, September 24, 2003.

Boyd, Brian. *On the Origin of Stories*. Harvard University Press, 2009.

Bradley, S.A. *Screaming for Pleasure*. Coal, Cracker Press, 2018.

Brody, Jessica. *Save the Cat! Writes a Novel*. Ten Speed Press, 2018.

Campbell, Joseph. *The Hero with a Thousand Faces*. Barnes & Noble, 1949.

Carroll, Joseph. *Literary Darwinism*. Routledge, 2004.

Clasen, Mathias. *Why Horror Seduces*. Oxford University Press, 2017.

Deacon, Terrence W. *The Symbolic Species*. Norton, 1997.

Diamond, Jared. *Guns, Germs, and Steel: The Fates of Human Societies*. Norton, 1999.

Fields, R. Douglas. *Why We Snap*. Dutton, 2015.

Gottschall, Jonathan. *The Storytelling Animal*. Mariner, 2013.

Gottshall, Jonathan, and David Sloan Wilson, eds. *The Literary Animal*. Northwestern University Press, 2005.

Hafdahl, Meg, and Kelly Florence. *The Science of Stephen King*. Skyhorse Publishing, 2020.

Hill, Thomas. Quoted in *Humans Aren't the Only Animals that Are Self-Aware, New Study Suggests*. Continuum, 2015.

Hills, Matt. *The Pleasures of Horror*. Continuum, 2005.

Panksepp, Jaak, and Lucy Biven. *The Archeology of the Mind*. Norton, 2012.

Schank, Roger. *Tell Me a Story*. Scribner, 1990.

Soper, C.A. *The Evolution of Life Worth Living: Why We Choose to Live*. C.A. Soper, 2021.

Wilson, E.O. *Consilience*. Vintage, 1998.

Appendix 2

Bibliography of Works about Stephen King

Anderson, James Arthur. *Excavating Stephen King: A Darwinist Hermeneutic Study of the Fiction.* Lexington, 2021.

_____. *The Linguistics of Stephen King: Layered Language and Meaning in the Fiction.* McFarland, 2017.

Beahm, George. *Stephen King A to Z: An Encyclopedia of His Life and Work.* Andrews McMeel, 1998.

_____. *The Stephen King Companion.* Rev. ed. Andrews McMeel. 1995.

_____. *The Stephen King Story: A Literary Profile.* Andrews McMeel, 1991.

Bloom, Harold, ed. *Bloom's BioCritiques: Stephen King.* Chelsea House, 2002.

_____. *Bloom's Modern Critical Views: Stephen King.* Chelsea House, 2006.

Blouin, Michael J. *Stephen King and American Politics.* University of Wales Press, 2021.

Brown, Simon. *Screening Stephen King: Adaptation and the Horror Genre in Film and Television.* University of Texas Press, 2018.

Burger, Alissa. *The Quest for the Dark Tower: Genre and Interconnection in the Stephen King Series.* McFarland, 2021.

Clark, Chad A. *Tracing the Trails: A Constant Reader's Reflections on the Work of Stephen King.* Shadow Work Publishing, 2018.

Collings, Michael R. *The Many Facets of Stephen King.* Wildside Press, 2006.

Cowan, Douglas, E. *America's Dark Theologian: The Religious Imagination of Stephen King.* New York University Press, 2018.

Furth, Robin. *Stephen King's* The Dark Tower: *The Complete Concordance.* Scribner, 2012.

Gardner, Brighton David. *Stephen King: A Face among the Masters.* Independently published, 2014.

Hafdahl, Meg, and Kelly Florence. *The Science of Stephen King.* Skyhorse Publishing, 2020.

Held, Jacob M., ed. *Stephen King and Philosophy.* Rowman & Littlefield, 2016.

Hoppenstand, Gary, ed. *Critical Insights: Stephen King.* Salem Press, 2011.

Janicker, Rebecca. *The Literary Haunted House: Lovecraft, Matheson, King, and the Horror in Between.* McFarland, 2015.

Lant, Katherine Margaret, and Theresa Thompson, eds. *Imagining the Worst: Stephen King and the Representation of Woman.* Greenwood, 1998.

Magistrale, Tony. *A Casebook on* The Stand. Wildside, 2006.

_____. *Discovering Stephen King's "The Shining."* Wildside, 2006.

_____. *Hollywood's Stephen King.* Palgrave, 2003.

_____. *Landscape of Fear: Stephen King's American Gothic.* Popular Press, 1988.

———. *The Moral Voyages of Stephen King.* Wildside, 2006.
———. *Stephen King: The Second Decade.* Twayne, 1992.
McAleer, Patrick. *Inside the Dark Tower Series: Art, Evil, and Intertextuality in the Stephen King Novels.* McFarland, 2009.
McAleer, Patrick, and Michael Perry, eds. *Stephen King's Modern Macabre: Essays on the Later Works.* McFarland, 2014.
Northrup, Anthony. *Stephen King Dollar Baby: The Book.* BearManor Media, 2021.
Power, Brenda Miller, Jeffrey D. Wilhelm, and Kelly Chandler, eds. *Reading Stephen King: Issues of Censorship, Student Choice, and Popular Literature.* National Council of Teachers of English, 1997.
Riekki, Ron, ed. *The Many Lives of* It: *Essays of the Stephen King Horror Franchise.* McFarland, 2020.
Rogak, Lisa. *Haunted Heart: The Life and Times of Stephen King.* St. Martin's, 2008.
Russell, Sharon. *Revisiting Stephen King: A Critical Companion.* Greenwood, 2002.
Schweitzer, Darrell, ed. *Discovering Stephen King.* Starmont House, 1985.
Sears, John. *Stephen King's Gothic.* University of Wales Press, 2011.
Simpson, Philip L., and Patrick McAleer, eds. *The Modern Stephen King Canon: Beyond Horror.* Lexington, 2019.
———. *Stephen King's Contemporary Classics.* Rowman & Littlefield, 2015.
Spignesi, Stephen. *The Complete Stephen King Encyclopedia: The Definitive Guide to the Works of America's Master of Horror.* Contemporary Books, 1991.
———. *The Essential Stephen King.* Career Press, 2003.
———. *Stephen King: American Master.* Permuted Press, 2018.
———. *The Stephen King Quiz Book.* Signet, 1990.
Strengell, Heidi. *Dissecting Stephen King: From the Gothic to Literary Naturalism.* Popular Press, 2005.
Timpone, Anthony, ed. *Masters of the Dark: Stephen King, Clive Barker.* Harper, 1997.
Underwood, Tim, and Chuck Miller, eds. *Bare Bones: Conversations on Terror with Stephen King.* Underwood/Miller, 1988.
———. *Kingdom of Fear: The World of Stephen King.* Underwood/Miller, 1986.
Vincent, Bev. *The Dark Tower Companion.* New American Library, 2013.
———. *The Road to the Dark Tower.* New American Library, 2004.
———. *Stephen King: A Complete Exploration of His Work, Life, and Influences.* Epic Ink, 2022.
Wiater, Stanley, Christopher Golden, and Hank Wagner. *The Complete Stephen King Universe: A Guide to the Worlds of Stephen King.* St. Martin's, 2000.
Winter, Douglas. *Stephen King: The Art of Darkness.* New American Library, 1984.
Wood, Rocky. *Stephen King: A Literary Companion.* McFarland, 2011.

APPENDIX 3

A Chronology of Stephen King's Books

The following is a list of King's books arranged by publication date. This list includes only readily available editions, not collectables. Novellas are generally not included if they first appeared in part of a longer Stephen King collection.

N—novel
NV—novella
C—collection
NF—nonfiction
S—screenplay

Carrie, April 5, 1974. N
'Salem's Lot, October 17, 1975. N
Rage (as Bachman), December 1976. N
The Shining, January 1977. N
Nightshift, short story collection, December 1977. C
The Stand, October 1978. N
The Long Walk (as Bachman), December 1978. N
The Dead Zone, August 1979. N
The Mist (collected in anthology Dark Forces), August 29, 1980. NV
Firestarter, September 29, 1980. N
Danse Macabre, December 1980. NF
Roadwork (as Bachman), December 1980. N
Cujo, September 8, 1981. N
The Running Man (as Bachman), December 1981. N
The Dark Tower: The Gunslinger (Donald Grant edition), June 1982. N
Different Seasons, August 1982. C

Christine, April 29, 1983. N
Pet Sematary, November 1983. N
The Talisman (coauthored with Peter Straub), November 1984. N
Thinner, November 1984. N
Cycle of the Werewolf, April 1985. C
Skeleton Crew, June 1985. C
The Bachman Books, October 1985. C
It, September 1986. N
The Eyes of the Dragon, February 1987. N
The Dark Tower: The Drawing of the Three, May 1987. N
Misery, June 1987. N
The Tommyknockers, November 1987. N
The Dark Half, November 1989. N
The Stand: The Complete and Uncut Edition, May 1990. N
Four Past Midnight, September 1990. C
The Dark Tower: The Wastelands, August 1991. N
Needful Things, October 1991. N
Gerald's Game, May 1992. N
Nightmares and Dreamscapes, October 1993. C
Dolores Claiborne, November 1993. N
Insomnia, September 1994. N
Rose Madder, June 1995. N
The Regulators, December 1995. N
The Green Mile Part 1: Two Dead Girls, March 1996. N
The Green Mile Part 2: The Mouse on the Mile, April 1996. N
The Green Mile Part 3: Coffey's Hands, May 1996. N
The Green Mile Part 4: The Bad Death of Eduard Delacroix, June 1996. N

The Green Mile Part 5: Night Journey, July 1996. N
The Green Mile Part 6: Coffey on the Mile, August 1996. N
Desperation, September 24, 1996. N
The Dark Tower: Wizard and Glass, November 1997. N
Bag of Bones, September 22, 1998. N
Storm of the Century, February 1999. S
The Girl Who Loved Tom Gordon, April 1999. N
Hearts in Atlantis, September 1999. C
On Writing: A Memoir of the Craft, December 1999. NF
Secret Windows: Essays and Fiction on the Craft of Writing, December 1999. NF/C
The Green Mile: The Complete Serial Novel, October 2000. N
Dreamcatcher, February 20, 2001. N
Black House (coauthored with Peter Straub), September 15, 2001. N
Everything's Eventual, March 2002. C
From a Buick 8, September 24, 2002. N
The Dark Tower: Wizard and Glass, November 2003. N
The Dark Tower: Song of Susannah, June 2004. N
Faithful (coauthored with Stewart O'Nan), September 2005. NF
The Colorado Kid, October 2005. N
Cell, January 24, 2006. N
Lisey's Story, October 2006. N
Blaze (as Bachman), June 2006. N
Duma Key, January 22, 2008. N
UR (published on Kindle), February 12, 2009. NV
Under the Dome, November 2009. N
Blockade Billy, April 20, 2010. N
Full Dark, No Stars, November 2010. C
11/22/63, November 8, 2011. N
The Dark Tower: The Wind through the Keyhole, April 2012. N
Guns (published on Kindle), January 2013. NF
Joyland, June 2013. N
Doctor Sleep, September 24, 2013. N
Mr. Mercedes, June 2014. N
Revival, November 2014. N
Finders Keepers, June 2, 2015. N
The Bazaar of Bad Dreams, November 2015. C
End of Watch, June 7, 2016. N
Gwendy's Button Box (coauthored with Richard Chizmar), May 16, 2017. N
Sleeping Beauties (coauthored with Owen King), September 26, 2017. N
The Outsider, May 2018. N
Elevation, October 30, 2018. N
The Institute, September 2019. N
If It Bleeds, April 2020. C
Later, March 2, 2021. N
Billy Summers, August 3, 2021. N
Gwendy's Final Task (coauthored with Richard Chizmar), February 15, 2022. N
Fairy Tale, September 6, 2022. N
Holly, September 5, 2023. N
You Like It Darker, May 21, 2024. C

Index

Adams, Douglas 53, 114
addiction 23, 24, 27, 57, 113, 114, 155, 156, 180, 209, 210, 215, 216, 232, 234, 235, 237, 244, 245, 246, 257, 275
Albom, Mitch 267
alcohol (abuse) 13, 22-23, 24, 57, 112, 113-114, 115, 154-155, 180, 203, 216, 231, 232, 234, 241, 253, 290
Alice in Wonderland 198, 288
Alien (film) 46
altruism 9, 33, 42-43, 93, 104, 115, 156, 161, 182, 229, 242, 254, 259, 283, 294
American Horror Story 228
Anansi 91
Anderson, Poul 113
Apocalypse Now 179
Arabian Nights 108
autism 161, 258

Bachman Books 5, 17-18, 35, 37, 38, 52, 55, 62, 64, 66, 95, 99, 117, 120, 153, 158, 159, 162, 203
Bag of Bones 164-170, 262, 303
Barrett, William 233
Barrymore, Drew 51
Barsoom 198
Batman (film) 31
Beowulf 30, 73, 74
Bildungsroman 72, 73, 101, 174, 227, 276
"The Big Driver" 283
Billy Summers 280-285, 303, 304, 305
Biven, Lucy 61, 162
Bixby, Jerome 47
Blackwood, Algernon 85
Blaze 5, 203-206
Bloch, Robert 306
Blockade Billy 176
Bloom, Harold 146, 299
The Body 72-76, 107, 121, 225, 227, 283, 305, 307
Boyd, Brian 24, 75, 110
Bradbury, Ray 45, 46, 48, 63, 64, 127, 162, 220, 222, 228, 288, 298
Bradley, S.A. 26

brand names 44, 195, 305, 307
The Bridge over the River Kwai 69
Brody, Jessica 24, 292
Brown, Dan 292
bullying 5, 6, 8, 9, 10, 12, 74, 103, 303
Burns, Robert 149
Burroughs, Edgar Rice 198
butterfly effect 59, 97, 220, 222, 223

Campbell, Joesph 2, 29, 30, 74, 173, 289
cannibalism 74, 85, 96, 128, 293, 294
CARE (affective emotion) 50, 61, 65, 134, 168-169, 195, 253
Carrie 5-10, 11, 225, 47, 49, 103, 155, 203, 233, 255, 297
Cassandra 96
Castle Rock 39, 57, 58, 121, 122, 124, 125, 161, 210, 265, 266, 268, 307
The Catcher in the Rye 72, 227, 253
Cell 80, 192-196, 217, 219, 257, 304
chaos theory 32, 59, 222, 271
Chekhov, Anton 52, 69, 251
Child, Lee 240
Chinatown (film) 292
Christine 77-82, 185
Cinderella 7
Clasen, David 81
Clausen, Mathias 26
cleithrophobia (fear of being trapped) 217
clowns 31, 100, 103, 104, 299
collective unconscious 2, 7, 85, 101, 149, 248, 289
Coleridge, Samuel Taylor 209
Collins, Suzanna 35, 63
The Colorado Kid 1988-191, 274
The Comedy of Errors 118
coming of age story 7, 36, 226
confession story 133
Conrad, Joseph 178, 178
cosmic horror 103, 184, 185, 186, 187, 244, 246-247, 248, 302
Covid-19 28, 32, 34, 104, 217, 268, 280, 285, 286, 288, 289, 291, 292-293
Crane, Stephen 127

315

INDEX

creativity 24, 25, 63, 108, 114, 160, 179, 180, 182, 195, 200, 209, 211, 304
Crichton, Michael 31
Crimson King 141–142, 143–144
Cthulhu Mythos 246, 287, 288
Cujo 57–61, 79, 118, 121, 126, 127, 134, 156, 264, 303, 305
curses 95, 96, 97
cynophobia 58

Dahmer, Jeffrey 294
Danse Macabre 106
Darabont, Frank 71
The Dark Half 106, 117–120, 121, 262, 304
Dark Tower series 3, 11, 15, 31, 73, 89, 91, 93, 103, 104, 138, 141–142, 143, 144, 145, 155, 185, 198, 210, 212, 231, 246, 288, 289, 290, 307
The Da Vinci Code 292
The Day of the Triffids 179
The Dead Zone 28, 31, 39–44, 45, 47, 48, 58, 121, 180, 233, 255, 256, 297, 303, 304
death of the author 210
death taboo 86
Deaver, Jeffery 240
Deconstructionism 14
Derry 58, 100, 101, 104, 141, 142, 161, 177, 307
Desperation 62, 153–157, 158, 159, 160, 163, 264
Diamond, Jared 33
Different Seasons 68, 72
Doctor Sleep 25, 217, 231–237, 303, 304, 305
Dolores Claiborne 126, 131–135, 136, 156, 283, 303, 305
domestic violence 24, 136, 138, 143, 220, 304
doppelganger 118, 260, 262
Dreamcatcher 177–182, 302
Dumas, Alexandre 69
Duma Key 207–212
Du Maurier, Daphne 24, 165, 292
Dylan, Bob 187
dynamic characters 22
dystopian novel 35, 36, 62, 63, 302

El Cueo 260
Elevation 265–268, 303
11/22/63 42, 44, 59, 98, 185, 219–224, 228, 271, 280, 281, 283, 289, 303, 307
Eliot, T.S. 149
Ellison, Harlan 118, 262
eminent domain 52, 54, 55
End of Watch 238, 255–259, 261, 303
evil place 11, 13, 15, 24, 25, 27
The Exorcist 79
Eyes of the Dragon 89–94

A Face in the Crowd 176
Fairy Tale 286–290
fairy tales 7, 14, 58, 84, 89, 90, 91, 101, 174, 254, 288, 289
The Faithful 102
Faulkner, William 1, 282, 301, 307

Faust 123
FEAR (affective emotion) 2, 26–27, 47, 155, 161, 181, 187, 217, 236
Feminism 10
Fields, R. Douglas 10, 20, 55, 65, 124, 129, 139, 284
Finders Keepers 238, 250–254, 291
Finney, Jack 154, 159
Firestarter 32, 37, 41, 45–51, 156, 181, 195, 233, 270, 301, 304
Fischer, Bobby 230
Fisher, Roland 229
Floyd, George 64
The Flying Dutchman 208
The Fools of Time 233
foreshadowing 2, 6, 9, 12, 40, 63, 64, 84, 90, 122, 132, 148, 159, 173, 214, 232, 239, 256, 261, 270, 275, 306
free will 59, 61, 144, 221, 222–223, 303
From a Buick 8 183–187, 188, 189, 171
The Fugitive (television series) 46

game theory 33, 41, 50, 151
Genesis 31, 79, 91
Gerald's Game 57, 126–130, 131, 133, 136, 303
Ghost Town (film) 154
Gilgamesh 306
Ginsberg, Allen 301
The Girl with the Dragon Tattoo 292
Golding, William 214
"A Good Marriage" 283
Goodwin, Doris Kearns 224
gothic 13, 16, 23, 166, 302
Gottschall, Jonathan 194
The Graduate (film) 227
Grafton, Sue 240
The Great Gatsby 22
The Great God Pan 245
The Green Mile 146–152, 162, 283, 302, 303, 305, 307
GRIEF (affective emotion) 104, 168–169, 201, 264, 290, 304
Grimm Brothers 58, 91, 101, 289
Groome, Francis Hines 96
Guns (essay) 217

Hamilton's Rule 156
Hamlet 22
Hansel and Gretel 174
Hardy, Thomas 166
Harry Potter 7, 270
Haven (television series) 188
Haven Foundation 203
Hawking, Stephen 230
Hawthorne, Nathaniel 23, 24, 96, 301
The Heart of Darkness 178–179
hermeneutic code 40, 148, 159
hero's journey 2, 29, 31, 73–74, 101, 173, 240
Hill, Thomas 263
Holly 238, 291–295, 305

Hughes, Langston 301
Hughes, Thomas 270
The Hunger Games 35, 63, 288
Hunter, Stephen 281
Hurkos, Peter 44
Huxley, Aldous 63, 302

I Am Legend 193
If It Bleeds 238, 258
The Iliad 96
in-group 98–99, 104, 151, 267–268
incest taboo 129, 134–135, 277, 278
Insomnia 141–145, 185, 271, 303, 307
The Institute 37, 41, 180, 195, 269–273, 302, 303, 304
Invasion of the Body Snatchers 154, 160
It 100–105

Jackson, Shirley 13, 24, 37, 45, 306
Jacques, Brian 209
Jane Eyre 72
James, Henry 24, 301
Jaws 30
Joyce, James 7, 38, 73, 74, 76, 277, 300
Joyland 188, 225–230, 249, 274, 303
Jung, Carl 27, 149, 289
justice 29, 46, 50, 66, 68, 69–70, 71, 92, 93, 97, 131, 132, 134, 139–140, 150, 151, 242, 254, 261, 284, 300, 302–303

The Karman Lane (film) 266
ka-tet 104
Kiernan, Caitlyn 301
King, Tabitha 5, 16, 168, 203, 206
King Arthur 30
King Tut's curse 96
Kinsella, W.P. 172
Kirkman, Robert 194
Kubrick, Stanley 21, 22, 26, 27

L.A. Confidential 202
Larsson, Stieg 292
Later 58, 188, 274–279, 305
LaVey, Anton 233
Lee, Tanith 91
Lévi-Strauss, Claude 91
Lewis, C.S. 198
LIFEMORTS 20
Lisey's Story 73, 192, 197–202, 252, 283, 303, 307
Loki 91
The Long Walk 5, 35–38
Lord of the Flies 214
Lovecraft, H.P. 1, 23–24, 75, 79, 81, 103, 104, 113, 128, 161, 167, 184–185, 186, 244, 245, 246, 247, 248, 277, 287, 288, 297, 298, 301, 306
Lumley, Brian 234, 275, 301
LUST (affective emotion) 169, 224

Machen, Arthur 245, 306
magical realism 148

"The Mangler" (short story) 56
Marlowe, Christopher 123, 240
Martin, George R.R. 215
Matheson, Richard 193, 222
McVeigh, Timothy 241
mental health 10, 20, 24, 27, 54, 139, 165, 199, 201, 205, 206, 253, 303
metafiction 132, 275, 281
Mighty Morphin Power Rangers 160
Milgram, Stanley 272
Mill, John Stuart 271
Minotaur 137
Misery 25, 89, 106–111, 170, 252, 253, 304, 306
"The Mist" 195
Moby Dick 22
"The Monkey" 79
monomyth 74, 289
Moore, Ward 209, 222
Morrison, Toni 301
Mr. Mercedes 238–243, 251, 253, 256, 292, 295
music 80–81

Naked and Afraid (television series) 37, 63, 64
Narnia 198, 210
narrative determinism 84
Nash, John 230
Naylor, Gloria 167
Necroscope 275
Needful Things 121–125, 132, 305
neuroscience 104, 168, 283
The Night of the Living Dead 193, 256
Nightshift 21, 56, 297
noble savage 204
nostalgia 43, 54, 74, 75, 81, 185, 219, 220–221, 227–228, 305

objective correlative 13, 149
O'Brien, Tim 282
The Odyssey 2, 29, 59, 74
Oedipus 22
Of Mice and Men 149, 204
Offutt, Andrew J. 297
On Writing 2, 8, 22, 57, 92, 279, 282
1001 Nights 24, 108
Orwell, George 32, 36, 46, 63, 64, 213, 302
out-group 98–99, 104, 267–268
The Outsider 118, 238, 258, 260–264, 302
Overlook Hotel 21, 23, 25, 27, 49, 79, 210, 231, 232, 233, 234, 307

Pandora's Box 75
Panksepp, Jaak 25, 26, 61, 75, 115, 139, 162, 190, 211, 224, 247
Persephone 207, 208
Pet Sematary 1, 50, 83–88, 264, 303
PLAY (affective emotion) 66, 115, 211, 258
Poe, Edgar Allan 79, 118, 127, 133, 251, 262, 277, 300, 301, 306
point-of-view 79, 125, 126, 132, 137, 148, 172, 178, 187, 214, 270, 274, 287, 306

Prison Break (television series) 69
private language 200
prolepses 40
Prometheus 91
psychic phenomenon 22, 255, 304
psychic vampire 233–234

RAGE (affective emotion) 3, 9–10, 20, 50, 55–56, 65–66, 124, 139, 155, 284, 304
Rage 5, 11–16, 55, 299, 303
Raven 91
reality television 37, 63, 64
The Regulators 153, 154, 156, 158–163
religion 8–9, 10, 14–15, 98, 155, 156, 187, 216, 230, 244, 246, 248, 304
revenge story 9, 155, 185, 244–249, 277, 283, 303, 304
Revival 240
"Rhyme of the Ancient Mariner" 240
Rice, Ann 301
Rip Van Winkle 40
Rita Hayworth and the Shawshank Redemption 59, 68–71, 92, 302, 307
Roadwork 11, 17, 52–56, 302, 303
Romero, George 117, 193–194, 256
Rose Madder 136–140, 283, 303, 304
Roth, Philip 254
The Running Man 17, 37, 46, 50, 62–67, 266, 302

'Salem's Lot 11–16, 25, 121, 122, 154, 155, 161, 297, 302, 306, 307
Salinger, J.D. 227, 253, 254
Sand Kings 215
The Satanic Bible 233
Schank, Roger 92, 110
The Science of Stephen King 85
school shootings 18–19, 20, 299
Seabrook, William 193, 256
Secret Window, Secret Garden 106
SEEKING (affective emotion) 75, 104, 186, 190–191, 202, 247
SELF (affective emotion) 263
selfish gene 119, 195, 236, 253
Shakespeare, William 1, 69, 91, 118, 167
Shelley, Mary 84, 150, 235, 246, 248, 301, 306
The Shining 1, 15, 21–27, 41, 48, 150, 154, 161, 179, 231, 233, 237, 297, 302, 304
"The Shop" 31, 45, 46, 47, 48, 114, 121, 122, 181, 270, 273, 302
The Silence of the Lambs (film) 292
Simmons, Dan 160, 234, 301
social Darwinism 32, 33
Somewhere in Time (film) 232
Song of Susannah 11
The Sound and the Fury 282
Stanford Prison Experiment 272
The Stand 2, 9, 28–34, 37, 46, 49, 150, 161, 195, 213, 215, 217, 246, 258, 297, 304, 307
Star Wars 2, 29, 30, 74, 306
Steinbeck, John 149, 204

Stevenson, Robert Louis 118
Stockton, Frank 189
Stoker, Bram 13, 79, 306
storytelling 24, 37, 40, 75–76, 92–93, 108, 110, 132, 167, 184, 191, 194, 196, 289
Stowe, Harriet Beecher 301
stream of consciousness 53, 74
suicide 256–257, 258
"Survivor Type" 127, 128

The Tempest 69, 91, 167
Tetris effect 257
textual code 120, 275
Theseus 137
The Things They Carried 282
Thinner 95–99, 266
To Kill a Mockingbird 72, 227
Tolkien, J.R.R. 28
Tom Brown's School Days 270
The Tommyknockers 112–116, 177, 178, 304
trickster 31, 91, 93
tragic flaw 22, 23, 24, 60
Tuesdays with Morrie 267
The Twilight Zone 39, 47, 118

Under the Dome 213–218, 246, 302, 304
underdog narrative 8, 102–103
Updike, John 254
UR 73, 219
utilitarianism 181, 271

vampires 11–13, 14, 15, 233–234, 276, 302
Van Gogh, Vincent 42
Vandermeer, Jeff 64
Vonnegut, Kurt 299

The Walking Dead 30, 194
Wall Street (film) 121
War of the Worlds 178
Wells, H.G. 178
wendigo 85
The White Zombie 194, 256
"whydunit" 291, 292
Whitman, Walt 301
Wilde, Oscar 85
Wilder, Thornton 306
Wilson, David Sloan 93
Wilson, E.O. 9, 33, 43
The Wind Through the Keyhole 73
The Wizard of Oz 288
The Wolves of Calla 11
Wyndham, John 178

Yarbro, Chelsea Quinn 130

Zamyatin, Yevgeny 63
Zimbardo, Philip 272
zombies 192–194, 195, 196, 256, 257, 259

www.ingramcontent.com/pod-product-compliance
Lightning Source LLC
Chambersburg PA
CBHW032031300426
44117CB00009B/1023